THE TRAINING DESIGN MANUAL

THE COMPLETE PRACTICAL GUIDE TO CREATING EFFECTIVE AND SUCCESSFUL TRAINING PROGRAMMES

TONY BRAY

KOGAN PAGE

London and Philadelphia

Acknowledgements

Thanks to all the companies I've worked with, especially Allied-Dunbar, BAT, BE, BNG, BT, Rolls-Royce, Sun Microsystems and Van den Burgh Foods; in addition Guys, Barts, Kings College and ELC Mental Health NHS Trusts. Thanks also to John Thacker for his valuable contributions on course design and training needs analysis. Finally, a big 'thank you' to my partner, Tessa Simpson, for her support, inspiration and belief in me.

Publisher's note

Every possible effort has been made to ensure that the information contained in this book is accurate at the time of going to press, and the publishers and author cannot accept responsibility for any errors or omissions, however caused. No responsibility for loss or damage occasioned to any person acting, or refraining from action, as a result of the material in this publication can be accepted by the editor, the publisher or the author.

First published in Great Britain and the United States in 2006 by Kogan Page Limited

120 Pentonville Road
London N1 9JN
United Kingdom
www.kogan-page.co.uk

525 South 4th Street, #241
Philadelphia PA 19147
USA

© Tony Bray, 2006

ISBN 0 7494 4570 X

British Library Cataloguing-in-Publication Data

A CIP record for this book is available from the British Library.

Library of Congress Cataloging-in-Publication Data

Bray, Tony.
   The training design manual : the complete practical guide to creating effective and successful training programmes / Tony Bray.
      p. cm.
   Includes bibliographical references and index.
   ISBN 0-7494-4570-X
   1. Employees—Training of—Handbooks, manuals, etc. 2. Instructional systems—Design—Handbooks, manuals, etc. 3. Employee training personnel—Handbooks, manuals, etc. I. Title.
HF5549.5.T7B638 2006
658.3'12404—dc22

                              2005037495

Typeset by JS Typesetting Ltd, Porthcawl, Mid Glamorgan
Printed and bound in Great Britain by Bell & Bain, Glasgow

Contents

Activities

Figures

Introduction

- Welcome
- Structure of the book
- What is 'learning'... and 'training'?
- The benefits of good design
- Focus on designing a real course

WELCOME

Welcome to *The Training Design Manual: The complete practical guide to creating and delivering effective and successful training programmes.*

You may be wondering if you should add this manual to your already extensive library of learning resources. Well – if you can answer 'Yes' to any of the questions in Activity 1.1 then you should be taking this book away with you.

Helping people to acquire new knowledge, skills or behaviours, or to build their confidence and tackle previously daunting tasks, is a real privilege that everyone in the training profession shares. No matter how the training is delivered, at some stage someone will have had to sit down and plan *what content or course material*

```
                                                        ┌──────────┐
                                                        │   0.05   │
                                                        └──────────┘

    Activity 1.1 How this book might benefit you

    I have been delivering training courses that other people have designed,
    and I'd like to be able to do it myself. Yes/No.

    I have been told that I'll soon be asked to design a course and I haven't
    a clue where to start. Yes/No.

    I am an experienced training course designer and perhaps feel the need
    to refresh my existing skills. Yes/No.

    I've designed many courses but, if I'm honest, several are a bit 'jaded'
    or need re-energizing. Yes/No

    I am taking on a new role as a training 'consultant' and want to be able
    to project a more professional image with my client departments. Yes/No.
```

will be covered, the *order* it's to be done in and exactly *how* it's to be delivered – all the basics of good training design.

That's what this book will give you. It will take you through a step-by-step design process, presented in a user-friendly and practical way. To ensure you get the greatest benefit from your investment we suggest you take an active part in the learning experience, and not just read it (more of this later in this chapter). Of course if you want to simply read it you'll still get lots of ideas – the choice is yours.

STRUCTURE OF THE BOOK

We've broken the journey into separate chunks, and you can see the broad direction each one takes from the chapter listings. So, if you only want to join us for a specific part of the journey, that's fine.

Like every good training course, each chapter contains elements of theory interleaved with practical exercises, where you get the opportunity to try it out on your own course design project. The activity boxes ask you to complete specific tasks that will build towards your complete course design. Each activity box also shows an estimate of how long the task could take – the digital display shows hours and minutes.

There are some examples of materials or course peripherals that would not sit easily in the main body of the text, so they are reproduced on the attached CD ROM.

As with most other subjects there is a wealth of information available on the internet that you can easily access using the popular search engines. To avoid cluttering the text with endless lists of websites we have only provided those that you may not readily be aware of, for example in the chapter dealing with accessibility.

WHAT IS 'LEARNING'... AND 'TRAINING'?

Learning

Before we start on our design journey we should perhaps clarify what we mean by 'learning' and 'training'. A pure definition of 'learning' could be: 'Learning is a process that enables someone to acquire new attitudes, skills or knowledge.'

To justify all the direct costs in providing learning opportunities, not to mention the lost revenue-earning time, a business must be able to see a direct benefit resulting from any learning its staff experience. So, for learning taking place in a commercial or business setting, we should perhaps expand the definition of learning to: 'Learning is a process that enables someone to acquire new attitudes, skills or knowledge... _so that they can do something they couldn't do before, or do it more effectively.'_

When we consider someone being able to work more effectively the four main parameters usually considered are:

1. Quality – deliver new levels of quality.

2. Quantity – process or handle more orders or items.

3. Cost – do more for the same cost, or the same output for less cost.

4. Time – take less time in basic handling, or work to earlier deadlines.

It's being able to apply the learning to make a difference to performance which differentiates learning in the commercial sense from pure education.

Training

So now we've defined 'learning'… how do we define 'training'? Building on the definition we used earlier for 'learning' we could define 'training' as follows: *'Training is any form of process designed to facilitate learning in the target audience.'*

As before we've kept the definition as wide as possible and not limited ourselves to the strictly commercial setting. The important thing to remember throughout the whole training design process is to always jump into the shoes of the target audience and ask yourself: 'How will this exercise or task feel for them?', 'How will this section of the course or activity facilitate learning?'

THE BENEFITS OF GOOD DESIGN

Please take a few minutes to think back on the training courses you've attended … then think of the best one. Please write down five things that made it so special.

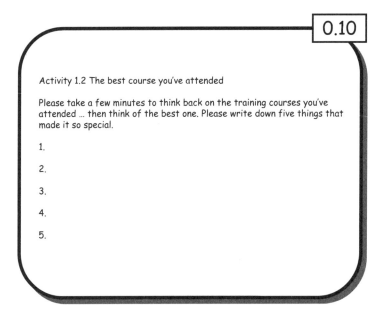

0.10

Activity 1.2 The best course you've attended

Please take a few minutes to think back on the training courses you've attended … then think of the best one. Please write down five things that made it so special.

1.

2.

3.

4.

5.

At least one of the items you've written will describe the trainer. You may have used words like:

- knowledgeable;

- organized;

- inspirational;

- focused;

- approachable.

The list could go on and on. We all recognize the importance of a good trainer or teacher to make any subject come alive. But the focus of this book is not on the trainer but on the *design* of the training, so let's look at some of the other items you've written. Your list may include:

- well structured;

- varied training methods;

- logical flow;

- appropriate models or concepts used;

- ideas I can take back and use straight away;

- appropriate balance of theory and practice;

- good handouts, visual aids or workbooks.

This list, which could also go on and on, clearly shows the benefits of good design. Given a well-designed course even an average trainer can deliver an acceptable learning experience. But if you start with a poorly designed course you need an exceptional trainer to turn it into anything worthwhile. It's rather like the old saying: you can't make a silk purse out of a sow's ear – unless you are exceptional!

FOCUS ON DESIGNING A REAL COURSE

We made a conscious decision to make this book participative rather than just a good read because we believe participation is one of the cornerstones of designing training that works. To make the participation *meaningful* (another of our cornerstones) we would strongly suggest that, as you work through the book, you focus on a real piece of training design you have to do.

Ideally, if you have a course to design soon then use the tools and techniques in the book on the actual design. That way you get to grasp the theory and to design a course at the same time. That'd be novel, wouldn't it? Doing some real work whilst having some training. Please take a few minutes to identify the course, or part of a course, which you will focus on as we progress through the book.

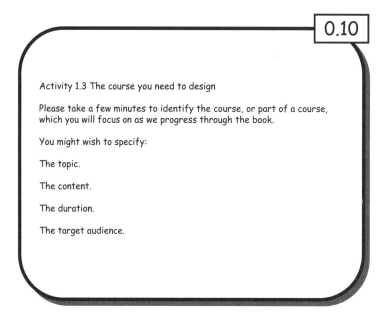

0.10

Activity 1.3 The course you need to design

Please take a few minutes to identify the course, or part of a course, which you will focus on as we progress through the book.

You might wish to specify:

The topic.

The content.

The duration.

The target audience.

Are you ready to begin the rest of the journey? Then let's make a start.

2

The training design project

> - Identify your stakeholders
> - Project dashboard
> - The initial planning meeting

IDENTIFY YOUR STAKEHOLDERS

So you've been asked to design a course – where do you start? It's tempting to get stuck into the detailed design of the course but there are more important aspects to get to grips with first.

You need to establish your training design team. Start by identifying all the key people who have an interest in the project – in current jargon the 'stakeholders'. This sounds obvious but, if you don't involve all the right people, you can end up wasting days of effort, not to mention damaged reputations! Here's a cautionary tale.

I once worked in a freelance capacity for a team of independent consultants who had designed and delivered an intensive quality initiative programme for one of the UK's leading FMCG companies. Following the success of this initiative the company's Quality Director asked the consultants to design and deliver a follow-on programme, which would take the quality initiative to a deeper level in the client's organization.

The consulting company spent several days designing the initiative and practising the presentation, which was to be made to the Managing Director and the Quality Director. On the due day the consulting team arrived, loaded down with OHP slides and handouts, and, after the usual preliminaries, started their presentation.

Within a few minutes the MD called the presentation to a halt saying, 'I never expected an extension of the Quality Initiative – what I wanted was a Management Development programme.'

'No,' countered the Quality Director, 'When we spoke the other week you said you wanted to see Quality Improvement teams established in the company.'

So the whole thing ended in chaos. Clearly the MD and QD had failed to agree between them what they really wanted but, more fundamentally, the representative from the consulting firm had failed to identify this rift between the two key stakeholders and work to resolve it.

We walked away from this valuable learning experience with our self-esteem and professional image damaged, and have never repeated the same mistake again. The lesson is clear – before you start any design work you must identify the key people who will have an impact on your project and who you need to involve from the very beginning. Your list will probably include some or all of the following.

A project 'champion' or sponsor

A champion or sponsor needs to be someone well known in the company who is able to influence a wide range of key people, especially operational and financial 'movers and shakers'. The champion will promote your project and, if things get tough, argue why it should not be abandoned in favour of other projects.

Your champion will almost certainly have an operational interest in the successful outcome of the training initiative, probably contributing to the success of corporate objectives with which they are personally associated.

Budget holder

You will need to gain (and keep) the active support of the budget holder to ensure that irritating budgetary approvals or delays do not hold up progress.

Topic 'owner'

Each topic in the training portfolio will have someone who is recognized as the 'owner' of that project and who will have the power to 'sign off' changes to the strategy or the content of any materials related to it.

Subject matter experts

For the training to be credible you need to enlist the support of acknowledged experts in the field to provide up to the minute advice or guidance on the way the topic is being implemented, or how it may change in the light of future techno-logical developments or legislative changes.

This may be you or, depending on the topic, may be someone in an operational department. You also have another issue to consider – do you employ internal or external people?

Internal people will have extensive knowledge of current initiatives, be soaked in the culture and need no introduction to current processes or procedures. They will also be less expensive than external subject matter experts or designers, but may not have so much flexibility in terms of availability.

External people bring a fresh approach and are able to share best practice from other companies, unencumbered by all the internal politics or 'baggage'. The downsides are that they will need to spend time familiarizing themselves with your internal procedures or initiatives and, of course, they generally cost more than internal people.

So the choice may simply come down to costs, time or availability to enable a project to be completed in a given timescale.

Line managers and staff

You also need to gain the commitment of the managers and staff who are likely to be affected by the training, and you need to keep them actively involved throughout the whole development life cycle. Listen to what they say and build their ideas into the programme as it develops.

Please take a few minutes to identify who your key stakeholders will be.

> **0.15**
>
> Activity 2.1 Who are your stakeholders?
>
> Please take a few minutes to identify who your key stakeholders will be. Please write their names or job titles below.
>
> Project champion
>
> Budget holder
>
> Topic owner
>
> Subject matter experts
>
> Line managers
>
> Staff
>
> Others?

PROJECT DASHBOARD

Now that you've identified your stakeholders it can be useful to clarify in your own mind the status and influence each of them has. A useful technique to help at this stage is the 'project dashboard' – let's talk you through the main elements.

First of all you will need to prepare a blank dashboard for each of your stakeholders so that you can enter the key information for each person individually. Figure 2.1 shows what it looks like.

The dashboard enables you to record:

- Their name.
- The amount of influence they can exert, classified as:
  - high;
  - moderate;
  - low.
- The role they will probably have in the project, using the mnemonic CUTIE:
  - Champion

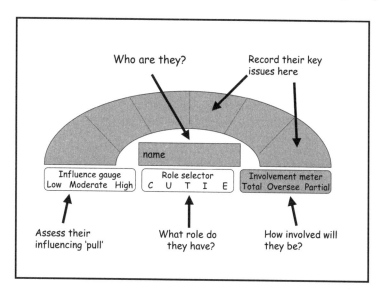

Figure 2.1 Project dashboard

- User
- Technical
- Inhibitor
- Economic.
- Their involvement meter, using three categories:
  - total;
  - oversee;
  - partial.
- Issues or concerns.

Finally, the dashboard enables you to summarize some of the key issues or concerns the stakeholder may have.

As you start doing some preliminary research around the organization to assess people's reaction to the proposed course you will quickly realize that people fall into one of three broad categories:

0.30

Activity 2.2 Develop your project dashboards

Having identified your stakeholders, you may now wish to develop a project dashboard for each of them, so that you have a ready reference for each person.

1. Those who are basically supportive of the idea.

2. Those who are neutral. They must be encouraged to at least stay that way, or ideally become 'lukewarm' about supporting the project.

3. Those who are 'anti' the project.

Possible antagonists

For most of us the last person we would choose to speak to is anyone who is likely to object to or oppose our ideas. But speaking to them at an early stage can help you in one of two ways. First, a neutral reaction. Discussing your ideas may encourage them to adopt, at the very least, a neutral response, when they do nothing to inhibit or harm your project. Second, a positive reaction. Spending time with them *may* turn their attitude around and encourage them to adopt a positive attitude towards the project, in which case you now have an ally rather than an enemy – and a very strong ally at that.

In any event, spending time with people who have different views from your own, and exploring why they think that way, can give you valuable insights or other perspectives on the way the company operates or how things get done. Let them know you're speaking to them early because their opinion is important to you. Very often we put off difficult discussions until last, by which time these individuals are aware that you've spoken to everyone else first. This can make a challenging situation worse.

THE INITIAL PLANNING MEETING

It's important to get the whole project off to a good start and, to ensure that there are no misunderstandings, it's worthwhile getting all the key stakeholders together for an initial planning meeting. That way you can ensure that all the key issues are fully discussed, and that everyone's in agreement at least once during the project life cycle!

As you draft your agenda you may wish to include some or all of the following items:

- Confirm the membership of the training design team.

- Discuss roles, responsibilities and accountability.

- Discuss how the learning needs will be assessed.

- Discover any limitations.

- Establish links to other business initiatives or products.

- Discuss company standards.

- Set realistic deadlines.

- Agree the review process and set key dates.

- Agree budgets, funding and resources.

- Agree the 'signing off' process.

Let's briefly explore each one in turn.

Confirm the membership of the training design team

While this should be quite an easy topic to resolve, you may find it takes more time than you expect. You want people on the project team who are really prepared to give their full commitment, not just an occasional passing visit. Think back to the ratings you've given people on the project dashboard and be prepared to really challenge someone's commitment and interest.

How many people should you have on your training design team? Ideally aim for about 6 to 10 people in total. Fewer than 6 people will make for snappy meetings, but will place extra demands on the creativity of those present. It may also mean that there is limited 'ownership' of the resulting programme across the business. Having more than 10 people enables you to draw on a wide range of experience and knowledge across the business. However, it may be difficult to schedule meetings, and they may last longer than you would wish.

Discuss roles, responsibilities and accountability

Once you've agreed who's going to contribute, it's important to discuss and agree these three interrelated aspects:

1. What roles do people expect to play? Do they see themselves as sources of knowledge or expertise to be consulted on critical points?

2. What specific responsibilities are they prepared to accept?

3. Who is accountable for the overall success of the venture, and how is that cascaded down to you?

Clarifying these issues early on will avoid much heartache later in the design cycle!

Discuss how the learning needs will be assessed

First of all, why have we called this section 'learning needs' and not by the more familiar name 'training needs'? The reason is simple – what we have to discover first is what people need to learn. Once we know that, we can decide the most appropriate way for them to learn, and training is but one of the available options.

At this early stage you may not have a clear idea of how and where the learning needs will be assessed, let alone who will do it. But it's useful to have some discussion about the overall methodology that could be adopted, and gain some commitment on time and resources. However the learning needs analysis is to be done, there will inevitably be some disruption to work and that needs to be agreed at the highest levels:

- Who will do the learning needs analysis?

- On what sites, locations or shifts will it be carried out?

- Are there any other sources we can call upon?

- How will the results be processed and analysed?

- What's the timescale?

Learning needs analysis is a complete topic by itself – please see the next chapters.

Discover any limitations

Before you start any serious design work you need to know if any decisions have been taken that place any restrictions on what your final training solution might look like. I know this sounds a bit like 'putting the cart before the horse' but you need to know if there are any constraints you must work within before you start designing.

For example, having completed an exhaustive learning needs analysis, you might design a two-day training course only to be told, 'Sorry about this. We'd decided right at the start that the longest the staff could be away from their desks is half a day', or 'At the last Board Meeting it was decided to cascade these key global training messages using DVD', or 'Oh, didn't you hear? It was agreed that this topic was ideal for e-learning, so can you design it in that format?'

Whatever the cause, you will then have to go away and redesign the training programme and materials – it's a waste of your time, so why not ask before you start?

Establish links to other business initiatives or products

Now we come to a very important issue. Depending on the topic there will be a varying amount of company-specific information, processes, standards or policies that must be included, and you need to find and use them. For example, if you're designing a course on selling your company's products, you must use exactly the same materials used elsewhere in the sales process. Contracts, specifications, conditions, prices, terminology, brand images, etc will all be defined by the relevant marketing or procurement teams and you must use them all.

However, if you're designing a course on, for example, performance management, the situation will be more fluid. There will be many standard procedures and policies that are implemented across the company, and which will have to be incorporated into the course. An example is the company discipline procedure. There will also be many other aspects of performance management that are more generic, such as soft skills, which can be imported as best practice from outside the company. Examples could be asking open questions and helping an individual to boost his or her self-esteem.

If you're designing a presentation skills course then the situation is likely to be different again. Apart from some general advice about using standard PowerPoint templates there will probably be little mandatory material to be incorporated.

You will need to have access to all these materials, ideally in electronic format so they can be used in the course design with the minimum amount of effort. In many organizations these materials can be found on the company intranet, so they are readily accessed electronically.

One further aspect while we're on this section is to identify any content that *must* be included in your training package. Perhaps there has been a directive about some important issue, or there may have been some recent legislation that places onerous responsibilities on employers, which has to be stressed to all employees. For example, one can't imagine a recruitment and selection course that doesn't include a section on diversity.

Discuss company standards

Another different, but linked, issue is the need to ensure that the materials you develop in your course are consistent with other company materials, such as existing initiatives, buzzwords, images, logos or templates.

So, if you were developing a recruitment and selection course you would need to ensure that all the terms and content related to 'job descriptions' or the 'short-listing process' were consistent with the words and concepts used anywhere those concepts were discussed.

This may take some persistence as you will need to contact a wide range of people in the company to see if anything they have, or are responsible for, may impinge, however slightly, on the topic you are developing. Again it is time well spent – better to change something now than when many hours of development have been committed.

Set realistic deadlines

We all realize the importance of setting deadlines but they're not always *realistic*. Don't be pressurized into agreeing deadlines if, even as you're saying them, there's a little voice inside your head saying: 'You'll never meet that!'

Of course if you're designing a training programme linked to another initiative, like the launch of a new company product or service that has a high-profile 'go live' date, then you may not have too much choice. But the pressure to meet the publicized date may free up some extra resources that you might otherwise not have.

Inevitably your design process will take longer than expected:

- People won't always be available when scheduled.

- People change their requirements part way through the design process.

- Other departments suddenly announce changes to their part of the business, which have an impact on your course.

- Market forces may bring about changes in priorities or focus.

- Key people go on holiday, just when you need them.

So, when you're discussing the timescales, do remember to build in some additional time to allow for the unexpected.

Agree the review process and set key dates

Another important element is to discuss and agree how progress will be reviewed, and how any necessary corrective action will be scheduled and monitored.

Look ahead and set the key dates by which the various elements of the programme need to be in place. Getting these dates into people's diaries early is the only way you can be sure they'll be available at the critical moments. If it turns out that the meetings aren't needed they can always be cancelled, magically freeing up spare time.

Consider using project management software to keep everyone involved in the development of what will become a complex project. You may also wish to discuss and agree a standard review template that you can use to drive the agenda for each review meeting.

Agree budgets, funding and resources

Yet another vital aspect of managing your project is to secure the all-important financial support. Prior to the initial meeting prepare an outline budget that includes all the costs you can anticipate, plus some contingency.

Things always cost more than you expect and take more time than you budget for. Ensure that any changes that are requested as the project develops are fully documented so that you can justify any budget overruns.

You need to ensure that the budget appears on the agenda for the periodic review meetings, so that no one can accuse you of allowing costs to spiral out of control.

Agree the 'signing off' process

An important issue to clarify is who has the authority to 'sign off' the course and the associated documents at critical stages. This sounds easy, but I have had several challenging situations that arose because this hadn't been clarified.

On one occasion I was developing a performance management course for a client and had reached the final 'sign off' stage. At that point the manager who throughout had claimed to be the authority on the topic casually announced: 'I suppose I ought to run it past X, who is the topic owner for the company's discipline and capability procedures.' And of course the other manager, who had not been at all involved in the design process, quite reasonably declined to 'sign off' the materials, so we had to virtually start all over again.

To avoid this happening to you spend a few minutes agreeing:

- Who will 'sign off' the design.

- Provisional milestones for the various stages of the design.

- How changes will be agreed. Will you meet to discuss them? Will you do it by e-mail? Tele-conference?

- A process whereby, if no changes are sent within an agreed time, agreement can be assumed.

0.10

Activity 2.3 Your initial meeting agenda

Having considered the various issues you need to discuss during the initial planning meeting of your design team, please take a few minutes to draft the agenda.

The message is clear. To be successful you must prepare for every stage in your course design process. Don't just cruise along only to find that events collapse around you. Take heed of the well-known adage: *proper professional preparation prevents poor performance!*

3

Designing for global diversity

- The DESIGN process
- DESIGNing for global corporate diversity
- Why diversity is important
- Accessibility for trainer-led courses
- Accessibility for web-based materials
- The employer's 'two tick' commitment

THE DESIGN PROCESS

This chapter introduces you to three further important aspects of design:

1. A six-step DESIGN process you can use to manage any training design project.

2. How you can use this process to design training that takes account of global corporate diversity.

3. How you can provide for individual diversity by designing-in wider accessibility for course delegates and web-based materials, so meeting statutory requirements for disability.

Even if you are unlikely to be operating globally we would recommend reading this chapter, as DESIGN is a rigorous design methodology that you can apply to the way you manage your programme design, no matter at what scale you're operating. First of all then, let's introduce you to the DESIGN process before looking at the detail.

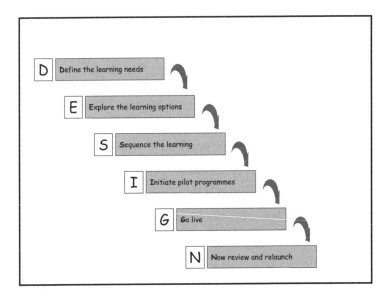

Figure 3.1 DESIGN for global corporate diversity

DESIGNING FOR GLOBAL CORPORATE DIVERSITY

Recent years have seen amazing changes in the way that many businesses operate, brought about through mergers, acquisitions and alliances, coupled with an explosion in the capability to exchange data electronically through the internet and intranets. For many training designers the advent of truly global operations presents many opportunities, including:

- The ability to achieve cost savings through economies of scale.

- Because of the wider potential markets for any particular training programme it's possible to design and stage programmes that any one company might not be able to justify.

- By pooling training budgets from companies operating around the globe, there are opportunities to develop programmes hitherto thought too costly.

- With the introduction of 'virtual' teams, designers can call upon the expertise of fellow professionals worldwide, and so share knowledge and expertise on a previously unheard-of scale.

- The ability to share development tasks across the world has the potential to reduce development lead-times.

- The capacity to exchange huge amounts of data electronically gives the opportunity to share existing courseware and design materials between operating companies, so potentially reducing design costs.

- The easy sharing of information and course materials means that important messages can be delivered to a worldwide audience in a very short space of time.

It all sounds very positive – 'But there must be some down-sides,' I hear you say. And of course there are, including:

- The traditional 'not invented here' resistance to courses designed somewhere else still applies.

- Operating companies still like to give any training programme a local 'spin' to reflect the conditions in their culture and market.

- Local market forces will drive different priorities for the development and delivery of training programmes. What one country may see as 'top priority' may be second or third elsewhere.

- It's essential to design-in the capability to easily switch languages in any aspect of the course.

- A course designed for the UK market may need to be subtly amended for delivery in mainland Europe, more drastically modified for the North American market, and need major surgery for the Far East. We're talking about cultural issues here, not just language.

- Forming a 'virtual' team may be relatively easy but getting people to commit to timescales, and then deliver on them, may be harder.

As you can appreciate, on balance there are more advantages than disadvantages, which is just as well because the corporate culture will 'encourage' you to work with your colleagues across the globe. Developing a programme suitable for global markets is complex and we suggest you use the following DESIGN process to give a standard, logical format you can work through no matter where you are located. Many of the issues are covered in depth in individual chapters and we're not intending to duplicate the material here. We simply aim to give you an overview of the six steps so you can see how they all fit together, and decide how you might adapt them for your own use.

Step 1. Define the learning needs

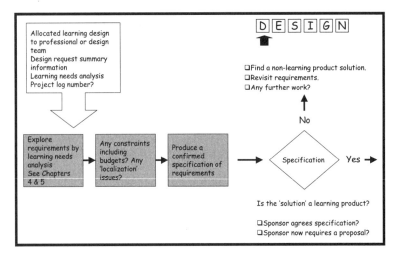

Figure 3.2 Define the learning needs

Purpose

The purpose of this step is to:

- Define, in consultation with the sponsor and their organization, the human performance requirements in terms of learning needs.

- Identify constraints, localization issues and budget limits.

- Validate any existing needs analysis.

- Confirm that a learning solution is appropriate.

Inputs

The inputs to this step in the process might include:

- Allocated learning design professional or design team.
- Design request summary information.
- Learning needs analysis.
- Do you have a project log? If so, allocate a number.

Actions

The actions you might expect to take include:

- Explore requirements – carry out learning needs analysis (see Chapters 4 and 5 for more detail).
- Discuss any constraints you might identify, including budgets.
- Are there any 'localization' issues – for example, what languages would be required? Are there any 'cultural' issues that need to be reflected in the courseware?
- Summarize what you find and draft an initial specification of requirements.

Outputs

The outputs from this step might include:

- Confirmed requirements specification.
- Updated project log (if appropriate).

Decision point

The key decision point before moving on could be:

- Is a learning product the right 'solution' to the performance issue?
- If the answer is 'Yes':
    - Does the sponsor agree the specification?
    - Does the sponsor now require a proposal?
- If the answer is 'No':

- Find a non-learning product solution.

- Revisit the requirements.

- It's possible there may be no further work.

Step 2. Explore the learning options

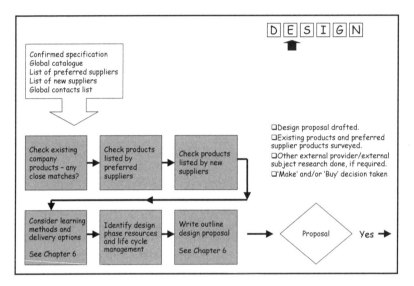

Figure 3.3 Explore the learning options

Purpose

Create an outline proposal highlighting options and the preferred course of action.

Inputs

- Confirmed specification from Step 1.

- The company global catalogue of existing course and resources.

- The list of preferred suppliers.

- The list of new suppliers and their products.

- Global contacts list.

Actions

- Are there any existing products in the company worldwide catalogue which are acceptable?

- If so, would they require significant language/cultural modification?

- Do any of our existing preferred suppliers have acceptable products?

- Do any other external providers have acceptable products?

- Consider learning methods and delivery options.

- Identify design phase resources – people, time and budgets.

- Consider 'life cycle management' – how long will it be 'on the shelf' and who will manage it?

- Write an outline design proposal.

Outputs

- Learning design proposal.

- Updated project log (if appropriate).

Decision points

- Outline design proposal drafted.

- 'Make' and/or 'buy' decisions taken.

Step 3. Sequence the learning

Purpose

- Design the overall flow of the training.

- Gain sponsor's agreement to the outline design.

Inputs

- Outline design proposal.

- Effective learning design techniques.

- Discussions with sponsor.

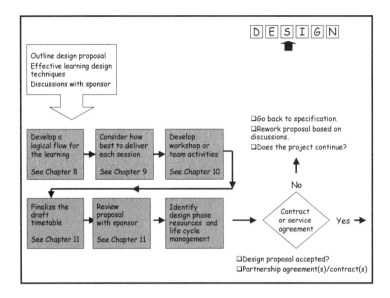

Figure 3.4 Sequence the learning

Actions

- Develop a logical flow for the learning.

- Consider how best to deliver each session.

- Develop any workshop or team activities.

- Are there any sessions requiring language or cultural modification?

- Must the programme be delivered by local trainers, or would 'foreign' trainers be acceptable?

- Finalize the draft timetable.

- Review proposal with sponsor.

- Identify design phase resources and life cycle management.

Output

Final design proposal.

Decision point

- Is the final design proposal accepted?

- If 'Yes':

  - Develop partnership agreement(s) and/or contract(s).

  - Draft contract or service agreement.

- If 'No':

  - Go back to specification.

  - Rework proposal based on discussions.

  - Does the project continue?

Step 4. Initiate pilot programmes

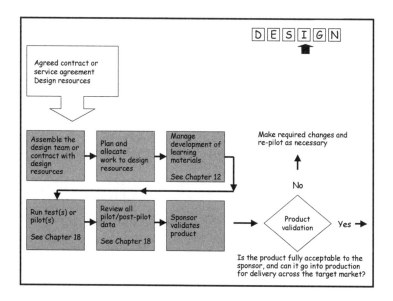

Figure 3.5 Initiate pilot programmes

Purpose

Turn the agreed design proposal into learning products ready for testing in the pilot/test phase.

Inputs

- Agreed contracts or service agreements.
- Design resources.

Actions

- Assemble the design team or contract with design resources.
- Plan and allocate work to design resources in the required timeframe.
- Manage development of learning materials.
- Run test(s) or pilot(s).
- Review all pilot/post-pilot validation data.
- Sponsor validates product.

Output

Product validation.

Decision point

- Is the product fully acceptable to the sponsor and can it go into production for delivery across the target market?
- If 'Yes':
  - Go ahead and make available to all operational training units.
- If 'No':
  - Make required changes and re-pilot as necessary.

Step 5. Go live

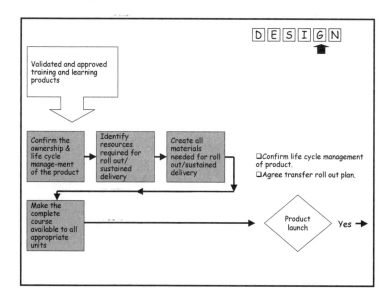

Figure 3.6 Go live

Purpose

To move a newly designed and tested product into sustainable delivery.

Input

Validated and approved training and learning products.

Actions

- Confirm the ownership and life cycle management of the product. Who will be responsible for it initially? Who will manage it in the longer term and make decisions about the product life cycle?

- Identify resources required for roll out and sustained delivery.

- Create all materials needed for roll out and sustained delivery.

- Make the complete course available to all appropriate units and departments.

Output

Complete learning and training programmes.

Decision points

- Has the life cycle management of the product been confirmed?
- Has the transfer roll out plan been agreed?

Step 6. Now review and relaunch

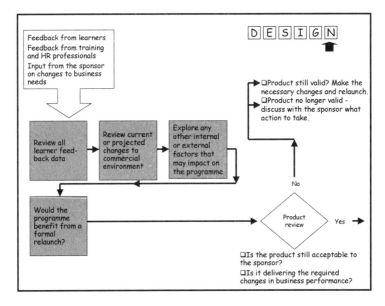

Figure 3.7 Now review and relaunch

Validation is a continuous activity enabling you to report back to the stakeholders on the success of the venture. If the required level of performance is not being delivered you can, if required, modify the training programme accordingly. So it's important to note that, although the review and relaunch step is the last in the cycle, you need to be working on this aspect throughout the whole design process. If you are always considering how you will measure the output from the programme, by the time you get to the end you will have produced some meaningful and workable measures.

Purpose

Review the continued relevance and effectiveness of the learning/training programme, and modify as appropriate.

Inputs

- Feedback from learners.

- Feedback from training and HR professionals.

- Input from the sponsor on changes to business needs.

Actions

- Review all learner feedback, and also feedback from training and HR professionals. Does it suggest any changes are required to the programme?

- Review current or projected changes to commercial environment – does anything impact on the overall programme?

- Are there any other internal/external factors that might impact on the programme?

- Would the programme benefit from a formal relaunch?

Output

Balanced review of the current state of the product, supported by factual and anecdotal evidence.

Decision points

- Is the product still acceptable to the sponsor?

- Is it delivering the required changes in business performance?

- Are there any other markets globally where it might be required?

- If 'Yes':

  - Consider relaunching the product to retain staff awareness of it.

  - Market the product more energetically using all internal communications media, focusing on benefits and sustained improvements to business performance.

- If 'No' then react appropriately:

> – If the product is still valid but in need of updating or a 'makeover', then make the necessary changes and relaunch.

- If the product is no longer valid, discuss with the sponsor what action to take.

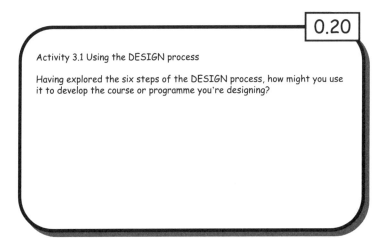

0.20

Activity 3.1 Using the DESIGN process

Having explored the six steps of the DESIGN process, how might you use it to develop the course or programme you're designing?

WHY DIVERSITY IS IMPORTANT

Diversity is about everyone – it's about creating working cultures and practices that respect, welcome and harness difference for the benefit of everyone. Some differences are visible, for example sex, ethnicity and some disabilities, while others are not visible, for example sexuality, nationality, religion, education, class and experience.

Valuing diversity is not about encouraging or forcing people to 'fit in', but it is about identifying aspects of the existing culture that prevent people from being naturally inclusive in the way that they relate to customers, existing or potential colleagues, partners or any other stakeholders. So, any training you design should help create an environment where people from different backgrounds, with different experiences and perspectives, feel valued for the positive benefits they can contribute to any organization.

Valuing diversity is not about saying 'yes' to everyone, or giving in to requests to accommodate a particular difference. All organizations have their own values and professional standards, and valuing diversity does not require those values or standards to change. However, everyone should be prepared to question their values and standards to ensure that these are not deliberately or unintentionally discriminating unfairly against people either within or outside the organization.

Why this is important to your business

You may be surprised to see a section on diversity so early in the book, but its position says volumes about the importance of the subject to anyone producing training, and especially web-based materials. The emphasis on providing wider accessibility has been mainly triggered by legislation.

Respecting people as individuals, and providing for their every need, is a fundamental part of any training design, and the extent to which your programme is successful will depend on several elements:

- the design of the training – which you can control;

- the attitude and style of the trainer – over which you have less control;

- the pervading culture within your organization – over which you have even less control.

Web-based products or services

Before we focus on training design let's take a step back and look at the wider scene. There are few large companies nowadays that don't offer some form of web-based access to their customers, and many others have internal websites or offer training involving web-based access. If your company is providing an e-learning course as part of a public programme (open to anyone), or to members of your organization who have accessibility problems (poor sight, dyslexia, mobility, etc) then you have to provide the content in a format that will be 'accessible' to all potential users.

This is an issue that affects everyone in a company from the board downwards and is particularly important for customer-facing staff. Many companies may say that their 'customer service to disabled people is great', but they may not have measured this belief against anything specific. Your company may actually be turning disabled customers off because it has not even identified who these customers are and their needs.

A common example is the perception of a disabled person being someone in a wheelchair, and ignores the remaining millions of people within the group who are not wheelchair users. Many disabled people are not disabled in as obvious a way as a wheelchair user – but their needs have to be met too.

Apart from the moral case, there is also a statutory duty. In Australia in June 1999, Bruce Maguire lodged a complaint with the Human Rights and Equal Opportunity Commission (HREOC) under the Disability Discrimination Act. His complaint concerned the website of the Sydney Organizing Committee for the Olympic Games (SOCOG), which Maguire alleged was inaccessible to him as a blind person.

According to the complaint, Maguire, unlike most blind people online, does not use a screen reader to read aloud the elements of a web page. Instead, he uses a refreshable Braille display. But neither technology can understand and turn into voice an image that lacks a text equivalent. Nearly all web pages online have some kind of graphics, including high-profile sites like those associated with major sporting events. Maguire contended that significant parts of the SOCOG website, Olympics.com, were inaccessible to him.

On 24 August 2000, the HREOC released its decision and supported Maguire's complaint, ordering certain access provisions to be in place on the Olympics.com site by 15 September 2000. This case demonstrates that the legal need for accessibility is so clear-cut, and the means of achieving basic accessibility so straightforward, that even a powerful international organization can lose in a judicial proceeding.

ACCESSIBILITY FOR TRAINER-LED COURSES

There are compelling reasons to ensure that all your training designs are fully accessible to all people, irrespective of their individual capabilities. Clearly the more you can design 'accessibility' into your courses or programmes the less opportunity the trainer has to dilute your good work. We'll explore two different aspects of designing improved accessibility – the practical issues associated with running a trainer-led course or workshop, and the separate, but related topic of designing web-based materials.

Much will depend on the attitude and flexibility of the trainer delivering the programme because, no matter how well designed the content, trainers are often confronted with unexpected situations. A good trainer will be aware of the way people react to situations or activities, and enable them to derive most of the benefit of a programme by helping them to adapt the situation or task to suit their own capability. All it takes is a bit of imagination and sensitivity:

- Many delegates arrive feeling anxious and simply need reassurance.

- A delegate on a presentation skills course, delivering a presentation from a wheelchair, required a few small changes.

- I've easily helped delegates with dyslexia to steer their way through a course and avoid being the flipchart scribe.

- I quickly adapted to a delegate with Tourette's Syndrome, though it was helpful that her colleagues already knew what to expect.

- Similarly, I quickly adapted to a delegate with exaggerated speech and behaviours caused by pronounced autism.

- Perhaps the most challenging situation was an (unexpected) blind delegate on a course that relied heavily on visual slides.

Wheelchair access

A fundamental issue is ensuring that everyone can reach the training room. This can sometimes be a problem for wheelchair users. It's certainly worth mentioning this in your venue specification. If you're planning any significant amount of desk-based work, for example IT training, it's also worth specifying that you need purpose-built office desks that have a work surface that can be raised or lowered to provide easy wheelchair access.

Course activities

When selecting activities or tasks for your course design, you will do so expecting that all delegates can play a full part in whatever is happening. But wherever possible try to give guidance to the trainer on how he or she might be able to adapt the task or delegate roles to allow for people who are unable to play their full part. For example, many activities depend on accurate feedback for the full learning to be gained, so the trainer might suggest someone plays the role of observer. Or a task might require some less demanding role, which someone would willingly take on. From personal experience I would always explain what the task involves, then ask the person what they would feel comfortable doing, rather than make the decision for them. You'll often be surprised by what people will volunteer for!

ACCESSIBILITY FOR WEB-BASED MATERIALS

International accessibility standards

Now let's turn our attention to any web-based materials you may be designing, as there are so many opportunities to improve accessibility, so long as you're aware of them. The World Wide Web Consortium's (W3C) commitment to lead the web to its full potential includes promoting a high degree of accessibility for people with disabilities. The Web Accessibility Initiative (WAI), part of the W3C, in coordination with organizations around the world, is pursuing web accessibility through five primary areas of work:

1. technology;

2. guidelines;

3. tools;

4. education and outreach;

5. research and development.

The current version of the WAI Web Content Accessibility Guidelines (WCAG) can be found at **www.w3.org/TR/WAI-WEBCONTENT**.

Recent legislation

Recent legislation in the UK, the Disability Discrimination Act, includes reference to the provision of goods, facilities and services. Interpreting the legal jargon reveals the following guidelines:

● All users should be able to operate the websites successfully.

● Content/controls should be understandable to as many users as possible.

● Websites should be developed using web technologies that maximize the use of current/future accessibility and assistive technologies.

● Changes to websites should be assessed in their own right and also for their impact on overall site accessibility before release.

● Usability should be considered along with accessibility but should not be compromised by accessibility features.

- The product development life cycle of all sites should be customer-centred, including accessibility testing with real users wherever possible.

The best thing to do is to look through all the relevant websites and decide what is appropriate for your own situation. Let's briefly explore some of the key issues for the different categories of users.

Physical accessibility

One obvious potential problem area is people who find using a mouse difficult. Many sites use access keys, which are essentially keyboard shortcuts on a website that give users of keyboards or screen readers quick and easy access to all the main areas of the site. The keys operate functions, just like they did in the DOS days, long before Windows!

Dyslexia

Advice from groups representing the interests of people with dyslexia is straight-forward and easy to implement, stressing the need for clear and uncluttered screen design. Follow these guidelines for success:

- Keep the use of text on any screen to a minimum.

- Use short paragraphs, with clear headings.

- Choose font colours carefully.

- Use pale backgrounds.

- Use sans serif font, 12 point.

In fact these guidelines follow the advice for good design of any visual aids.

Hearing difficulties

If you're designing an e-learning course it's relatively easy at the design stage to build in captions or subtitles, which someone who has hearing difficulties can easily access. Essentially you use the same text as would be spoken for the voiceover, but it would be displayed on request.

Visual impairment

Web designers can use a screen reader that converts the on-screen text to a voice-over to enable blind people to use web materials easily.

THE EMPLOYER'S 'TWO TICK' COMMITMENT

Many employers have signed up for the 'two tick' symbol system, which gives specific commitments to disabled people regarding employment. It's worth bearing these in mind as you design your courses, so you can incorporate them wherever necessary.

Commitment 1

To interview all disabled applicants who meet the minimum criteria for a job vacancy and consider them on their abilities.

The aim of this commitment is to encourage disabled people to apply for jobs by offering an assurance that, should they meet the minimum criteria, they will be given the opportunity to demonstrate their abilities at interview stage.

Commitment 2

To ensure there is a mechanism in place for disabled employees to discuss at any time, but at least once a year, what they can do to make sure they can develop and use their abilities.

The aim of this commitment is to ensure that disabled employees are getting the same opportunities as others to develop and progress within their job.

Commitment 3

To make every effort when employees become disabled to make sure they stay in employment.

The aim of this commitment is to make sure that employees know that, should they become disabled, they will have your support to enable them to continue in their current job or an alternative one. Retaining an employee who has become disabled means keeping their valuable skills and experience and saves on the cost of recruiting a replacement.

Commitment 4

To take action to ensure that all employees develop the appropriate level of disability awareness needed to make your commitments work.

The aim of this commitment is to provide awareness of disability issues to all staff in order to improve the working environment.

Commitment 5

Each year, to review the five commitments and what has been achieved, to plan ways to improve on them and let employees and Jobcentre Plus know about progress and future plans.

The aim of this commitment is for the employer to monitor its practices and achievements in meeting its symbol commitments and to identify areas for further progress or good practice to share with others. The commitment also helps managers to plan how to let people know initially that the company has become a symbol user, and to keep them up to date with developments.

Be positive about accessibility

The main point to emerge from this chapter is to be positive about accessibility as you progress through your training design project. It starts right at the beginning when it's much easier, and less expensive, to build these features in. So remember to put accessibility positively on the agenda for every step of the journey.

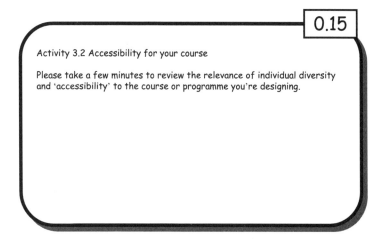

0.15

Activity 3.2 Accessibility for your course

Please take a few minutes to review the relevance of individual diversity and 'accessibility' to the course or programme you're designing.

4

Formal learning needs analysis

- The importance of learning needs analysis
- Who will you consult?
- Learning needs checklist
- Data collection techniques
- Practical examples
- Now focus on your course

THE IMPORTANCE OF LEARNING NEEDS ANALYSIS

Having assembled the project team, you're now ready to start the design journey by tackling the first step of the DESIGN process. Start by analysing how people need to change in order for them to deliver the new levels of performance required. Then, before starting any design work, get the recommended course of action 'signed off' by the key stakeholders.

Define the learning needs

The purpose of this chapter is to introduce you to a variety of formal methods for assessing how people need to change in order to be able to deliver the new level of performance required. In the next chapter we'll explore several approaches that teams can use, with your guidance, to carry out their own learning needs analysis. Hopefully you will find that using a combination of these approaches will enable you to discover the real learning needs, so that you can design an appropriate package of experiences, to deliver the required changes in performance in a timely, stimulating and cost-efficient manner. Spending time early on with the key people involved in the project may save you valuable design time later. Many years ago, as a young soldier, I was introduced to one of the Army's basic maxims – *time spent in reconnaissance is seldom wasted.* And it's true!

WHO WILL YOU CONSULT?

As you plan how to conduct your needs analysis, one of the first decisions you will have to make is *who* you will approach – whose views or opinions will you seek? There are many candidates, including:

- strategists – the 'movers and shakers';
- known 'champions' of specific initiatives;
- managers and team leaders;
- staff;
- internal specialists or experts;
- recognized industry or topic experts;
- customers or suppliers;
- government or regulatory bodies;
- professional institutions;
- trade unions;
- external consultants;
- independent specialist organizations;
- similar industries or professions.

As you develop the list of people within your organization who you intend to consult, it's important to remember that you need to be sensitive to their feelings and anxieties. Many people feel threatened if someone approaches them to ask about the way they or their team currently perform their jobs. At the very least they may see it as an adverse comment on their skill or commitment, and many may fear that it heralds future unwelcome changes, or even job losses.

Also ensure that you canvass views across a fully representative population, recognizing that some people work in remote locations or at unsocial hours. It will be much easier to get 'buy in' to your proposals if everyone can feel they have had an input to the needs analysis.

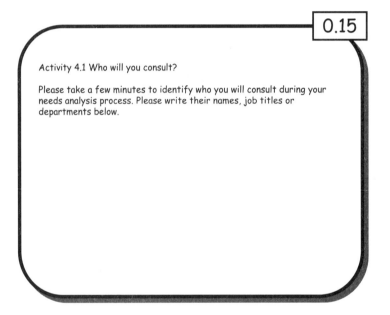

0.15

Activity 4.1 Who will you consult?

Please take a few minutes to identify who you will consult during your needs analysis process. Please write their names, job titles or departments below.

LEARNING NEEDS CHECKLIST

By this stage you've decided who you will approach but you may be a little uncertain about what you will ask them. To help you with this we've given you a detailed checklist of topics to cover and, although you may not need to discuss every item, this should give you a starting point. It's unlikely that you will be able to run through the set of questions in the sequence we've given, as people will often talk around the subject in an unstructured way. Listen carefully and capture the information they give, using the checklist as a prompt to ensure nothing is missed. Incidentally, the content and sequence are replicated in the chapter dealing with the training proposal, and both are on the CD ROM for easy reference. There are three main sections and we'll explore each one in detail:

1. Background to the problem/requirement.

2. Detailed exploration of the problem/requirement.

3. Delivery logistics and constraints.

1. Background to the problem/requirement

What is the problem/requirement?

Your aim is to produce a clear problem or requirement statement. This helps you and the sponsor to understand the problem in simple terms, eg: 'Our system users are having difficulty with many of the transactions on our new X software.' Where problems are more complex, and may have a number of contributory factors, it helps to isolate and define those that are likely to have learning and development solutions, and those that will require other solutions. It's useful to ask people to articulate what success would look or feel like, as this can give you ideas about how you can see or measure the impact of any learning or training interventions:

- What do people need to do that they currently cannot do or are not doing?

- What would success look like?

    - What would people be doing?

    - How would they be behaving?

    - What measures would change?

- What has given rise to the requirement?

Your aim is to understand the likely cause of the problem. Is it a short-term issue requiring a 'sticking plaster' (perhaps updating workshops or courses) or a more systemic issue that requires longer-term treatment (eg, a new starter skills development programme)? Specific issues to explore or discuss include:

- Operational, legislative, governance, technical, social or other 'big picture' drivers.

- Need to 'dovetail' the intervention with other initiatives within the company or industry.

- Changing market requirements.

- New systems/processes/procedures/work practices.

- Any other significant changes planned – for example new organizational structures.

- Externally driven timescales or criteria you need to take account of.

- Changing job roles.

- New people unskilled/untrained.

What is the impact on the business?

It's important to understand the relative importance and cost to the business for two reasons. First, it can help justify any expensive proposals you are likely to suggest using a cost/benefit approach. Secondly it helps you to prioritize your efforts and secure resources from your manager. Specific issues to explore or discuss include:

- What is the likely impact of doing nothing/what is at stake?

- What savings could be made by intervening?

- What would be the potential value of intervening?

2. Detailed exploration of the problem/requirement

Who is involved? It's important to establish as much as you can about the number, type and location of the people involved as this information will have an influence on the learning or training strategy proposed. Different groups of people may need different products more appropriate to their situation and role in the organization. Some groups may have a greater priority for the training, which may affect your roll out plan.

If they are scattered globally then an e-learning solution may not only be cost-effective but may be the only way of reaching everybody. Alternatively, you may need to partner with external training providers who operate in the locations. There are other issues related to the location, the most obvious being the language used. Even if English is officially spoken locally, not everyone will appreciate the subtleties of English words, phrases or expressions, which can so easily change the meaning of what's being said. This is especially important in self-study products where the trainer isn't available to explain any misunderstandings. Specific issues to explore or discuss include:

- Personnel company-wide?

- Personnel within a specific business sector?

- Personnel within a specific site/unit/department?

Are they:

- Managerial/supervisory?

- Non-managerial professional/technical?

- Operators?

- Support staff?

How many people are there in each category? Are they:

- Represented by a trade union or professional body?

- Does the trade union or professional body need to be involved in the design process?

What are:

- Their educational levels (eg degree, non-degree, craft qualifications, other recognized vocational qualifications)?

- Their nationality/nationalities?

- The language needs – is translation required?

- The major cultural sensitivities, if any?

- Their known personality characteristics or learning styles?

What type of performance is required?

The information you collect under this heading will influence the learning or training strategy you develop. You need to understand what performance is required by the individuals and the skills, knowledge and behaviours needed in order to perform effectively. The type of skills involved will also influence the training media and methodologies chosen. Finally, understanding the persistence and decay of the skills or knowledge will help you understand the frequency needed and whether certification, testing or accreditation is required. Specific issues to explore or discuss include:

- manual/operative/transactional skills;
- interpersonal or behavioural skills;
- technical or professional skills;
- the difficulty level of the skills;
- the required level of accuracy;
- the frequency with which they are performed;
- any safety-critical issues;
- whether there is a mandatory or legislative requirement;
- whether certification or accreditation is required;
- the need for regular reinforcement to prevent rapid decay of skills;
- the information required to underpin the skills;
- the behaviour required to underpin the skills;
- whether different groups will need different approaches or products.

3. Delivery logistics and constraints

Where does the learning/training need to be delivered?

You obviously need to discover where the learning or training is to be delivered and the preferred delivery methods, such as on site, on-the-job versus off-site, etc. The answers here are obviously closely linked to who is involved, where they are located and the relative costs of the options. Specific issues to explore or discuss include:

- Worldwide?
- National/geographical region?
- At work, on site?
- At a company learning/training centre?

- At a company learning resource centre?

- External venue?

- Home?

- A mixture? If so who, where, what and how?

When does the learning/training need to be delivered?

You need to determine the urgency of the requirement and the lead-time available before the first programme has to be delivered. This will obviously influence the design resources required and the make or buy-in decision. Specific issues to explore or discuss include:

- What are the timescales?

- What is the lead-time to the first event?

- Does it need to be completed by a specific date?

What are the potential delivery approaches?

At this stage the aim is to understand whether there are any preferred delivery approaches or constraints that will restrict or make certain approaches unacceptable. Specific issues to explore or discuss include:

- What approaches may be suitable and/or acceptable?
    - Common programme for all?
    - Bespoke versions for specific target groups?
    - Modular approach – mandatory core sections plus electives?
- Are there priorities for delivering learning to specific groups?
- Is a phased delivery strategy likely and/or appropriate?
- What would the phases be?
- What is the likely 'shelf life' of the product?

Preferred delivery methodologies

Discover if there are any strong preferences for or against a particular delivery strategy. Do staff have access to the company Learning and Development Centres, or can they access learning online? Specific preferences to explore or discuss include:

- Learning on or off site.
- E-learning.
- Training centre based.
- Learning at the workplace.

What funding is available?

It's important to establish early on whether the person commissioning the work has the budget to pay for the product or, if not, has access to someone who has. Clarifying how much money is available and when it could be released is vital as it may affect the choice of the learning methodology selected. Specific issues to explore or discuss include:

- Is there a budget for the project?
- What is it?
- Who is/are the budget holder(s)?
- What is the relationship with the sponsor?
- How will work be paid for?

Are there any other constraints?

Determine whether there are any other major constraints, either known or suspected, that may affect the overall project. Specific issues to explore or discuss include:

- Do all end-users have access to the company network/intranet/internet?
- Can concurrent training be provided across the time zones involved?

Transfer or wider application

Determine if this product might have wider application to other businesses. If it does, it might be possible to involve other prime users who will jointly sponsor the work to reduce the costs to any one business and maximize the use of the design work. Equally, a wider application may free up additional design resources and so speed up the design process. Specific issues to explore or discuss include:

- Could the product have relevance outside the target groups?

- Could it be used elsewhere in the business?

- Are there other business units with similar developmental issues?

So now we return to the question we asked at the beginning of this section – what information will you collect? Please take some time to gather your ideas before we move on.

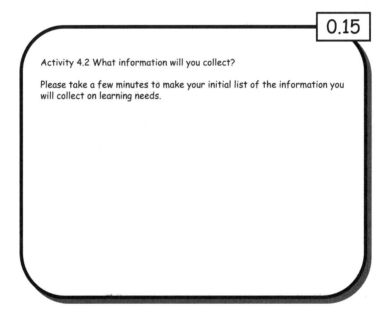

0.15

Activity 4.2 What information will you collect?

Please take a few minutes to make your initial list of the information you will collect on learning needs.

DATA COLLECTION TECHNIQUES

Now that you have a good idea of the information you need to collect you can consider how you will gather it. There are many ways to discover learning needs, some formal but many informal... and sometimes from unexpected sources. Let's illustrate this with a story.

Several years ago I was travelling by air from London to Paris. I arrived at the airport, as required by the airline, at 5.30 am – two hours before the scheduled departure time of 7.30 – and joined the other passengers at the departure gate. The

49

passengers waited patiently, watching the clock creep round towards the expected boarding time. As 7 am came and passed the passengers started to get restless. Finally at about 7.30 a member of staff abruptly announced that 'We've just been told that your flight has been delayed for four hours.' No reason was given, no apology was given and no alternatives were offered.

Immediately the previously quiet and orderly 100-odd passengers erupted into a noisy and unruly mob. The information desk was surrounded by passengers demanding explanations and transfers to other airlines. The staff gave out no more information and refused to organize transfers. Absolute chaos resulted and the staff had to placate scores of angry passengers, with all the resulting stress for everyone involved. I decided against joining in the fray and quietly stood back and let events unfold. Within an hour I learnt from another, more helpful member of staff, that all flights from London had been delayed because of fog covering Paris.

Back in the departure lounge, just before 10 am, I had a quiet word with the member of staff who made the original unhelpful announcement and discussed her approach. After some gentle questioning I got her to realize that if she had told people that the cause of the delay was fog, which would obviously affect every airline, her morning would have been a lot less stressful. Realizing that the delay was outside the airline's control, people would have reacted in a much more reasonable way. Hopefully she came out of that morning having learnt a valuable lesson!

So, 'observation' can be a very helpful way to discover learning needs – what other sources or methods can you call upon to discover them? You might wish to consider some of the following:

- interviews;
- questionnaires;
- focus groups;
- observation;
- feedback;
- customer complaints;
- fault reports;
- work samples;
- accident investigation;
- testing;

- skills audits;
- annual appraisals and performance reviews.

These sources can be placed in two main sub-groups – verbal or written, with varying degrees of interaction. Let's explore the advantages and disadvantages of the primary methods, leaving you to decide which will work best for you.

Verbal interactive methods

Overall – greater depth, detail and focus, but can lose accuracy and objectivity.

Interviews

- Structured interviews – consistency.
- Informal interviews – depth.
- Larger samples – accuracy.
- Face-to-face interviews – detail and candidness.

Advantages of interviews:

- Good for uncovering feelings and hidden causes.
- Non-verbal signals can indicate key issues.
- Spontaneity – follow the unexpected issue.

Disadvantages of interviews:

- Time-consuming.
- Unrepresentative sample can skew the results.
- Can be difficult to quantify.
- Very dependent on the skills of the interviewer.

Focus groups

A facilitated discussion with a representative group, which brings group dynamics into the analysis process.

Advantages of focus groups:

- Allows people to build on the ideas of others.

- Less repetition than individual interviews.

- Better use of time.

- Use the group to focus the training design effort.

- Develop group 'ownership' of the resulting programme.

Disadvantages of focus groups:

- Unskilled facilitator can allow the situation to go 'critical'.

- May be difficult to schedule.

- Quantifying the results may be difficult.

Written interactive methods

Overall – moderate depth of detail and easier to quantify. Moderate accuracy, objectivity and spontaneity.

Testing

- Structured analysis of skills and knowledge.

- Effectively follows broad needs analysis process.

- Presence of trainer may increase validity.

Advantages of testing:

- Good for uncovering specific skill deficiencies.

- Results easily quantified.

- Good for testing 'right' or 'wrong' solutions.

Disadvantages of testing:

- Limited availability of tailored, pre-validated tests.

- Testing may inhibit normal performance.

- Testing may build resistance to training.
- Inappropriate where there is no 'right' answer.

Questionnaires

- Larger samples – greater accuracy.
- The more random the sample, the more valid the results.
- Blend a variety of question formats.
- Give the option to remain anonymous.

Advantages of questionnaires:

- Option of anonymity may increase the accuracy.
- Portions of data easily quantifiable.
- Cost-effective – more people reached with less effort.
- Sample many people at the same time.

Disadvantages of questionnaires:

- Little opportunity for spontaneous clarification.
- Developing a valid questionnaire takes a lot of time.
- Low response rates.
- Inability to probe for root causes.

Semi-interactive methods

Overall – greater accuracy and objectivity. Moderate spontaneity, depth and relevance.

Observation

- Wide range of applications: time and motion studies or watching specific behaviours.
- Flexible approach – can involve one to many in the process.

Advantages of observation:

- Observer awareness does not alter performance.
- Resulting training should be highly relevant to the operational setting.

Disadvantages of observation:

- Observers must be well trained.
- They need the right skills, and awareness of what to look for.
- People may change their performance while being observed.

Work samples

Examples include:

- letters/proposals;
- product samples;
- job descriptions;
- design sketches;
- financial projections;
- project plans.

Advantages of work samples:

- Highly effective way to assess results currently produced.
- Easily obtained with little interruption to current work.

Disadvantages of work samples:

- Less able to reveal potential skills.
- Often require skilled analysis.
- Limited to internal factors.

Documents

Examples include:

- summaries of appraisals and performance reviews;

- third-party feedback and complaints;
- fault reports;
- training manuals;
- policy handbooks;
- budgets;
- employee records;
- management reports;

Advantages of documents:

- Easily obtained with minimal disruption.
- Extremely objective way to collect data.

Disadvantages of documents:

- Data may not be current.
- Skilled analysis may be needed.
- Less able to uncover root problems.

Deciding which techniques to use

As you can see, there is a wide range of formal techniques or approaches open to you, and your choice will depend on the operational constraints within which you have to work. If possible, opt for a blend of several methods, as this may help you to get more representative results, rather than relying on one method.

PRACTICAL EXAMPLES

Using questionnaires

A sample questionnaire is shown in Figure 4.1, which was designed to gather information about learning needs associated with speed reading. Alongside the text on the left we've shown the types of questions being used. Please record in the boxes to the right of the text which types of information you think each question is designed to target.

Types of Question	Speed reading questionnaire	Types of Information
	We are assessing the need for a course on speed reading and we would appreciate your responses to the following questions. It's purely voluntary and shouldn't take you more than a few minutes. Please be assured your answers are confidential.	
Open	1. Please briefly describe your role.	
Rating	2. Please rate your level of need for speed reading and comprehension with the following types of material:	

Reports/proposals   [no need] 1 2 3 4 5 [strong need]
Non-fiction books   [no need] 1 2 3 4 5 [strong need]
Fiction books   [no need] 1 2 3 4 5 [strong need]
Newspapers   [no need] 1 2 3 4 5 [strong need]
Technical manuals/documents [no need] 1 2 3 4 5 [strong need]
Letters/ promotional material [no need] 1 2 3 4 5 [strong need]
Magazines/professional journals[no need] 1 2 3 4 5 [strong need]

Ranking

3. Please rank the following skills in order of importance to you – '1' being the most important and '5' least important.

___ Remembering reading material more effectively.
___ Taking brief and effective notes of written material.
___ Deepening comprehension and understanding of written material.
___ Increasing reading speed.
___ Summarizing and applying written materials.

Open

4. Have you ever studied 'speed reading' before?

If 'Yes' please briefly describe what you did and the results you achieved.

Clarifying

5. Please tick any of these concepts you're familiar with.

__ Area reading   __ Multiple reading process
__ Recall patterns   __ Previewing reading material
__ Reading hand motions __ Subvocalization

Open

6. Please describe one or two specific methods you currently use to manage your reading load.

Open

7. Under what circumstances and with what types of material do you find it most difficult to read quickly and effectively?

Forced choice

8. How do you learn most effectively? Please select only one.
__ Studying underlying concepts   __ Step-by-step instruction
__ Observing others   __ Just getting 'stuck in'

Figure 4.1 Sample questionnaire

Learning needs analysis in action

One interesting assignment I undertook was to assess the learning needs of a group of staff who would be operating a new production line in a food factory. The production line would comprise a series of different machines from varied suppliers, and would process raw materials into sealed sachets, which would then be packed into cartons, which would in turn be loaded onto pallets before despatch to customers.

We got together a representative group of the operators, together with the design engineers. We posted the machine diagrams around the walls in the sequence they would operate in the new production line. Then we started at the beginning of the production line and worked through to the end. All I did was to ask questions:

- 'Where will that come from?'

- 'Who will do it?'

- 'Where will it go next?'

- 'What control will you have over...?'

- 'How will you monitor the quality?'

As the questions were answered we wrote the responses on Post-it Notes, which we stuck on the appropriate part of the engineering diagram. By the end of three hours we had achieved quite a lot. We had a very clear idea of the role of the different operators at each stage of the manufacturing process, which we later turned into a formal training plan. More specifically, we knew:

- how many operators would be required;

- what specific actions the operators would have to take at each stage of the manufacturing process;

- how the quality of the product would be maintained;

- how the operators would monitor stocks of the various ingredients and materials, and when to order more;

- which faults the operators could clear themselves, and which they would have to call the engineers for.

As a bonus we had also identified two major engineering conflicts in the production line, because it was the first time that anyone had 'walked' through the process from start to end. If we hadn't identified them the production line would have stopped within the first 30 minutes of operation on day one, with all the resulting chaos while the problem was sorted out under intense pressure.

NOW FOCUS ON YOUR COURSE

Having looked at this topic from a theoretical stance we'd now suggest you consider the course you're designing and decide how you'll carry out learning needs analysis yourself. Please take a few moments to make a preliminary selection of the approaches you think might work for you. In addition to the eight approaches we've shown above, we've also included space for two other methods that you may know of.

0.20

Activity 4.3 Discovering the learning needs

Please take a few minutes to identify which of the methods you might use to discover the learning needs for the course you're designing.

Method	Yes	Not sure	No
Interviews			
Focus groups			
Testing			
Questionnaires			
Observation			
Work samples			
Documents			
Other			
Other			

In the next chapter we'll explore some alternative approaches you can use for discovering learning needs – the extra bonus for these methods is that they can be used by team members themselves, leaving you free to adopt an advisory role.

5

Team-based needs analysis

> - Introduction
> - Functional competences
> - Core competences
> - Critical work processes

INTRODUCTION

In the previous chapter we looked at a variety of more formal methods for assessing learning needs, which involve you in collecting and analysing the data. But there may be times when this approach isn't appropriate:

- The team involved may be small and simply doesn't warrant a formal learning needs analysis.

- Your high workload may limit the number of projects you can personally get involved in.

- The team involved has a strong identity and may reject anything not generated internally. You know – 'not invented here'!

If any of these conditions apply, why not try one of the following 'do it yourself' approaches? The first group are competency-based, while the final approach is based on examining critical work processes.

FUNCTIONAL COMPETENCES

Let's assume you've been asked to assess the learning needs of a group of people who work together, in a specific team or shift. Get them together and set the scene by explaining that you wish to hear their ideas on the learning needs of the team before starting to develop a training plan. If the number of people is greater than, say, 10, you may wish to break them into two groups for this process. There are four simple steps to follow:

1. List the tasks or activities.

2. Define standards of performance.

3. List the team members.

4. Assess each team member's performance.

Step 1. List the tasks or activities

The team should start by listing all the main tasks or activities they need to be able to do to perform their jobs effectively. The tasks should be broken down into small enough 'chunks' to be meaningful, and listed vertically on flipchart sheets. To show how it works in practice let's consider the results developed by a team working in a financial services company. An extract from their list of tasks is shown in Figure 5.1.

Step 2. Define standards of performance

The next step is to agree standards of performance that can be applied across all the tasks or activities and, in this case, the team defined the following six levels of performance:

- Level 1. Has to refer a task or query to someone else.

- Level 2. Can process 25 per cent of the task being scored to a quality standard of 95 per cent right first time without referral.

Task						
Processing customers' orders						
Planning production						
Client detail changes						
Policy reviews						
Fund variation reviews						
Task X						
Task Y						

Figure 5.1 List the team's tasks

- Level 3. Can process 50 per cent of the task being scored to a quality standard of 95 per cent right first time without referral.
- Level 4. Can process 80 per cent of the task being scored to a quality standard of 95 per cent right first time without referral.
- Level 5. Can process 80 per cent of the task being scored to a quality standard of 95 per cent right first time without referral. Capable of planning and delivering training to others in these tasks.
- Level 6. Can process 80 per cent of the task being scored to a quality standard of 95 per cent right first time without referral. Capable of planning and delivering training to others in these tasks. Competent to perform quality checks on team members.

Step 3. List the team members

This is the easy bit – simply add the names of all the team members across the top of the matrix.

Step 4. Assess each team member's performance

Step 4 is when the team assesses the competence of each person on every task, using the agreed performance criteria. This may take some time because it's essential that everyone agrees with the rating system – but it's time well spent. The resulting matrix quickly reveals where the team has sufficient coverage on the key tasks, and also shows in which areas they are vulnerable. A training programme can then be developed to plug the critical gaps. The final matrix looks the one shown in Figure 5.2.

Task	Raj	Carol	Harry	Julie	Simone	Jill
Processing customers' orders	4	2	4	6	3	4
Planning production	5	3	5	6	4	5
Client detail changes	4	2	4	5	3	5
Policy reviews	4	1	4	5	4	5
Fund variation reviews	6	3	4	4	3	5
Task X						
Task Y						

Figure 5.2 The completed task analysis

Publicly displayed, the chart allows everyone to see at a glance who they should approach for advice or guidance, and it quickly shows the team's progress towards a better skills coverage. This general concept has been found to be very useful in a wide variety of industries and skill areas. Clearly the wording and actual task definitions are modified for each work area, such as machine operation, fork lift truck driving, processing customer orders, building maintenance, etc.

CORE COMPETENCES

The list of tasks the team developed above are, in effect, the functional competences required for each role within the team but, in addition, there are a number of generic competences, which can apply to all jobs. It's quite likely that the team members will need to improve these generic competences as well as the purely functional ones, so you may wish to consider the following approach. It's based on a list of 16 typical core competences, which you can find on the CD ROM. The full list is:

1. Customer focus.

2. Breadth of vision.

3. Judgement.

4. Influencing.

5. Company networking.

6. Achieving results.

7. Communication.

8. Developing people.

9. Team building.

10. Empowerment.

11. Managing performance.

12. Safety management.

13. Commercial success.

14. Managing finances.

15. Project management.

16. Managing change.

Your own organization may already have its own list of competences – if so, it would be wise to use them. Although they may change from time to time, the broad basket of competences will remain fairly constant. If you don't have a company competency model then you may find this one helpful. Just like the functional competences, which the financial team identified, each of these generic competences is described in six levels, to enable performance to be precisely assessed. For example, the 'customer focus' competency could be classified as follows:

- Level 1. At the lowest level the person understands that everyone has customers.

- Level 2. Understands who the main customers are and the standard of service required.

- Level 3. Assesses and reacts quickly to customer needs, delivering to time specification and cost.

- Level 4. Ensures the team retains a clear focus on customer service.

- Level 5. Improves the existing level of service, prioritizing needs and keeping customer focus.

- Level 6. At the highest level they anticipate major changes in customer needs, and drive the business to meet them.

As before, the levels described are cumulative, so that someone who is assessed at, say, level 4, is also displaying all the attributes of levels 1 to 3. How could a team use this approach? Basically they could adopt the same four steps as before, except that most of the work is already done:

1. List the competences – use either the company list or the one given here.

2. Confirm standards of performance – are they happy with the six levels of definitions?

3. List the team members as before.

4. Assess each team member's performance.

Looking at the list of competences, you can appreciate that each job will require varying levels of performance – some may not feature very highly, while others will feature a lot. Similarly, in general, the higher the level of a job within an organization, the higher will be the required competence level. To enable people to focus on the essential competences it wouldn't be necessary to rate all 16 but just those that are deemed to be vital for the specific job.

Practical example

Let's see how it works in practice using a typical job – an administrator at a visitors' centre, who also conducts occasional tours for visitors around the site. The manager for this post might have decided that the core competences shown in Figure 5.3 were essential, and that the job-holder would be required to display the performance levels shown.

Over a period of time the manager would discuss performance with the individual and, from a mixture of observation, performance measures and third-party feedback, he or she might conclude that the actual levels of performance being displayed were as shown in Figure 5.4. We can see that, while the individual is performing on or above the required level for competences 1, 3, 6 and 7, competences 2, 4 and 5 require some development. It's a simple step to formulate a personal development plan to address these learning needs.

Competence	Desired level	Current level	Action plan
1. Customer focus	3		
2. Influencing	3		
3. Company networking	3		
4. Communication	4		
5. Team building	3		
6. Safety management	4		
7. Commercial success	2		

Figure 5.3 Core competences part 1

Competence	Desired level	Current level	Action plan
1. Customer focus	3	4	
2. Influencing	3	2	Attend next training course.
3. Company networking	3	4	
4. Communication	4	3	Report writing weak – to receive coaching for 1 month
5. Team building	3	2	Can sometimes be a 'loner' – needs to build relationships
6. Safety management	4	4	
7. Commercial success	2	2	

Figure 5.4 Core competences part 2

By adding the selected generic competences to the list of functional competences the team can quickly identify the learning needs for the whole team, and have it displayed in a visual and easily understood format.

Can you identify any situations where you might use either of these competency-based approaches for helping a team to identify its learning needs?

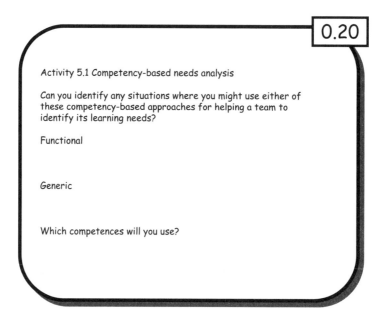

0.20

Activity 5.1 Competency-based needs analysis

Can you identify any situations where you might use either of these competency-based approaches for helping a team to identify its learning needs?

Functional

Generic

Which competences will you use?

CRITICAL WORK PROCESSES

This next approach helps a team to identify its learning needs in an innovative way, by looking at their work processes and deciding which are critical for business success. The method goes direct to the core of learning needs analysis by focusing on what's required to improve business performance. It involves three main phases:

1. Identify all the team's work processes.

2. Identify the 'critical' work processes.

3. Focus on the learning needs.

To show how it works, we have used a freelance trainer's role for the inputs, outputs and critical work processes. When you come to explain it yourself you'll no doubt use jobs and terms with which the team is familiar, before embarking on the actual process with them.

Phase 1. Identify all the team's work processes

Phase 1.1. Create a template

Use the template in Figure 5.5 for the first part of the process – the three columns are used to record inputs, critical work processes and outputs.

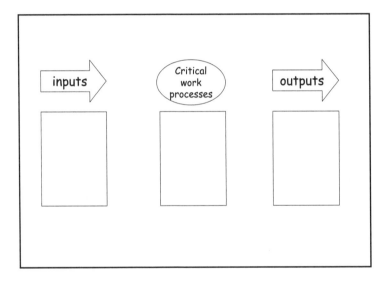

Figure 5.5 Critical work processes Phase 1.1

Phase 1.2. List your inputs

Start by focusing on the left-hand column headed Inputs. Working with the team you would ask them to list everything that prompts them to do their work. It's important that they use nouns like 'Phone calls' or 'Meetings' and not verbs! Using our example of the freelance trainer, the template could look like the one shown in Figure 5.6.

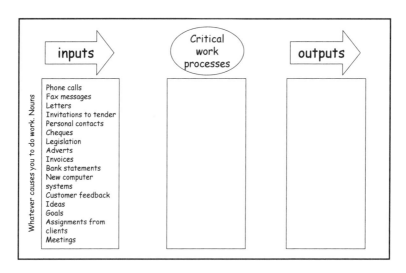

Figure 5.6 Critical work processes Phase 1.2

Phase 1.3. List your outputs

The next step is to focus attention on the right-hand column headed Outputs. You would ask your team to identify what they produce, using nouns again – words like 'Satisfied clients' or 'Motivated people' and not verbs! Using our example of the trainer, the template now looks like the one shown in Figure 5.7.

Phase 1.4. List the critical work processes

The final stage of phase 1 is to identify the work processes, which are recorded in the central column. The team should ask themselves, 'What do we do to turn inputs into outputs?' This time they should use action verbs like 'Planning' or 'Consulting'. You're not trying to link specific inputs and outputs with work processes – just to identify a full list of all the work processes involved. So, using our example of the trainer, we might see the list of critical work processes shown in Figure 5.8.

Review what you've done

Once you have reached this stage with the team, ask everyone to take a few minutes to reflect on the information they've recorded in the three columns. Although the main focus will be on the critical work processes, it's worth examining the other two elements to see if there are any opportunities for improvement. Start with the

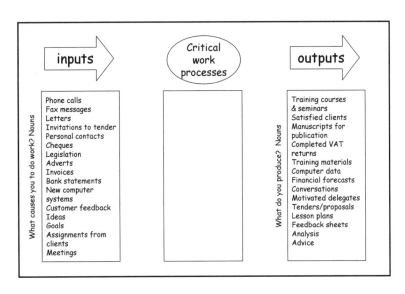

Figure 5.7 Critical work processes Phase 1.3

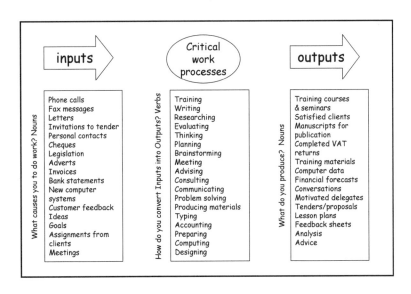

Figure 5.8 Critical work processes Phase 1.4

inputs, many of which will be from their key suppliers:

- What are their relationships like? Could they be improved?
- Do they have service level agreements, or their equivalent, with them all?
- Which causes most hassle on a day-to-day basis?
- How do they measure supplier performance?
- Could their suppliers modify the inputs they supply to reduce processing work?

Then ask the team to consider the outputs they produce, many of which will be to key customers:

- What are their relationships like? Could they be improved?
- Do they have service level agreements or their equivalent with them all?
- Which causes most hassle on a day-to-day basis?
- How do they measure the service they give their customers?
- How do they react to feedback from customers?
- Could they modify their outputs to reduce the processing which their customer perform?

Now you can focus on the critical work processes they've identified, the action verbs listed in the centre column, as this is where they will start to discover the team's learning needs. Before going into any deeper analysis you might ask them whether the list contains any surprises. Does everyone agree with the list?

Phase 2. Identify the 'critical' work processes

Phase 2.1. Create a template

Check they're ready to move on to the next part of the process, when they will identify the work processes which, for whatever reason, they're not doing as well as they should. Now you need to work with a different template, which looks like the one in Figure 5.9.

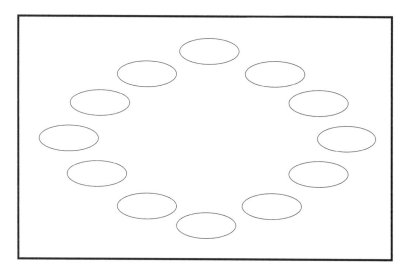

Figure 5.9 Critical work processes Phase 2.1

Phase 2.2. Transfer the critical work processes

To use this template the team transfers the critical work processes they have just identified to the ovals on this diagram. If they need more than 12 then draw in extra ovals. Using our example of the trainer, the template could look like the one shown in Figure 5.10.

Phase 2.3. Record the flows between processes

Having listed all the critical work processes, the team should now consider which processes lead to others. For example, 'Brainstorming' could lead to 'Planning', and 'Meeting' could lead to 'Designing'. As you determine the flow, you draw an appropriate arrow on the diagram between the two ovals. You can appreciate that some arrows will flow in both directions between two processes – so, for example, 'Planning' could also lead to 'Brainstorming'.

Very quickly the diagram will come alive with arrows showing the flow of activity between the various critical work processes, but eventually you'll realize that you've captured the main flows. The resulting template could look like the one in Figure 5.11 – you'll appreciate that we've deliberately kept this simple to demonstrate the concept. In a real example there will be many more arrows flowing all over the diagram!

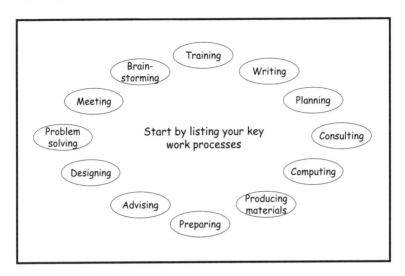

Figure 5.10 Critical work processes Phase 2.2

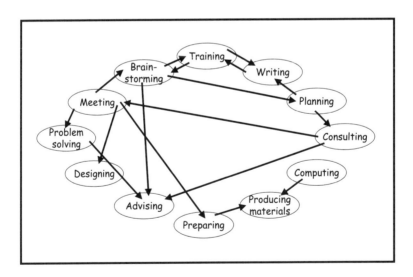

Figure 5.11 Critical work processes Phase 2.3

Phase 2.4. Identify the 'leading' work processes

Now you're ready to start the penultimate part of the process in which you identify those work processes that are 'leaders' and those that are 'followers'. It's a simple matter of counting the arrows both in and out of each process. The numbers show which processes 'lead' and which 'follow'. A process with a higher 'in' number and lower 'out' number is a 'following' process, and will probably have less impact on overall success. A process with a higher 'out' number and lower 'in' number is a 'leading' process and will probably have greater impact on your overall success.

In our example, the results would look like Figure 5.12. By the way, please remember this example is purely to show how the process works – the diagram your team develops will be much more complex!

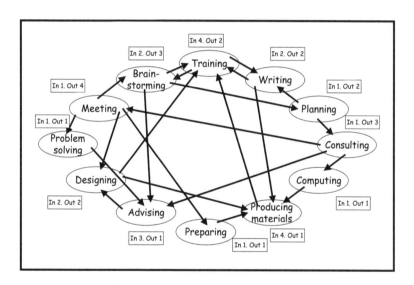

Figure 5.12 Critical work processes Phase 2.4

Meeting	4 Out, 1 In.
Advising	1 Out, 3 In.
Producing materials	1 Out, 4 In.
Training	2 Out, 4 In.
Planning	2 Out, 1 In.
Consulting	3 Out, 1 In.
Brainstorming	3 Out, 2 In.

Writing	2 Out, 2 In.
Designing	2 Out, 2 In.
Computing	1 Out, 1 In.
Preparing	1 Out, 1 In.
Problem solving	1 Out, 1 In.

Once you have reached this stage working with the team, ask them to reflect on the outcome. What does it tell them about where they inject their main efforts? Do the results reflect reality?

- Do they currently tend to focus on 'leading' or 'following' processes?

- If they focus on 'following' processes, are they happy with the situation?

- If not, what could be changed?

- How do they compare their confidence or competence with the 'leading' or 'following' work processes? Do they see any imbalances?

Phase 3. Focus on the learning needs

For the third and final phase of the process, delegates relate the achievement of business objectives to the team's critical work processes, to determine their underlying learning needs.

Phase 3.1. Relating processes to business objectives

This is how to do it, using the template in Figure 5.13 to facilitate the analysis.

Phase 3.2. List the business objectives

The team should start with the right-hand column and list their current key objectives – they can either do this on a team basis or individually. Suggest they reduce the words to the minimum necessary to understand the objective. Our template could look like Figure 5.14.

Phase 3.3. Add 'critical' work processes

The next step is easy – simply transfer into the left-hand column the key 'leading' work processes they identified in phase 2. These were the work processes that had a higher number of 'out' that 'in' arrows. The template now looks like Figure 5.15.

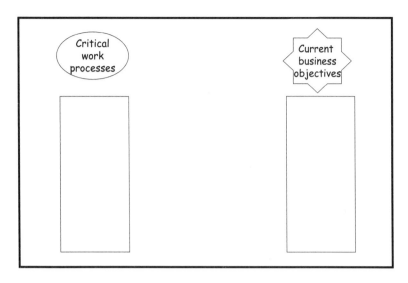

Figure 5.13 Critical work processes Phase 3.1

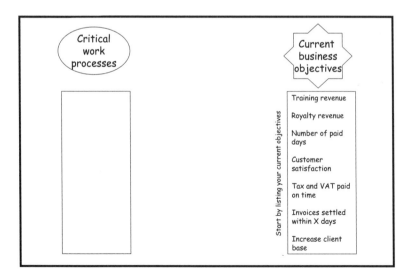

Figure 5.14 Critical work processes Phase 3.2

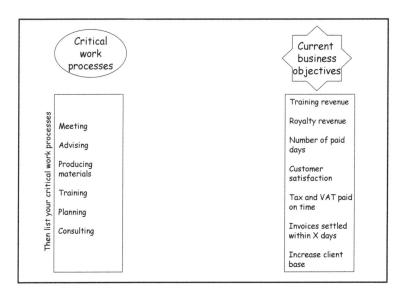

Figure 5.15 Critical work processes Phase 3.3

Phase 3.4. Relate success to work processes

Now comes the interesting bit – relating success or failure in achieving objectives to the key underlying work processes. The team should now look for relationships between Current Objectives (listed in the right-hand column) and the Critical Work Processes (listed in the left-hand column).

Phase 3.5. Define the changes in behaviour needed

Draw arrows from each Objective to the Critical Work Processes that feed into it, so highlighting interdependencies. They should ask themselves, 'If an objective is not achieved, which key process(es) has failed?' Accept that the diagram may become very messy and that you might wish to use a different colour for each objective.

If the team is failing to achieve results in particular objectives, this analysis should help to identify what specifically they need to improve, as it focuses on improving underlying 'enabling' processes, rather than the final objective.

For example, if your team worked in sales and wished to improve their revenue earning ability, the traditional approach might be set an objective like: 'To increase sales by 10 per cent.' But setting this objective doesn't actually help the team members to do better. It simply tells them 'what' is required, without helping with the 'how' to do it. The approach we're recommending here helps the team to focus on, and thus improve, the processes that lead to getting more sales.

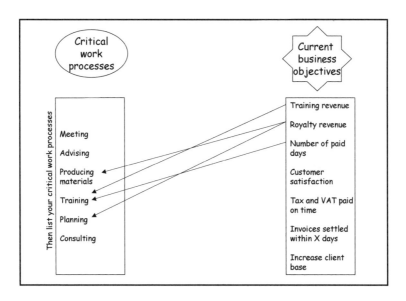

Figure 5.16 Critical work processes Phase 3.4

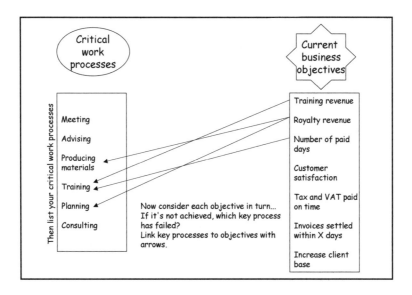

Figure 5.17 Critical work processes Phase 3.5

Using this approach the team might come to realize that they are under-performing in two of the enabling processes essential for achieving more sales: increasing client contacts and interrogating databases. So the objectives could be redefined as: 'To increase the number of client contacts by 20 per cent' and, 'To improve our ability at interrogating database information.' The final step would be to translate these objectives into specific learning needs.

Where might you use the critical work processes approach?

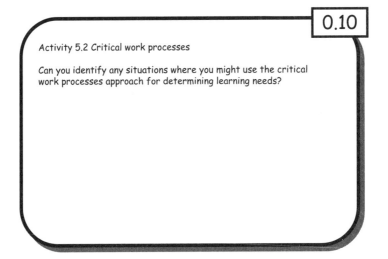

0.10

Activity 5.2 Critical work processes

Can you identify any situations where you might use the critical work processes approach for determining learning needs?

6

What do you propose?

- Training may not be the solution
- Define the overall course 'envelope'
- Internal or external designers?
- Write your proposal
- Sunflower analysis

TRAINING MAY NOT BE THE SOLUTION

By this stage you've collected lots of data from a variety of sources, so now you need to analyse what you've got and then persuade someone to give you the authority to do something about it. This is where you need to remember why we called the earlier chapters *'learning* needs analysis' and not *'training* needs analysis'. You may have uncovered many performance gaps – where the current performance fails to meet the required level of performance. And, because we're trainers, it's tempting to think that training is the most appropriate solution. Let's use the flow chart in Figure 6.1 to walk through the next piece.

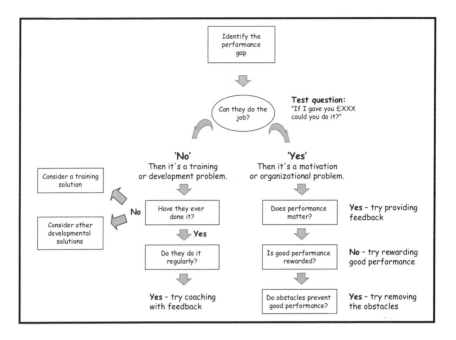

Figure 6.1 What's the gap?

So you've identified a performance gap. The starting point is to imagine yourself asking the person with the performance issue: 'If I gave you £XXX could you do it?'

'Yes – I could do it'

If you think the answer would be 'Yes', then his or her under-performance is a matter of willingness, and no amount of training will change things. The solutions for these performance-related problems will go much deeper than you can probably deal with. Some of the questions that need to be asked include:

- Does performance matter? If the answer is 'Yes' then try providing feedback.

- Is good performance rewarded? If the answer is 'No' then try rewarding performance differently.

- Do obstacles prevent good performance? If the answer is 'Yes' then try removing the obstacles. Get the rocks off the runway!

The managers of the departments concerned will need to search for other solutions, which may include motivation, different equipment, new processes, changed working practices, organizational changes, environmental issues, etc. As you can appreciate, these won't be a 'quick fix' and must be in place before any training starts, or it will be a complete waste of time.

On several occasions I have been asked to recommend a training solution for an organization and, after conducting a learning needs analysis, I have reported back to the managers that I have revealed an underlying issue that needed to be addressed before the focus could switch to training. On some occasions I was able to help the company to address these issues, before turning to the training solution, but several other times I had to walk away – if the training had been delivered as requested, the only observable change would have been to my reputation!

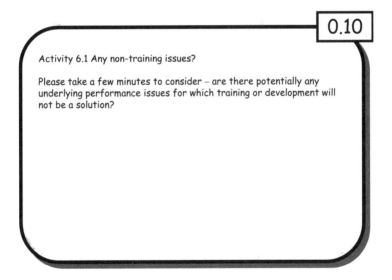

0.10

Activity 6.1 Any non-training issues?

Please take a few minutes to consider – are there potentially any underlying performance issues for which training or development will not be a solution?

'No – I can't do it'

If, however, you think the answer might be 'No', then you can go down the left-hand side of the flow chart and look for training and development options. Don't get too excited yet – you've still some other solutions to consider before you recommend 'training' as *the* solution. Depending on your situation, you may be able to offer some or all of these additional developmental opportunities:

- secondments;

- project work;

- temporary promotion;

- self-study using books or multimedia;

- watching video or DVDs;

- surfing the net;

- coaching;

- open learning;

- shadowing an experienced person;

- professional development or qualification;

- on-the-job development;

- being mentored;

- learning from other people or companies doing a similar role.

Which of them looks promising depends entirely on the situation. Your role is to recommend a package of solutions that represent the most productive, stimulating and cost-effective way of developing people's abilities in the required areas. Referring back to your own situation, can you see any development opportunities, other than training, which might be appropriate?

Analysis not paralysis!

Confronted with all the data you've collected, it's very easy to feel overwhelmed and to not know where to start. I am a great believer in Post-it Notes whenever I feel 'information overload' coming on.

As you look through all the data you've collected, write the key points of each element on its own Post-it Note. At this stage don't try to make sense of anything, just keep writing until you've got a rash of Post-it Notes on the wall. Now stand back and look for themes, moving the Post-it Notes so they form groups of related topics. Gradually you will begin to see patterns emerge and that could be the start of your training plan and, ultimately, your proposal, if you have to do one.

Sifting through the data and developing your ideas on how the training can be designed and delivered is not a cold, mechanical process but one that involves reflection and discussion. By the way, don't try to do this alone – you will get a much better result by working with others. Using the Post-it Notes enables ideas to be moved and grouped, and then regrouped as different thoughts emerge.

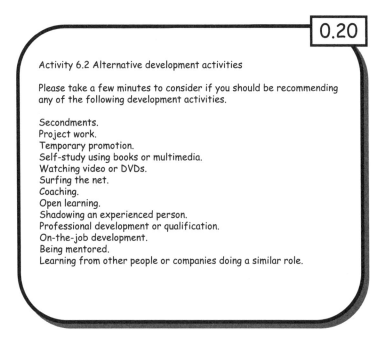

0.20

Activity 6.2 Alternative development activities

Please take a few minutes to consider if you should be recommending any of the following development activities.

Secondments.
Project work.
Temporary promotion.
Self-study using books or multimedia.
Watching video or DVDs.
Surfing the net.
Coaching.
Open learning.
Shadowing an experienced person.
Professional development or qualification.
On-the-job development.
Being mentored.
Learning from other people or companies doing a similar role.

DEFINE THE OVERALL COURSE 'ENVELOPE'

One of the key issues to clarify as you ponder your data is the overall course 'envelope'. Aeronautical engineers use the phrase 'envelope' to describe the whole set of performance criteria within which an airframe must stay if it is to be safe, so we can use the same term to bring together all the criteria for your training event. You know the sort of issues – the objectives, the duration, how many people, residential or day course, trainer-led or e-learning, etc.

Learning outcomes

Early on you will need to confirm exactly what the sponsor expects delegates to gain from the training, and this needs to be 'signed off' by the topic owner before you can start to formulate your proposal. Once this is clear you can start to fix the overall design 'envelope' within which your course needs to fit. Let's consider each of the key elements individually.

Duration

An important decision will be how long the course should last. In an ideal world you would collect your thoughts about what the course should include, arrange the topics for the best flow, and strike the optimum balance between theory and practice. Once you have done all that you might decide, for example, 'This is a two-day course.'

Generally the real world isn't like this anymore. Instead, it's quite likely that your sponsor will tell you in the first minutes of your discussion: 'The longest we can spare people away from their workplace is…' The challenge for you is then to get the best fit between what you would like to do, and what you realistically can do, in the available time. Very few organizations nowadays can afford the luxury of generous, or even adequate, time for courses.

Early on you will spend time discussing how long the course should last, and expect pressure from the sponsor to minimize the time people spend away from their primary role. You might wish to bear in mind these guidelines:

- Half a day is great for 'refresher' sessions, or some topics like minute-writing skills where you can cover all the concepts and still give time for practice.

- One day is ideal for many topics as it allows a fast-paced course to cover key theory, with some time for participation and interaction, for example time management and writing skills.

- Two days are essential for courses where you need to cover theory and provide a greater amount of time to practise skills, for example presentation skills or recruitment interviewing.

- Three days and more are required for courses where there is a greater amount of theory to grasp, probably coupled with the need to demonstrate mastery of the skills.

Start and end times

An important decision is when to start and end your course, and you need to recognize that you will be largely constrained by people's normal working hours.

If you schedule the start time earlier than they are used to, you will find people drifting in over an extended period, which makes it difficult to make a high-impact start. Similarly, if you plan to end later than they are used to, you will find people's concentration starting to lapse, or some individuals needing to leave before the end because of travel or child-care arrangements.

So listen to the advice given to you and plan accordingly.

Residential or not?

For many courses, especially the short ones, there is no debate about a course being non-residential, but the question will arise for longer courses, or in situations where delegates need to travel from geographically dispersed sites.

Advantages of residential courses

- More time available as you can work into the early evening, or start earlier on subsequent mornings.

- People get to know each other better.

- People often relax more as their domestic issues can be put aside.

- More relaxed pace as there's less pressure to cram it all in.

- People travelling from afar have time to adjust before the course starts.

- Opportunity to build teams and break down barriers.

Disadvantages of residential courses

- Costs will be much higher as you are housing and feeding people overnight.

- Some people will be unable to stay overnight due to personal circumstances.

- The temptation to work too late into the evening.

- Some people feel threatened or uncomfortable with the continual social immersion with the other delegates.

Number of delegates

As you're discussing the number of delegates for your event you may wish to bear in mind the following guidelines developed from past experience. It's important to agree this upfront, as much of your design will hinge on the number of people attending. If the sponsor suddenly decides that the number of delegates needs to increase, say, from 8 to 12, you may have to redesign whole chunks of the course:

- One-to-one. This may be the only way for the most senior managers or professionals in an organization to receive feedback on their performance. It's very intensive as you don't get a break from each other.

- Up to three delegates. Good for advanced presentation skills or similar courses where you need to give a small amount of theory, but most of the course is devoted to individual presentations, followed by in-depth feedback.

- Up to six delegates. Ideal for standard, two-day presentations courses as it gives the optimum balance of theory, presentations and feedback.

- Up to eight delegates. Ideal for most interpersonal skills courses, as it gives a good balance between the variety of ideas and experience the delegates bring, and a comfortable number for the trainer to give individual attention to.

- Up to 12 delegates. The maximum I will normally work with on a conventional training course.

There are of course exceptions to these guidelines, including:

- Networking sessions. Courses on networking work much better the more people you have in the room because it not only allows them to practise the skills you're exploring, but enables them to do some real networking.

- Complete teams. When you're asked to run an event for a complete team, for example the management team at a particular location, or a complete department, then obviously you have to take the whole team. Leaving just one person out gives people a let-out clause for not having to change.

- Open courses. You may be asked to design an open course, which may last from several hours to a full day, when an unlimited number of people may attend.

The fundamental issue is that, in general, the more people you have, the less interaction there is between the trainer and the delegates, leading to more theory and less opportunity for participation. But it's not always the case.

Method of delivery

This is an important topic to clarify with the sponsor and, put simply, you have three main choices: trainer-led, self-study or a blend of the two. Let's examine the pros and cons of each choice.

Trainer-led courses – Advantages

- Gives opportunity to practise skills and receive feedback.

- Delegates interact with each other – discuss common issues and concerns.

- The trainer can modify the content or flow to meet the delegates' needs.

Trainer-led courses – Disadvantages

- The pace is determined by the slowest delegate.

- Delegates will have varying levels of knowledge of the underlying theory.

- Expensive in terms of person-hours and venue costs.

Self-study – Advantages

- People can acquire new skills when they need them, instead of waiting for the next scheduled training course.

- Students can choose their own learning path to suit their prior knowledge of the topic.

- Minimum disruption to normal work, as people can study at times convenient to them.

- Students can revisit sections they find challenging.

- You can use multimedia – text, sound and vision.

- You can build in clever animations to explain complex topics.

- You can train a lot of people in widely spread sites in a short time.

- Delegates receive a consistent message irrespective of when or where they are trained.

Self-study – Disadvantages

- Can feel very lonely, especially if the student is struggling with a section.

- You're reliant on people completing all sections of the work.

- Take care about using 'right' answers.

- E-learning solutions – the upfront investment can be high so use it for carefully selected topics.

- E-learning solutions – once designed the course is expensive to modify.

- E-learning solutions are very dependent on the quality of your IT network.

Blended learning

Increasingly, companies are looking to bring together the best of trainer-led and self-study solutions, particularly using e-learning. These 'blended learning' courses typically offer the learner a two-stage learning experience. First of all, they study an e-learning package, which covers all the theory they need to know about the topic. Then they experience a short, normally one-day, trainer-led course when they get to practise the key skills they acquired through the e-learning.

Blended learning – Advantages

- Keeps delegates' non-revenue-earning time to a minimum.

- Allows key skills to be practised.

- No need to devote time to covering underlying theory.

Blended learning – Disadvantages

- Not all delegates will have completed the e-learning course or, if they did, it may be some time ago.

- There's limited time for discussion about delegates' issues or concerns.

- The time pressure means that there's no time to introduce new concepts or models.

- Without some follow-up coaching, whether 'live' or online, it's easy for the newly acquired skills to wither.

Venue and equipment considerations

Although the choice of venue will be more of an issue when it comes to the actual course delivery, there may be specific equipment or facilities that must be available for the course to be effective, and these may have to be defined in the course design. For example, you may need to:

- ensure your venue can welcome delegates irrespective of their mobility or visual capabilities;

- have access to IT or other specialist training equipment to enable the delegates to develop their skills;

- select venues with suitable outdoor training facilities if that's part of the course design.

How many trainers will be required?

This is an important issue to consider early on as it will affect the way you design the course. In general, if you follow the guidelines on numbers of delegates we outlined above, one trainer should be able to manage quite satisfactorily. However, there may be situations when additional trainers are justified:

- The course design may require delegates to work in small teams that require trainer input, facilitation, observation or feedback and one trainer simply can't manage, for example development centres.

- There may be parts of the course that require specialist knowledge the 'main' trainer doesn't have, for example managing outdoor activities safely.

- The course may involve fast changeovers to different tasks or activities so, while one trainer is managing the group, the other can be preparing the next activity.

Will you need any guest speakers?

There may be topics that are so specialized that few people have the required level of knowledge or expertise – so you need to invite a guest speaker along. There may be other topics where, although your own trainers could do equally well, bringing along a guest speaker with acknowledged expertise or reputation will dramatically enhance the acceptability of what they have to say.

If you're considering using guest speakers there are some additional points to consider:

- Do you have the budget? Guest speakers will cost you, and not just the direct fees but also the additional items associated with travel, accommodation and 'meeting and greeting'.

- You will need to get the dates into their diary early – many months ahead of the planned date.

- Have a 'fallback' position in case you can't get the person you want, or circumstances change and their involvement would no longer be acceptable or desirable.

Considering any 'unusual' events or activities?

Sometimes it's decided to include 'unusual' events or activities, such as go-karting, rock climbing, walking on hot coals, horse whispering – the list is endless. If you're considering any of these, a few additional considerations are:

- Time – it will certainly eat into precious time.

- Cost – involving specialist activities will hit your budget hard!

- Travel – you may need to travel to a different location.

- Distraction – will everyone see the relevance of the experience?

- Threats – some people may see the activity as threatening.

You need to carry out a ruthless cost/benefit analysis before committing to these types of activity. I can remember very clearly meeting some delegates from a work conference who had been out the previous evening for a team-building session at the local go-kart track. The evening had ended rather early when two karts collided, injuring both drivers, who then spent most of the night in the casualty department of the local hospital!

> **0.20**
>
> Activity 6.3 Define your course 'envelope'
>
> Please take a few minutes to consider the factors that will define your course 'envelope'.
>
> Learning outcomes
>
> Duration
>
> Start and end times
>
> Residential or not?
>
> Number of delegates
>
> Method of delivery
>
> Venue and equipment considerations
>
> How many trainers?
>
> Any guest speakers?
>
> Any 'unusual' events or activities?

INTERNAL OR EXTERNAL DESIGNERS?

When exploring the options with your sponsor, one of the key decisions is whether to develop the courses or workshops internally, or to buy in resources from an external training provider. External suppliers could either provide you with an existing course or, for extra cost, design something new especially for you. If you struggle with this issue, why not use these selection criteria to guide your decision? You could allocate a weighted score to each factor, and total the final result.

Credibility

Buy in existing external products. The external facilitators who run the courses are more familiar with the issues and possible solutions than internal facilitators might be.

Develop internally. Your staff will attribute more credibility and relevance to the event if it is obviously developed internally.

Costs

Buy in existing products. The cost of buying in the programmes is less than the cost of resources and staff development time required to produce a programme of the same quality.

Develop internally. Consider the price of the course you're planning on a cost-per-person basis. If you need to train a significant number of staff a programme developed internally would be significantly cheaper.

Content

Buy in existing products. The content and objectives of the course under review might provide such a close fit with your needs that you could not justify developing a programme yourselves.

Develop internally. A workshop to meet your training objectives may require frequent revisions or updating, which is easier to do with an internally developed programme.

Time

Buy in existing products. You can't afford the time to develop and refine an internal programme. The courses you'll be buying in are fully proven and validated, and will be fully effective from the very first event.

Develop internally. Developing a course to meet the specific needs of your staff is more valuable than the staff time and other costs you would save by buying in an existing programme.

Design capability

Buy in existing products. The people who designed the event being considered have more design experience for this topic/objective than your internal training designers have.

Develop internally. Your internal course designers have enough resources and experience to develop a programme that will satisfy your training objectives in every way.

Specific

Buy in existing products. Buying in one of the programmes under review will free up staff development time for courses you will have to develop internally.

Develop internally. The training objectives you have are so specific to your organization that it would be difficult to modify any packaged training programme to meet them.

Culture

Buy in existing products. The programmes being considered are developed from resources that are more sophisticated or specialized than internal resources.

Develop internally. Management policy or organization culture strongly supports internal development of training programmes.

Before moving on, you may wish to consider whether you will be using internal or external resources for the course you're considering.

0.20

Activity 6.4 Internal or external designers?

Please take a few minutes to consider which sources you might use and record them using this Merit Matrix.

Criteria	Internal new design	External existing design	External new design
Credibility			
Costs			
Content			
Time			
Design capability			
Specific			
Culture			

WRITE YOUR PROPOSAL

At some stage you will need to seek someone's authority to convert the learning needs analysis into some form of training intervention. Who you are, where you work and the scale of the project will determine how much energy and thought will have to go into your proposal:

- If you're really lucky you may simply have to explain the situation to the sponsor to gain their agreement, perhaps having e-mailed an outline in advance.

- At the next level you may have to produce a formal proposal, which you explain to the key stakeholder during an informal meeting.

- The most demanding requirement is to produce a formal proposal, accompanied by a presentation, which you deliver to a group of decision makers.

Many are called – few are chosen!

If you have to produce a formal proposal, don't regard it as a waste of time or something to be dashed off quickly while you focus on 'more important things'. Remember your proposal may be one of many presented to busy senior managers and if your proposal doesn't grab them at the first pass, it will probably fail. And that's it. Your only chance will be gone! So spend time, spread over several days, writing a proposal that not only is complete and correct, but also grabs their attention right at the start and makes them want to read to the end. So write a proposal that:

- Highlights the benefits to the business.

- Is structured, so the reader can quickly reach the parts that interest them.

- Has that optimum balance between 'completeness' and 'conciseness'.

- Is written in plain English – clear and to the point.

- Has an 'assumptive close' embedded in it. Instead of saying: 'If the proposal is approved ...' write instead: 'Once the proposal is approved . . .'.

- Offers clear, costed options to carry out the design work which will deliver the required changes in business performance.

- Leaves the reader feeling compelled to go ahead with the proposal.

Your proposal

Even if you do not have to produce a formal proposal we'd suggest you look through the following checklist as a reminder of the topics you need to consider. If you do have to produce a proposal then this list could give you a structure, which you can 'flesh out' with the appropriate details. To ensure consistency, we've used the same broad headings for the proposal as the chapter on learning needs analysis. You might wish to refer back to the detailed questions and issues raised there. Your proposal could include these main sections.

'Topping':

- Distribution list – which says who it's going to, divided into two categories:
  - action addressees – who need to take action;
  - information addressees – who only need to be aware of it.
- Contents list
- Executive summary – which gives a brief overview of the proposal. Write this last of all.

Section 1. Background to the problem/requirement:

- The problem/requirement and what has caused it.
- The impact on the business.
- Who initiated the project?
- Terms of reference.
- Membership of the training design project team.
- Outline the learning needs analysis process.
- Internal and external drivers for change.
- Other linked initiatives.

Section 2. Summary of details of the problem/requirement:

- Who is involved?
- What type of performance is required?

- Performance gaps identified.

- Issues identified for which training will not be the solution.

- Where and when learning/training needs to be delivered.

- Corporate, departmental or individual issues.

Section 3. Options:

- Options with relative advantages/merits/disadvantages and associated through-life costs (where appropriate).

- Suggested optimum solutions to deliver the requirement within constraints.

- Framework design strategy/intervention design.

- How learning/effectiveness of the programme will be evaluated.

- Suggestions on how the operational impact of the programme will be measured by the organization/business.

The programme in detail:

- Who is it aimed at? Grade/location/function?

- Proposed duration, number of events, maximum participants, etc.

- Total population to be trained.

- Sites and locations.

- Give an overview of the content and flow.

- Mention specific models or concepts.

- Delivery method – trainer-led/self-study/blend.

Design process:

- Design team members.

- Outline how the design will be done.

- Agree the 'sign off' process.

- Discuss compliance with brands, logos or procedures.

- Propose key milestones.

Resources:

- Budgets.
- Buy in or design in-house?
- IT implications.
- Other resources, eg other training materials or equipment.

Timings:

- Schedule for design work.
- Pilot course – when/where/who?
- Review and modification process.

Roll out:

- Train the trainers.
- Launch strategy.
- Communication and publicity.
- Venue requirements.

Evaluation:

- Return on investment for the business
  - short term – end of course;
  - medium term – changes in behaviour;
  - longer term – business success.

Section 4. Way forward/next steps:

- Say why this approach is the best.
- Outline the key benefits for the business.
- Propose an outline action plan – who will do what and by when.
- Say what is required by the designer/design team from the sponsor in order to move forward.

- Itemize the next steps to be taken to mobilize design resources, leading to develop and test the pilot design.

- Quote a specific date by which approval will be assumed unless objections are raised.

'Tailing':

Signature, Job Title and Department
Date
Contact details
Supporting documents (attach any supporting documents or information the reader may find interesting).

0.15

Activity 6.5 Ideas into action!

Please take a few minutes to consider these three questions:

1. Whose authority do I need to go ahead with the training design?

2. What facts or information will I need to share with them to get their agreement?

3. What's the most effective way of gaining their agreement? Informal meeting; e-mail proposal; formal written proposal; formal presentation; other?

SUNFLOWER ANALYSIS

Working through this chapter will have made you aware that you need help or support from a wide variety of people to enable you to get the design process under way. To help you plan effectively you may wish to use Sunflower Analysis – it's called that because the final diagram vaguely resembles a sunflower.

This is how you use it. Start by drawing a circle in the centre of a sheet of A3 paper, in which you write the project or task; see Figure 6.2.

Figure 6.2 Sunflower Part 1

The next step is to draw a ring of 'petals' in which you write the names of the people, departments or organizations whose help or support you'll need. We've shown eight petals but you don't need to be limited to that number. The diagram starts to grow and now looks like Figure 6.3.

Figure 6.3 Sunflower Part 2

The next step is to draw a further ring of 'petals' in which you'll write exactly what help or support you'll need, for example:

- topic 'owner' – accurate advice and quick responses to 'sign offs';
- budget holder – frequent updates, fight for the project and flexibility;
- the design team – commitment, creativity, enthusiasm, and time management;
- line managers and staff – honest input on work processes and genuine feedback;
- HR department – up-to-date advice and quick responses to 'sign offs';
- IT department – accurate advice and quick solutions to problems;
- course trainers – honest input, open attitude to new approaches and creativity;
- reprographics – timely, cost-effective, attractive and functional materials.

By now your sunflower looks like Figure 6.4.

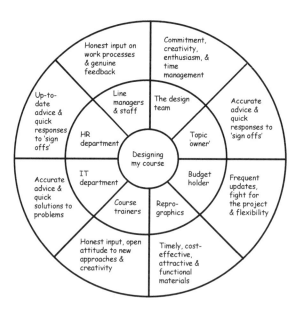

Figure 6.4 Sunflower Part 3

You can see how on one sheet of paper you can quickly develop a master plan for your design project. In many ways it's simply another form of mind mapping, with the ideas being collected on the petals. Now you've got the idea, why not try it out on a topic related to your course design?

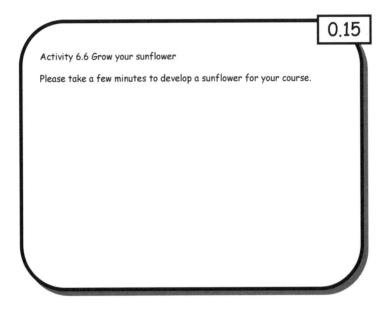

0.15

Activity 6.6 Grow your sunflower

Please take a few minutes to develop a sunflower for your course.

7

The impact of learning styles

- How people learn
- Climb the learning ladder
- The impact of learning styles
- Fight the filters
- So what does it mean for me?

HOW PEOPLE LEARN

So far you've made a good start on the training design journey. Having established the training design project you considered how your design could best meet the various diversity needs. You then conducted and analysed the learning needs, before defining what the course should look like, which led to proposing a specific course of action to the sponsor. The next logical step, surely, is to start the actual design itself?

Yes, but before we do that we need to refresh our ideas about how people actually learn, otherwise we can easily fall into the trap of designing training that fits with the way that *we* learn best, which isn't necessarily the best for our delegates: 'That must be the best way, after all, that's how I learn.' Just think back when you learnt to do something new or different – perhaps it was:

- struggling with the new package on your personal computer;

- assuming new responsibilities at work, perhaps involving promotion;

- learning a new hobby or sport;

- adopting a new role in life, for example becoming a husband, wife or parent.

What did you feel like as you found yourself in the new situation? How did you learn the new range of skills or knowledge? If you were to compare your experiences with a friend or colleague who had been through the same experience, you would probably find they tackled it in a totally different way.

For some years I enjoyed cruising the sky in a high-performance sailplane. Those of you who have experienced gliding will immediately feel a smile spread across your face as you relive that wonderful feeling of being thrown up into the air at 1,000 feet/minute, riding a wild thermal. One evening in the clubhouse, while discussing the skills of flying instructors, I asked one of them, Tony Mells, how many people he had taught to fly. Tony replied: 'None.' I immediately challenged him: 'Come on – you've done loads of flights in the back seat with me' (where the instructor traditionally sits). 'Ah,' said Tony, 'I didn't teach you to fly. You taught yourself. I just sat in the back and stopped you from killing yourself while you did it!' Later, as I drove home, I realized that Tony had defined the role of the effective instructor perfectly, which is to facilitate other people to learn. So we, as training designers, must create learning experiences which:

- enable our delegates to acquire their new attitudes, skills or knowledge…

- in such a way that they build confidence and competence…

- without harming themselves or others in the process.

It's made more interesting, some would say 'challenging', because we all tend to learn in different ways. There have been many schools of thought when it comes to learning theory, and we're not intending to reproduce them all here. But it's useful to visit some of the key concepts so that we have a common starting point for the actual design journey.

Behaviourist

The behaviourist approach, one of the early schools of thought, was based on the way we react and learn from circumstances when we are motivated to do so. The classic story of Pavlov's dogs illustrates this approach. A generalized view of this 'one size fits all' training process is 'explain, demonstrate, imitate and practise'.

Structuralist

Using this approach we would present learners with the end goal and allow them to teach themselves how to achieve that goal. This is based on a form of psychology where learners teach themselves by thinking of what has to be achieved and breaking the learning journey into its composite parts.

Cognitive

Adopting the cognitive approach we would design the training environment to meet the individual learning traits of learners, recognizing that people have unique thought and mental processes that affect their learning. When designing the learning environment we should take account of five key mental processes: attention, memory, language, reasoning and problem solving.

CLIMB THE LEARNING LADDER

Taking on something new

Another useful perspective on the way people learn is to consider the emotions and feelings experienced as we undertake a new task or adopt a new role. While someone may appear quite confident, most people experience a range of emotions, which have been likened to climbing a ladder. To be an effective training designer you need to be aware of these steps, and the impact they may have on your design.

First rung of the ladder

When we tackle something new we generally don't appreciate what's involved in doing it. No matter how simple or sophisticated the task may be, things generally look easier than we imagine. At this stage we are incompetent at performing the task – we simply cannot do it. Worse still, we don't know how much we don't know. So, in a nutshell, we are *unconsciously incompetent*.

We're sure you can recall experiences as you've undertaken new tasks – you may even be feeling unconsciously incompetent as you begin to design training. To bring the concept alive let me recount some learning experiences I shared with my elder daughter Jane.

Many years ago, when Jane was about 8 years old, she decided she would like to go roller-skating. Roller-skating was a totally new experience for me – I had never done it myself as a child. Anyway, we found that the local community centre had roller-skating sessions on Wednesday evenings so we turned up, hired some skates and had a go.

The rink was full of people of all ages confidently gliding around. They looked so elegant and it all looked very easy so I confidently moved out onto the rink – and immediately fell over! I struggled to my feet and promptly fell over again! I couldn't control my feet at all – they simply wouldn't do what I wanted them to! By the end of the evening I realized there was much more to roller-skating than I had ever imagined. I had gone to the first session in the blissful state of *unconscious incompetence*.

Second rung of the ladder

The next stage we move through is *conscious incompetence*. Having decided to start a venture we begin to grasp new skills, ideas or concepts. At this stage we are still incompetent but we become aware of how little we know, and what the journey ahead may entail. So we progress into the conscious incompetence stage.

The story continues. The following week Jane and I were still recovering from all the bruises we had developed during the first roller-skating session. The critical question hovering around the house was – would she want to go again? Well, she decided to give it another try and, being a devoted dad, I agreed to go along with her. Of course this week it was a little easier than the first time; we were both becoming aware of how to control the skates by applying varying pressure and generally starting to feel more in control of things.

We were still very much incompetent and were very conscious of how little we knew – the state of *conscious incompetence* prevailed for a few weeks. Of course as time went by, Jane raced ahead of me, eventually gliding elegantly around the rink demonstrating dance routines.

Third rung of the ladder

The next stage we progress through is *conscious competence*. While we now may be able to carry out the task, we have to do it step-by-step, and apparently with a lot of concentrated effort. This stage lasts for varying amounts of time – for some people and some situations it may pass quickly, whilst for others it may take a little longer.

> Many years later my younger daughter, Andrea, passed her driving test. When she proudly drove us around town in the family car she was so obviously at the *conscious competence* stage. Every move was positively considered and deliberate. We were able to see her progressing through the 'decision–mirror–signal–change gear–manoeuvre' process.

Top rung of the ladder

Finally all the hard work at the earlier stages starts to pay off and you move into being able to perform a task with little conscious thought or effort. After a period of time, and almost without knowing it, you are delivering the required perform-ance standard consistently and with confidence. You have reached *unconscious competence*.

> Andrea now drives safely and smoothly, with movements and decisions flowing quite naturally though a continuous, elegant process. I often wonder how she will react should one day a child of hers asks, 'Mum, will you take me roller-skating?'

Snakes and ladders

You can now visualize the four rungs of the learning ladder, but it's also important to imagine a 'snake' running down from the top rung (unconscious competence) to the lowest rung (unconscious incompetence). Using the analogy of the 'snakes and ladders' game reminds us that it's easy to slide from the top step to the lowest one. How? There are at least two ways.

You become complacent and, without realizing it, take shortcuts which steadily reduce the quality of actions or decisions. Alternatively, while you may continue to perform consistently, the world around you changes continuously and, if you don't change the way you do things, you will be left behind.

Applying the learning ladder

Understanding the learning ladder is all very well, but how can this help you when you're designing training? If we can explore the feelings people experience at the different steps, we will begin to see how our design can help our delegates to climb the ladder successfully.

Unconscious incompetence

Starting with unconscious incompetence, people may feel blissfully unaware, complacent or quietly confident. They may be saying to themselves, 'It won't affect/worry me!' or, 'I can do it easily!' As a designer you need to help people through these feelings in a positive way, so your design may need to:

- provide opportunities for people to realize themselves what's involved;
- break people in gently;
- let people assess the situation for themselves;
- allow them to talk with others who've recently started on or with it.

Conscious incompetence

As people try the new challenge or task themselves they move into the conscious incompetence state, and begin to experience some of the following emotions:

- Frustration – 'Why can't I do this?'
- Inadequacy – 'I'll never do this!'
- Denial – ' I never wanted to do this anyway!'
- Challenge – 'I'm not going to let this defeat me!'
- Realization – 'There's more to this than I ever realized!'

As you can imagine, this is a critical moment in the learning experience. If people feel overwhelmed by their initial failures and they don't get the right support, they may well walk away, convinced that they will never, ever be able to acquire the new skills or abilities. You need to ensure that your design allows time and/or opportunity for the trainer to coax people positively through this critical stage of the learning process. Some key guidelines to bear in mind are:

- Give people reassurance that they will be able to do it.
- Stress that their reaction is perfectly normal.
- Be patient and offer coaching or guidance as appropriate.
- Ask people to reflect on how they have tackled new situations in the past.
- Encourage those who look as though they might give up.

Conscious competence

Given the right support and encouragement, people struggle through the conscious competence state and slowly begin to develop the skills and abilities required of them. The pace at which people move through this phase depends very much on the individual – some racing through while others need more time. The feelings generally associated with the conscious competence stage are:

- Relief – 'So I can actually do it!'
- Frustration – 'I can do it, but why am I so slow?'
- Doubt – 'Will I ever be able to perform at the required speed or quality?'
- Satisfaction – 'After all my hard work I have got there.'
- Realization – 'I never realized there was so much to it.'

To allow learners to move through this phase successfully, your design will need to allow the trainer to do some of the following:

- Praise success.
- Encourage those who are feeling they still have a long way to go.
- Reassure people who doubt their ability to reach required standards.
- Gently but firmly coach the 'cocky' ones who think they know it all.
- Patiently help people gradually improve their ability to required standards.

Unconscious competence

Finally, people reach the unconscious competence state and a new set of feelings abound, including:

- Achievement – 'It's taken some time but I've finally reached it!'
- Arrogance – 'I always know I could do it. What was all the fuss about!'
- Satisfaction – 'How good it feels to be able to do it.'
- Complacency – 'I can just cruise now.'
- Laziness – 'How can I cut corners and achieve the same result?'
- Thoughtfulness – 'How can we make it easier for others learning how to do this?'
- Striving – 'What's next?'

A good design will encourage the trainer to be constantly aware of the variety of emotions learners will be experiencing, and what they need to do to ensure that people exit this phase successfully. The ideas could well include:

- Praise the successful.

- Cautious guidance to those cutting corners or taking shortcuts.

- Encouragement to those who found it a struggle.

- Remind the complacent of the changing world.

- Stimulate and challenge those who see the wider picture.

- Engender a sense of continuous improvement.

The changing role of the trainer

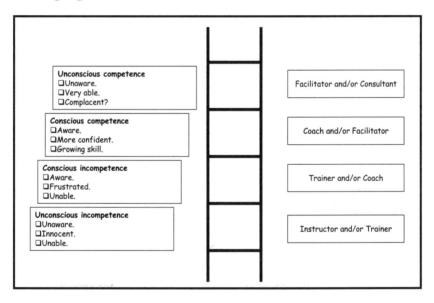

Figure 7.1 The learning ladder

It's worth reminding ourselves of the ways the trainer's role changes as learners climb the ladder, for you will need to reflect this in your design. Figure 7.1 shows the four rungs and, alongside, the roles the effective trainer needs to adopt. Stress in your design that a good trainer needs to be able to adopt these roles instantly as they will probably have people in their learning group on different rungs of the ladder. Before moving on, you may wish to reflect on this model to see how it resonates with you.

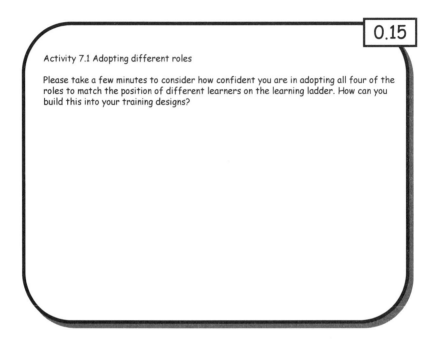

0.15

Activity 7.1 Adopting different roles

Please take a few minutes to consider how confident you are in adopting all four of the roles to match the position of different learners on the learning ladder. How can you build this into your training designs?

THE IMPACT OF LEARNING STYLES

Kolb's learning cycle

We'd like to explore two of the popular theories about the way people learn, starting with the work of David Kolb. He proposed that people progress round a cycle of learning events, the starting point being determined by their own preferred style. You may be familiar with the four elements, which are shown in Figure 7.2.

- Many people like to learn by having a concrete experience, often with limited preparation. Example – how many people when faced with a new software program will say: 'Just let me try it myself – I shouldn't need any help if it's good software.'

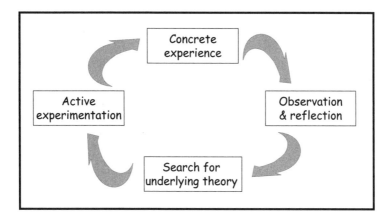

Figure 7.2 Kolb's learning cycle

- Others learn by watching someone else performing the task or reflecting on what they've seen. Using the software analogy, many people will ask: 'Would you show me how to do it before I try it myself?'

- Yet others will need to understand the underlying theory before attempting the task themselves. Back to the software: 'Can you let me read the manual first, please?'

- Finally, there are those who prefer practical experimentation to learn: 'I wonder how it might help me to complete that task?'

While most people progress round all four stages in the cycle, we tend to spend more time at some stages than others, depending on our own preferred learning 'style'. Over recent years David Kolb's work has come in for some criticism as it was based on limited research, and can be taken to imply that everyone progresses round all four stages of the cycle. But many people can relate to the underlying concepts, especially when we consider the model alongside the work of Peter Honey and Alan Mumford.

Four learning styles

Peter Honey and Alan Mumford proposed that there are four distinct learning styles:

1. *Activists.* Like having a new experience, and will tend to learn best from solving problems, opportunities, involvement, games, or practical exercises. These learners like to 'get stuck in' so, as a designer, provide concrete experiences and keep the pace lively and energetic. They often tend to find theory unhelpful.

2. *Reflectors.* Like watching others, or reviewing what's happened. They need time to think and absorb information before 'doing'. Your design should give them opportunities to reflect on events. They are impartial and observant, and like to discuss ideas and thoughts, so the pace should allow them time.

3. *Theorists.* Will probably find themselves developing concepts, theories or systems to apply to a problem. They like structure, order and clarity. Your design should allow them to explore underlying theories with their analytical and conceptual approach. They thrive on detail and extended discussion, and may have a reduced emphasis on urgency.

4. *Pragmatists.* Will be attracted to activities that have an immediate application, or offer the development of transferable skills. They like activities and learning that clearly relate to the real world, so provide practical experimentation, as they learn best by projects, tasks, etc. Provide space for small group discussions when they can search for practical applications.

Put the two together

It's easy to see from Figure 7.3 how Kolb's learning cycle can be combined with Honey and Mumford's four learning styles to develop a learning cycle, which many people will be able to relate to.

We can appreciate that each of the learning styles relates to a preferred way of learning and, if our training design is to be effective, each style has to be catered for. Most of us actually experience all four steps – personal style dictates how much time we spend at each stage and hence where our main learning occurs. Let's illustrate the four steps using a very real experience I had several years ago whilst gliding.

Some years ago I was gliding on a less-than-ideal day. There was plenty of lift around but the winds were very strong. After soaring for an hour I decided to land, but quickly realized that I had been blown downwind and would probably not make it back to the airfield.

Activist

You have some form of new experience – it may be good, bad, thrilling, frightening, inspiring or depressing.

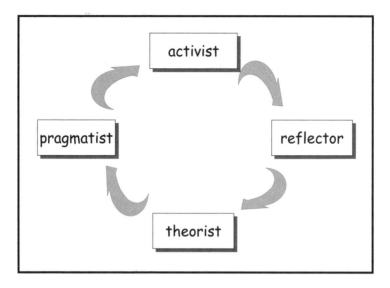

Figure 7.3 Combined learning cycle

Concrete experience. Although trained in field landings I wasn't expecting to do my first one that day. I finally landed in a field of cabbages just short of the airfield, having narrowly avoided a line of tress. As the glider came to rest, one wing tip caught the tops of the crops and slewed the glider around through 90 degrees.

Reflector

You reflect on what happened, and review all aspects of the experience. What did it feel like? How long did it last? What did it cost? Who else was involved? What was the end result?

Review the experience. As the glider skidded to a halt my mind went over all that had happened since it was launched. How long had I been flying? How could I have misjudged the strength and direction of the wind? Why did the wing catch and spin the glider around?

Theorist

You draw some conclusions from the experience. How did it happen? What might cause it to happen again? Do I want it to happen again? What might be a better outcome?

Conclude from the experience. What caused me to misjudge the situation? Should I have flown at all that day? How well had I managed the unexpected field landing? How did I honestly feel about my ability to cope with a wide range of flying conditions?

Pragmatist

What can I do differently as a result? Do I need any help? Do I need any extra skills? What materials, equipment or other resources may I need?

Plan the next steps. The first thing I had to do was to report the field landing to the farmer and assess whether any damage had been done (luckily none to either crops or glider – but much to my self-esteem!). Then I returned the glider to the airfield and resumed the day's flying, having apologized to my companions for their loss of flying time. In the longer term, I planned to ensure that this would never happen again. I reassessed my criteria for flying on windy days and being more vigilant about the effect of upper-air winds.

If you or your delegates are interested in learning more about their own learning styles, you may wish to consider using the 'learning style questionnaire' that was developed by Peter Honey and Alan Mumford (www.peterhoney.com). A less sophisticated but generally reliable method of discovering someone's learning style is to simply ask them before you start: 'How would you like to learn this?'

Before moving on, let's undertake a short activity on learning styles.

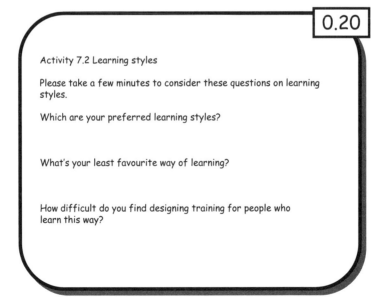

0.20

Activity 7.2 Learning styles

Please take a few minutes to consider these questions on learning styles.

Which are your preferred learning styles?

What's your least favourite way of learning?

How difficult do you find designing training for people who learn this way?

FIGHT THE FILTERS

As a designer you need to be aware of yet another set of potential hurdles your training design needs to overcome. We each have our own view of the world, which we tend to reinforce by creating a set of 'filters' that only allow through information that accords with our preconceptions and mindsets. The filters allow other information to be 'filtered out' and ignored. The VAKBASIC model shows the filters every trainer delivering your courses will need to fight through just to reach the processing areas of the delegates' brains.

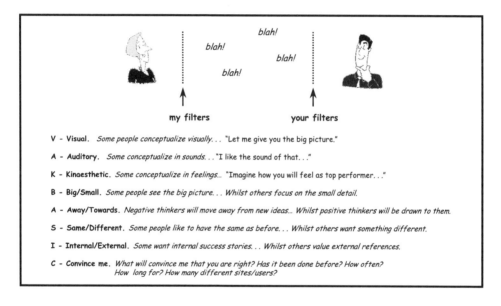

Figure 7.4 Fighting the filters

Visual, auditory, kinaesthetic

Let's go through the filters one by one. The first filters are those associated with personal communication preferences – visual, auditory or kinaesthetic. As you design your training it's worth remembering that some 80 per cent of the UK population have a strong preference for visual language, with auditory and kinaesthetic being secondary preferences.

Visual people will tend to retain experiences in the form of pictures, so their language will be mainly words associated with images. They'll say:

- I need to cast light on the subject…

- It's getting clearer…

- I can see what you mean…

Auditory people will tend to retain experiences in the form of sounds, so their language will be mainly words associated with hearing. They'll say:

- That rings bells for me…

- I like the sound of that!

Kinaesthetic people will tend to retain experiences in the form of feelings, so their language will be mainly words associated with sensations or feelings. They'll say:

- I'm under pressure.

- Keep in touch.

- I can't grasp that yet…

Having considered the three primary filters, visual, auditory and kinaesthetic, now let's look at the rest.

Filter B

This continuum runs from big to small.

People at the 'big' end of the spectrum will tend to see the big picture. They are 'big chunkers' and will be irritated by being asked to focus on details. People at the 'small' end will tend to focus on the smaller elements, the details. They are 'small chunkers' and will find it hard to see the bigger picture.

Filter A

This continuum runs from away to towards.

People at the 'away' end of the spectrum will tend to see the negative aspects of a situation. They will tend to focus on what they don't want to happen and can move away from. People at the 'towards' end will tend to focus on the positive outcomes they can see. They will talk about the things they want or hope to achieve and can move towards.

Filter S

This continuum runs from same to different.

People at the 'same' end of the spectrum will tend to look for things being the same or similar to what they currently have. They feel threatened by change or new developments. People at the 'different' end will tend to seek outcomes that are different from the current situation. They value new experiences or approaches.

Filter I

This continuum runs from internal to external.

People at the 'internal' end of the spectrum will tend to rely on internal references. They will base decisions on their own personal experience, and will be suspicious of changes until they have proved it themselves. People at the 'external' end will tend to welcome the results of external trials or how other people are using a particular approach.

Filter C

The C stands for 'Convincer Strategy', and tells us about what will be needed to convince the person to change the way they do things. There are two common variations: 1) Times – how many times will they need to see a result repeated to be convinced? 2) Duration – how long will they need to see the proposal in operation before they are convinced?

To show you've grasped the VAKBASIC concepts before moving on, why not try the short activity shown on p 118 (Activity 7.3)?

SO WHAT DOES THIS MEAN FOR ME?

Guiding principles

Whichever of the learning styles, models or concepts you subscribe to it's clear that you need to design your training events to catch and maintain the interest of everyone who attends. So what does this all mean in practice? We have deliberately covered just a few of the theoretical models associated with adult learning, but this limited coverage enables us to pull together some basic guidelines for you to follow.

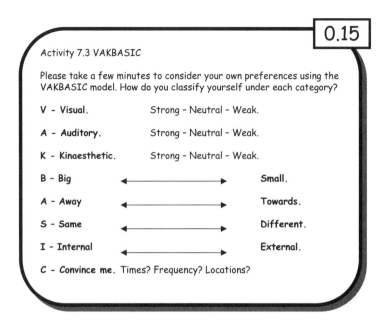

The underlying principle is to constantly visualize yourself in the target audience and imagine how you would feel moment by moment, taking part in the process you're designing. Then strive for a balance in everything you design:

- Balance the time spent discussing concepts or theories with trying things in practice.

- Balance the time you spend giving formal input with the time delegates have to formulate their own ideas or share their experiences.

- Balance the time spent working as a whole group with working in small teams.

- Balance the 'big picture' with small detail.

- Ensure you provide stimulation for all four learning styles.

- Encourage the trainers to use language and examples that will appeal to all three communication styles – visual, auditory and kinaesthetic.

- Vary the pace – ideally change the activity or the way you are processing it every 30 minutes.

Designing course materials

As you design the materials to support your sessions you'll realize that some options work better for specific learning styles. In general you may wish to consider the following:

Material or approach	Learning style
Reference guide	Theorist
Worksheets	Activist, Theorist
Student notes	Activist, Reflector
Scenario cards	Reflector, Pragmatist
Video/DVD	Reflector, Pragmatist
PowerPoint slides	Theorist
Quizzes	Activist, Pragmatist
Flash cards	Activist, Theorist
Practice sessions	Activist, Reflector

0.15

Activity 7.4 The impact of learning styles on your course

Having explored some of the issues on learning styles, take a few minutes to consider how they might affect the way you design your course and jot down the key points here.

8

Go with the flow

- Process-map the flow
- Learning methodologies
- Four ways to communicate
- Timing the course outline
- 'Sign off' by the project sponsor

PROCESS-MAP THE FLOW

Now you're ready to start the design, you may be feeling that familiar sensation of panic. 'Where do I start?', 'What should I include?', 'Will I be able to fit it all into the available time?' From experience, the most effective way to tackle the initial design work is to employ a method that frees you from any preconceptions or limitations. We would recommend using Post-it Notes, or their equivalent, as they're so flexible:

- You can move ideas around any number of times until you are happy with the result.

- You can easily insert new ideas as they occur to you.

- You can use them anywhere. My partner and I have often designed courses on plane journeys – you'd be amazed how many fellow passengers join in with ideas! You may be one of them.

- Portability. Once completed, the Post-it Notes can be plucked off the surface and popped into a pocket, to be reconstructed anywhere.

- Colour coding. Use different colours to denote varied activities, for example input sessions, teamwork, guest speaker 'slots', etc.

- You can start anywhere – you're not limited to starting at the 'beginning'.

- You can work solo or with a team.

An alternative to Post-it Notes is the range of commercially available planning hexagons, which have a yellow surface on which you write with dry-wipe pens. They are made in different sizes, and have a magnet on the reverse side so they stick to most whiteboards, meaning you can group them and move them around just like Post-it Notes. The high initial cost is offset by their long life. Like everything there are downsides – their reusability is countered by their lack of flexibility – you don't have the wide choice of surfaces to use that you do when using Post-it Notes.

Get a rash of ideas

Using Post-it Notes, or the hexagons, for course design couldn't be easier – the first task is to get a rash of ideas on your planning surface. Grab a stack of yellow stickies, find yourself a suitable surface (glass is ideal) and get going. As you think of any idea write it on a Post-it Note and stick it on the wall or glass. The only rule is that you need a separate Post-it Note for each idea. Once you get started the ideas will quickly flow, so just go with the flow and keep writing until the ideas dry up. Depending on the complexity of the topic and the depth of coverage, you may end up with between 40 and 60 Post-it Notes.

Theme the ideas

Once you've got a good rash of ideas the next phase is to consider the ideas and group them into themes or families. This process will help you to identify the topics that will ultimately be included in your course, and eventually lead to the development of the detailed timetable.

Start moving individual Post-it Notes into groups of similar topics or themes and you will gradually see a picture or flow begin to emerge, which is the embryo of the final programme. Here are some tips:

- Move from simple ideas or concepts to more complex ones.

- Move from individual skills to a combination of skills.

- Move from moderate to more demanding complexity.

- Look for natural sequences, such as processing a customer's order, or the life cycle of a product.

- Perhaps follow a chronological sequence – past, present and future.

Have you considered developing the entire programme around a central theme, case study or analogy (a principle of accelerated learning)? For example, one quality management programme I was involved in was based on the theme of making a journey, so we had a 'railway' theme for the course:

- The course had a proper timetable.

- The key tools and techniques were sited at various 'stations' that the delegates visited.

- The facilitators wore appropriate railway kit.

- And the Managing Director was dressed as the Fat Controller (his choice)!

When delivering recruitment courses I start by asking delegates to chart the whole recruitment process using Post-it Notes – from initial vacancy through to the new team member joining. We quickly have more that 40 tasks or individual activities plotted, which the delegates order into the appropriate sequence. The sheer number of interdependent tasks comes as a surprise to them, as well as demonstrating why an effective recruitment process takes so long. We then work through the process, spending time on the critical steps along the journey.

Working with the Post-it Notes may prompt you to add further ones as you realize that you have gaps. The final outcome is a wall that has several well-defined groups of Post-it Notes that represent the main themes for your course. Once the initial grouping is completed, stand back and reflect on what's appeared:

- Does it make sense?

- Can you see an overall pattern or flow emerging?

- Are there any obvious gaps or duplications?

- What do you feel about the overall flow – how will the course delegates react to it?

If you intend to do this initial planning with others then remember to allow time for them to reflect on the outputs. Their 'buy in' at this stage is most important so give them time and space to discuss the outcomes. With lots of people suggesting ideas you can expect to have some duplications. Ask the respective authors to explain what they had in mind when they wrote their idea – you may have two apparently similar ideas which, on further exploration, are quite different. If there are genuine duplications then invite one of the authors to remove theirs.

It's time for an activity, don't you think? This is a good moment for you to develop the initial rash of ideas for your course using Post-it Notes.

0.30

Activity 8.1 Initial planning for your course

Please use Post-it Notes to develop your initial ideas for the design of your course.

Start by getting a rash of Post-it Notes – remember each idea has its own Post-it Note.

Once the ideas dry up, put the Notes in groups or families so you start to see a pattern emerge.

Go away and do something else, then come back and evaluate what you've done. Happy with the results so far?

LEARNING METHODOLOGIES

Now that you have identified the content for your course the next step is to decide how each element is to be delivered. There are two main choices: trainer-led or self-study. The decision may already have been made for you by, for example, the sponsor who may have to work within internal political or commercial constraints. But if the choice is yours then consider the following guidelines:

- Trainer-led – when a group learns in a training room; it is essential for developing skills or shaping behaviours, and the success is very dependent on the knowledge, skills and style of the trainer.

- Self-study on the other hand is good for acquiring knowledge, especially as the learner can select which materials to explore, and work at his or her own pace and at the most convenient times.

- Self-study isn't limited to e-learning, and you will quickly realize that you probably already have a wealth of learning resources available, including books and training packs; published articles; video tapes; DVDs; audio tapes; interactive videos; one-to-one discussions and visits.

For ease we've referred here to the training being delivered in a 'training room' but in practice the training could be delivered in any environment – it just depends on the topic and the industry. As a young soldier, my training 'environments' ranged from the classroom to the simulated battlefield, from rifle ranges to bleak moorlands in the dead of night in the hissing rain!

Wherever possible, try to identify more than one resource for each chunk of the course. For example, the variety of learning styles in your target audience means that a video that interests one group may be a real turn off for others. Before moving on, let's briefly explore the advantages and disadvantages of these different methodologies, starting with trainer-led.

Trainer-led conference

Advantages

- Very large numbers – 100+.

- Good for imparting information or knowledge.

- Learners can choose sessions or subjects relevant to them.

- Lots of opportunity for informal learning and networking.

- Design time to delivery ratio quite high (in the order of 5:1 to 10:1).

Disadvantages

- Can be 'samey' if all sessions are given in a lecture format.

- Little opportunity to test understanding or application.

Trainer-led lecture with Q&A

Advantages

- Imparting large quantities of information or knowledge quickly.
- Should be current, based on the trainer's up-to-date expertise.
- People get learning direct from a high quality source.
- Large numbers of people.
- Low design time to delivery ratio (in the order of 3:1).
- Some opportunity for interaction.
- Low cost per head.

Disadvantages

- Not useful for demonstrations or practical application.
- Difficult to check understanding or ability to apply knowledge.
- Not good for behavioural or interpersonal skills.
- Trainer-centred – can be dull if variety is not designed in.

Trainer-led structured skills training

Advantages

- Learning practical, technical or interpersonal skills and practising them in a structured and controlled way.
- Good opportunities for trainer and delegate feedback.
- Testing can be easily incorporated.
- Reasonable design time to delivery ratio (in the order of 5:1 to 10:1).
- Moderate cost per head.

Disadvantages

- Practising the skills is often not in a real-world environment.

- Must keep the delegate numbers down to ensure optimum feedback.
- Can be too trainer controlled or centred.
- Less opportunity for learners to drive the agenda.

Trainer-led behavioural simulation

Advantages

- Excellent for interpersonal and behavioural skills.
- Gets as close to the real world as possible.
- Opportunity to practise what the learner wants to practise in a safe environment.
- Lots of opportunity for feedback.
- Design time to deliver ratio quite high (in the order of 5:1 to 10:1).
- Moderate to high cost per head.

Disadvantages

- Sometimes difficult to assess individual capability.
- Limited to small groups – 10 to 20.
- Resource intensive – can be higher cost to stage.

Self-study

Having looked at the group learning methodologies now let's briefly explore the advantages and disadvantages of self-study, which might be any combination of the traditional distance learning resources or a more sophisticated computer-based learning system. Later in the book we'll consider how to design these sessions in more detail.

Advantages

- Learner controls the pace of learning and when it's done.
- Good for acquiring knowledge and information, and certain levels of skills, eg language.

- Can be done during or outside working hours.
- Good for geographically dispersed or isolated learners.
- Can cover large numbers of people – 100 to many thousands.
- Delivers a consistent message.
- Costs are largely upfront, with low ongoing delivery costs.
- Can be combined with other methods to create pre- and post-learning opportunities.

Disadvantages

- Little opportunity for skills practice, so not good for interpersonal skills.
- No opportunity to question or debate the material unless combined with some form of face-to-face or telephone support.
- Once the design is completed there is no opportunity to make quick changes.
- Materials require more effort and cost to update.

Time for decision

By now you'll have some idea of which parts of your course will be delivered in trainer-led sessions and which might be appropriate for self-study, so it's time for an activity.

> **0.25**
>
> Activity 8.2 Session selection
>
> Please refer to the Post-it Notes you developed in the last activity.
>
> Start by selecting those you think would be most appropriate for self-study, leaving behind those you'll incorporate into the conventional group learning sessions.
>
> Now break and do something else for a while. When you return evaluate your earlier choices and confirm you're happy with the result.
>
> Carefully store the Post-it Notes you've selected for the self-study part of the course – you'll return to them later.

You have now reached a significant milestone in your course design, so number each Post-it Note to preserve the sequence, and ideally write down the order or transfer it directly to a PC. This outline will form the basis of the design of the course and, while it will need refining to allow some small changes to the overall flow or sequence, the basic 'spine' of the course is now in place.

FOUR WAYS TO COMMUNICATE

Now you have developed the basic flow for your course the next significant task is to allocate time to each chunk so you can start to finalize the overall timetable. But before you can do that you will need to consider the way that each session is delivered, as this will have an impact on the time each session needs. The ideas we introduce in this section build on the concepts from the last section and focus on the four main communications styles you can design in.

1. Telling

One popular approach is to use the telling style and the key characteristics of this approach are:

- The trainer or presenter delivers the message with little active involvement from the delegates.
- He or she is explicit about what needs to be done, and how it is to be achieved.
- The delivery will be well prepared, well rehearsed and perhaps involve multimedia visual aids.

This style of communication is most effective in situations when:

- There are specific management or performance messages to be passed on, which allow little or no scope for debate or discussion.
- There are urgent or timely responses needed to deal with specific situations.
- The delegates are new or inexperienced staff who would be able to contribute little to the discussions.

2. Selling

Another approach is to use the selling style, of which the key characteristics are:

- The trainer 'sells' the idea or concept.

- He or she provides limited opportunities for delegates to raise issues or concerns to gain their partial 'buy in'.

- The delivery will again be well prepared, well rehearsed and perhaps involve multimedia visual aids.

- There should also be time for some small-group discussions.

This style of communication is most effective in situations when:

- It's important that you gain some degree of 'buy in' to new initiatives or ideas.

- You're dealing with medium-term initiatives and there's not quite as much time pressure.

- The audience comprises staff with growing confidence and/or skill who would be able to contribute meaningfully to the discussions.

3. Involving

Now let's explore the involving style; the key characteristics of this approach are:

- The trainer essentially leads the delegates through a well-defined decision-making process.

- There is a high level of participation, which ensures the full commitment of all delegates to the resulting outcomes.

- Preparation will focus on defining the desired end results and the process to be followed.

- There should be plenty of opportunity for small group discussions and capturing the resulting outputs.

This style of communication is most effective in situations when:

- It's important that you gain a high degree of 'buy in' to new initiatives or ideas.

- You're dealing with medium-term initiatives and there's not quite as much time pressure.

- The audience comprises experienced staff with high levels of confidence and/or skill who contribute meaningfully to the development of the business.

4. Facilitating

Now let's move on to the facilitating style and explore its key characteristics:

- The trainer acts as a facilitator leading the delegates through a journey of discovery.

- There is maximum participation and control by the delegates, which ensures their full commitment.

- Preparation will focus on the process to be followed, since the facilitator will need to respond 'on the hoof' as the discussions develop.

- There should be plenty of opportunity for small group discussions and capturing the resulting outputs.

This style of communication is most effective in situations when:

- You're breaking new ground – a 'blue sky' type of approach.

- There are longer time scales with no immediate time pressures.

- The audience comprises seasoned professionals who contribute meaningfully to the development of the business.

Which to use?

In reality you will probably use a variety of these approaches during any one course – what you have to decide is which is most suitable at any particular moment. And of course they each eat up course time at different rates – telling being the quickest and facilitating being the slowest.

TIMING THE COURSE OUTLINE

Look at each session

By now you've got a better idea of how you intend each session to be delivered – is the trainer simply going to deliver the concepts, or will he or she involve the delegates to a greater or lesser extent? Having settled this you can move onto the next major step in the design process, which is to allocate a time to each chunk in the outline timetable. So it's time to go back to the Post-it Notes and consider each one in turn. Decide how much time each session will need, then write the time (in pencil) on each Post-it Note.

Employing 'unusual' activities

This early stage of developing the timetable is a good moment to consider if you are intending to incorporate any 'unusual' activities into the design. You recall we mentioned this earlier in Chapter 6. If you've decided to include any of these 'unusual' events or activities, such as go-karting, rock climbing, walking on hot coals, or horse whispering you will now need to decide how to build them into your timetable.

There are two time issues to consider. First, the actual activities will take a finite amount of time, which will eat into the precious time you have available. Secondly, you will almost certainly need to travel to a different location, so you will have to build this in as well. It will take longer than you expect – getting everyone on and off the bus, for example, takes a surprising amount of time.

Working into the evening

It can be very tempting to schedule work into the evening, especially if delegates are being invited to stay overnight in a hotel or residential conference centre. 'They can't complain – after all they're being put up in a nice hotel!' You'll often hear managers saying this, but it can be self-defeating as most people's energy levels quickly flag.

A pattern that is often suggested is to break from the day session sometime before dinner, then expect people to re-energize themselves after their meal and work late into the evening. Of course a lot comes down to company culture but, given a choice, it's better to work on to, say, 6.30 then close for the day. This approach also allows delegates to enjoy the leisure facilities that most residential conference centres offer – a bonus most delegates relish.

If evening working is to be scheduled then try to make it a fun activity. I once had to facilitate a challenging team-building workshop for a team who managed the sales of duty-free products in Europe. The sessions during the day were tense and conflict-laden so we had to lighten the mood for the evening. So, for the after-dinner event we divided them into four teams, and their challenge was to produce a fun, 5-minute video marketing a new duty-free opportunity for their products in Europe. To add an extra bit of fun each team selected at random two fancy dress costumes, one male and one female, which had to be woven into the story somehow. The teams chose from:

- Mexican bandit.
- Panto 'Dame'.
- Olive Oyl.
- Nun.
- Dennis the Menace.
- Cleopatra.
- Fred Flintstone.
- Convict.

The cost of hiring the costumes was modest and greatly enlivened the activity. Afterwards we had an Awards Ceremony when 'winners' from various categories were awarded miniature Oscars for their efforts. One of the most notable was the guy who squeezed into Cleopatra's dress – he looked quite stunning and never lived the event down!

Ebb and flow of energy levels

People aren't machines, so as a designer you must recognize and work with human energy peaks and troughs. The evening isn't the only time you need to be wary of – there are other times throughout the day when people are more or less active, or more easily stimulated. Some of the obvious guidelines are:

- Try to limit sessions of input or theory to the morning.

- Certainly avoid less-active sessions straight after lunch or towards the end of the afternoon.

- Devote after-lunch or late afternoon to active sessions or teamworking.

- Have shorter, more frequent breaks instead of infrequent, longer breaks.

- If using video have short bursts rather than longer sessions – otherwise you'll feel the energy levels sagging around the room.

- Keep to ambient light levels in the room – don't turn down the lights or people will fall asleep.

- Design activities that encourage people to get up, meet and work with different people.

Squeeze into the 'envelope'

All of these considerations will have an impact on when during the day particular activities are scheduled. So once you've done some adjustments, moving things back or forwards, gradually things will settle down and a pattern will emerge.

The next stage can often be quite a surprise! Add up the times from each session and compare it to the total time available for the course. In general you will find that the sum of the parts exceeds the time available. If that's the case you have several options:

1. Go back to the course sponsor and ask for the course duration to be extended.

2. Decide which sessions must stay and which must have the full time you've allocated.

3. Decide which sessions must also stay, but which you can reduce the time you devote to them.

4. Decide which sessions can be relegated to the 'nice to have' category and be delivered if you find you have extra time.

Assuming that you haven't had a sprinkling of 'magic dust' and had the course duration extended, by a combination of options 2, 3 and 4 you will be able to reduce the overall time to fit the time available. Let's turn theory into reality and return to your course design in the next activity.

0.40

Activity 8.3 Squeeze into the course 'envelope'

Now return to your set of Post-it Notes and total the time for the individual sessions and, by a process of adding and deleting, mould your outline so that it fits the overall time you have available.

'SIGN OFF' BY THE PROJECT SPONSOR

Before you undertake any further design work, this is an important moment to get the draft course timetable 'signed off' by the project sponsor. Don't proceed until you have his or her formal agreement, preferably in writing, or you may risk wasting your time. It may be that circumstances have changed, or that the sponsor knows something you don't that may have an impact on your course. In the initial design meeting you will have agreed how these milestones will be managed – will there be an exchange of e-mails, an informal meeting or a more formal presentation? Whatever you've agreed, present your case well but don't start on any further work until you get the go-ahead.

9

The STAR design model

- Follow the STAR
- 'S' is for stimulate interest
- 'T' is for transfer ideas or concepts
- Techniques for transferring ideas or concepts
- 'A' is for apply the learning
- Techniques for applying the learning
- 'R' is for review what's changed

FOLLOW THE STAR

You now know the overall flow for your course, how long each session will last, and when they start and finish. The next part of the journey is to explore the wide variety of options that exist to help you when you're ready to design each session in detail. In this chapter we'll introduce the STAR design model, and in the next chapter we'll look at designing workshop and team activities. Although

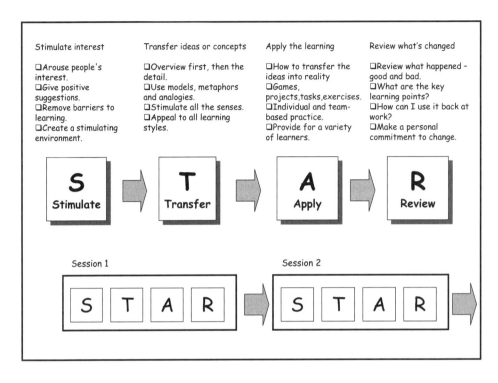

Figure 9.1 STAR training design

there may be some crossover between the two chapters there are some significant differences.

'S' IS FOR STIMULATE INTEREST

The first letter of the STAR stresses the importance of stimulating interest. If people aren't interested in learning, no matter how good the design and the materials are, it's unlikely that they'll get any real benefit from the training. So stimulating interest is something your design must do from the initial contact, through first arrival at the venue, and then throughout each and every session. Here are some things you can design in to arouse and keep your delegates interested.

Interesting joining instructions

Take a critical look at your current course joining instructions and, be honest, do they excite you? If you received them, would they really motivate you to attend one of your courses? If not – can you do something about it? You may wish to look at the example in Figure 9.2, which was used for an accelerated learning course. The document is printed on both sides of a sheet of A3 paper, which is then folded in a clever way so that, as the delegate unfolds it, gradually more detail about the course is revealed.

Look at some of the ingredients packaged in this example:

- It's addressed personally to the individual, making him or her feel special at the initial contact.

- The way it's folded is intriguing and arouses most people's interest.

- Printed in colour it says the course will be different – not boring 'business as usual'.

- It lists specific learning outcomes, at least one of which will hopefully appeal to the delegate.

- The informal 'overview' of accelerated learning looks different and interesting.

- It invites the delegate to do something constructive prior to attending.

- It says who to contact for more information.

- It gives clear directions about where and when the course will be held, and what to bring along.

Pre-course work

Does the subject lend itself to any meaningful pre-course work? Perhaps you can cover some of the underlying theory, or challenge delegates' pre-existing knowledge of the topic. Don't go overboard with this as you may cross that fragile line where people decide 'It's too much hassle!' and either don't finish it or, worse still, don't even start!

If you do use pre-course work, for goodness' sake make sure you refer to it sometime during the course, preferably earlier rather than later, and weave it into the whole programme. But don't expect that everyone will have completed it. In a typical group of, say, 10 delegates, one or two will have done it in full, six to eight

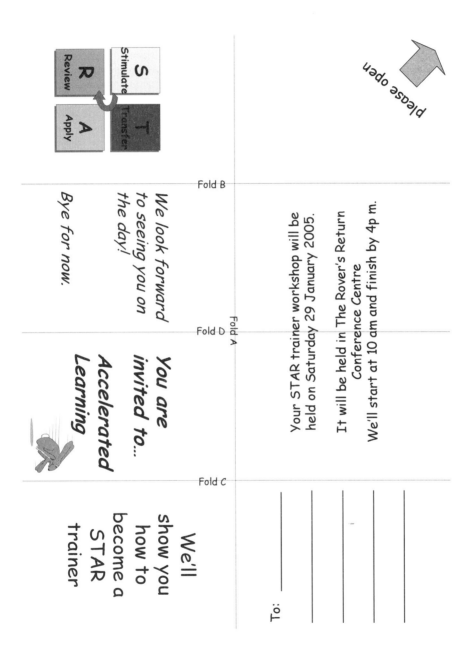

Figure 9.2 Interesting joining instructions

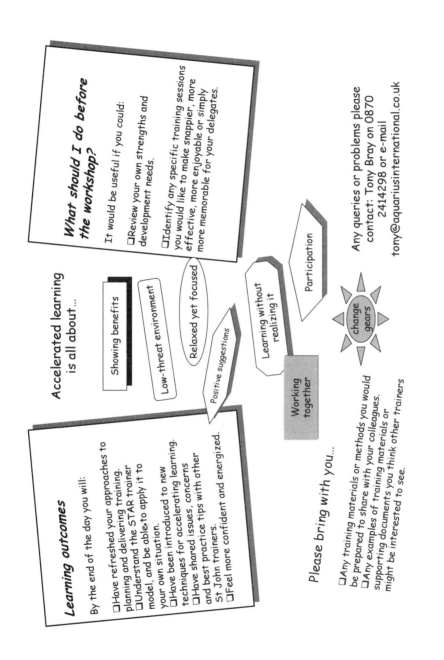

Learning outcomes

By the end of the day you will:

☐ Have refreshed your approaches to planning and delivering training.
☐ Understand the STAR trainer model, and be able to apply it to your own situation.
☐ Have been introduced to new techniques for accelerating learning.
☐ Have shared issues, concerns and best practice tips with other St John trainers.
☐ Feel more confident and energized.

Accelerated learning is all about...

Showing benefits

Low-threat environment

Relaxed yet focused

Positive suggestions

Learning without realizing it

Working together

change gears

Participation

What should I do before the workshop?

It would be useful if you could:

☐ Review your own strengths and development needs.

☐ Identify any specific training sessions you would like to make snappier, more effective, more enjoyable or simply more memorable for your delegates.

Please bring with you...

☐ Any training materials or methods you would be prepared to share with your colleagues.
☐ Any examples of training materials or supporting documents you think other trainers might be interested to see.

Any queries or problems please contact: Tony Bray on 0870 2414298 or e-mail tony@aquariusinternational.co.uk

Figure 9.2 Interesting joining instructions (*continued*)

will have done most or all of it but some time ago… and one or two will have done very little!

When we come to consider designing e-learning, this issue of completing pre-course work becomes even more critical as there is likely to be little time in a short trainer-led course to cover the basic theory. So it's ideal if the learning management system allows onto the trainer-led course only those who have actually completed all sections of the e-learning materials recently, or who have scored highly in the pre- and post-course tests. That way you have a sporting chance of ensuring your delegates have some grasp of the theory when they arrive.

Personal contact

If at all possible, make time to contact each delegate personally before the course – it doesn't take long but will have a huge impact. Don't send an e-mail – talk to them just like people used to – remember? Ask about issues or concerns they may have, and discuss their personal goals for the course.

Like going to the dentist?

I have always hated going to the dentist – I guess it all started when, as a child, I had a lot of trouble with my teeth and had to go the school dentist. Anyway, I eventually overcame my dread but still find it a worrying experience. I can remember sitting in the chair on one occasion, white-knuckled hands gripping the chair, dreading what would happen next – and I suddenly became aware of the dentist and his assistant chatting about the most mundane things. What they did at the weekend, where they were going on holiday, how the new car was running, etc.

They seemed to be quite unaware of the terror I was feeling – then I suddenly thought: 'How many people arrive for training courses feeling just like I do now?' And I would be as unaware of their sense of terror as the dentist is. Because I feel comfortable and at ease in a training room doesn't mean my delegates feel the same. So from that day onwards I resolved to put more energy into making people arriving for courses feel more relaxed and at ease.

Create a stimulating environment

A critical moment is when your delegates first enter the venue – what does it look, sound, smell and feel like? First of all, can they even identify the right room easily – is there a colourful, welcoming sign on the door? Then as people come in, what greets them? Stress in your design the need for trainers to 'meet and greet' delegates personally as they enter – make them feel special.

They should shake the delegate's hand, smile and make that first all-important eye contact. If they called them before the course, remind the trainer to try to remember what they discussed and bring it into the conversation. Have they been on holiday? Started a new job? Have they had some life-changing experience, like getting married, becoming a parent, or getting divorced?

Suggest that the trainers try to put themselves in the delegates' shoes as they enter the room – what will they experience? What will they be feeling? Try to stimulate as many of their senses as you can:

- Ensure the room looks welcoming and promises an interesting experience – table 'dressing' and room layout all contribute.

- Have colourful posters or charts on the wall, which change the feel of the average training or conference room.

- Provide challenging games or puzzles on the tables, which suggest that the course may be fun, and which get people talking and 'break the ice'.

- Play some appropriate music to take away that 'empty' feeling about a quiet room.

- If the air in the room is a little 'stale', light a joss stick to bring in a different aroma, but be careful that you don't site it under a smoke alarm, or you'll be out of the room in minutes!

- Arrange the furniture in a collaborative seating layout, which suggests that the delegates are more important than the trainer and encourages people to talk with each other.

Any plans for 'special effects'?

Sometimes you may be asked to design a course or workshop that has to create a high impact. If so you may consider employing 'special effects' that could highlight specific features, achievements or underlying principles to enhance the value of the event.

Can I share with you some examples that might fire your imagination? I helped to stage a conference for the IT function of a major international company, which was designed to get the IT specialists thinking beyond the technical aspect of their role, and see the contribution they made to the overall business. I suggested two ideas: one was adopted and the other was rejected.

One proposal was to set up an electronic counter that recorded the number of products the company made worldwide. It would be switched on when the conference opened and kept going throughout the duration of the event. In effect it was like a heart beat, giving the delegates a visible and constant reminder of what the business was about. This proposal was adopted and the counter set up in the main conference room. The impact was really effective and brought home to delegates the importance of the production they were supporting.

Another proposal was to construct across the entrance door into the conference centre a huge computer screen, complete with mock keyboard on the floor. As delegates arrived on the first morning they would smash through the screen and go through into the meeting hall to conduct the business. This would symbolize going through the technology to focus on the real business issues. This proposal was not adopted because, although the idea was in tune with the overall theme, the costs would far outweigh the impact, which would last for only a very short time.

0.15

Activity 9.1 How to stimulate interest

Can you identify any ways to stimulate extra interest in your delegates?

❑ Great expectations – arousing interest before they arrive at the course.

❑ Create a stimulating environment – removing the barriers to learning and making the venue feel, sound and look exciting.

'T' IS FOR TRANSFER IDEAS OR CONCEPTS

Now you have folks stimulated to learn, you're ready to move into the 'T' of STAR, when you begin to transfer some of the ideas or concepts you want to cover from your brain to theirs. First let's explore some of the overarching principles before looking at a selection of specific techniques. If you want extra ideas, surf the net and search for 'accelerated learning' – you'll find masses of sites!

Overview first, then the detail

Show people the wider perspective before you go into detail – that way people can see how the pieces fit together and the flow from one item to another.

Give positive suggestions

Ensure your design makes delegates feel positive about the learning experience they're about to undertake and that they'll develop both confidence and competence. Many course trainers seem to delight in telling delegates how difficult the subject is, or how few will manage to pass!

Use models, metaphors, stories and analogies

Constantly be searching for different ways to enliven familiar concepts or processes, especially those familiar, traditional or 'boring' topics.

Stimulate all the senses

It takes little imagination to use the two most common senses – hearing and seeing – especially with the easy availability of PowerPoint. But you can often build in ways to have delegates use their sense of touch – for example, handling materials, samples, models or parts of the 'real thing'. There are also many opportunities to use the sense of smell, especially with products or materials. Involving the sense of taste is a little more challenging – but it can be done, especially if you can use blindfolds as well!

Appeal to all learning styles

We've covered this already, but this is a good place to have a reminder – balance the active pace with time for reflection; balance the theory with the practical.

Reinvent approaches for familiar topics

There's no such thing as a boring subject – only boring designers or trainers! So always be on the lookout for new ways to put ideas across. For example, to illustrate the power of body language try showing delegates a short extract from a ballet, and ask them to summarize what they have learnt about the characters. You'll be amazed at what people can deduce from the dance, the gestures and the body language, all without a word being spoken! Bringing some wonderful music into the training room is an added bonus!

Change the processing method

Vary the way people do things – interleave trainer-led discussions with team exercises, paired discussions, solo work and challenges. Encourage delegates to constantly work with new people so they experience different ideas and approaches.

Change gears

As you design the programme, ensure that people don't do the same thing the same way for longer than 30 minutes. To keep their interest change the task, the focus, the grouping, or whatever.

Learning without realizing it

Whenever possible arrange your design so that delegates learn without realizing it.

The atmosphere

Strike the ideal balance between being relaxed and focused, although you need to recognize that much of the success of this will depend on the trainer running the programme. This is where the appropriate use of music can be so helpful – upbeat tempo when there's some energetic teamwork, or relaxing, reflective music for those quieter moments.

Working together

Design courses that encourage people to work together. Once we're adults we tend to do many work activities alone, which prevents us from benefiting from other's ideas and inspiration.

Make sure it's fun!

People will learn much more if they're enjoying themselves. To be effective training doesn't have to be serious, boring, intimidating, intense, etc. So build in fun and enjoyable tasks or activities.

Use humour carefully!

Don't tell jokes – for two reasons. First, most jokes rely on making fun of people in some grouping or other, and you may just have one of them in your audience! Secondly, jokes require good timing to deliver the punchline and, if you're nervous, you'll screw it up!

But have humour – it naturally oils the wheels of any course. And direct humour towards yourself – that way you can be sure that you won't offend anyone.

Participation

Overall, do everything you can to get people engaged with the course and the content physically, mentally, emotionally and spiritually. Make sure they see the course as something that is done with them and not something that's done to them!

TECHNIQUES FOR TRANSFERRING IDEAS OR CONCEPTS

1. Presentation

A straightforward way of transferring ideas is to deliver them in a focused presentation.

2. Demonstration

A demonstration is an expanded form of presentation, where the trainer demonstrates the skill or technique in action. This is particularly helpful when delegates will be expected to perform the skill or capability themselves.

3. Follow me

A variation on the traditional demonstration is to progressively transfer responsibility to the delegates as they build confidence. In the Army much of our weapon training was done this way, and a very effective approach it was. Breaking this method into its component parts, it looks like this:

- The instructor would first demonstrate the skill at normal speed to show what standard of performance was expected. To the uninitiated it all looked like a blur!

- The instructor would now do it again slowly to show the individual steps in more detail. Each step was given its own number.

- The recruit would now attempt each step in turn, with the instructor giving appropriate feedback, and sharing the tricks of the trade.

- Finally, the recruit does the whole process alone, slowly at first, then building up speed.

4. Visualization

Another valuable way to transfer learning is to use the power of visualization, especially if you're trying to implant apparently random information. If you don't believe this works, can you take a few minutes to try it yourself? You can? Good.

Before we start we'll ask you to do something we'll recommend later in this chapter, which is to undertake a pre-test to assess your current level of knowledge on the topic. This will take you about two minutes. Ready? On a sheet of paper please write down the names of the planets in our solar system in order from the sun. Done that? Then you're ready to start the visualization journey:

- First of all I want you to imagine that hanging from the ceiling is the base of a huge thermometer and, as you know, in the bulb of a thermometer there is Mercury. That's our first planet.

- The bulb suddenly bursts, spewing globules of mercury around. I want you to imagine that some of the mercury is caught by a really beautiful woman. Try to visualize her in as much detail as you can. Her name of course is Venus. So now we have Mercury and Venus.

- She throws some of this mercury over towards the garden, where it lands with a loud thump as it hits the Earth. So that is our third planet. We now have Mercury, Venus and Earth.

- As the mercury lands, it throws up a shower of earth and it rattles against the fence that you share with your neighbour. Can you imagine the violent drumming noise? This makes your neighbour angry and you suddenly see this bright red face pop over the fence shouting at you. And what is the planet with the red face? Mars. So we have got so far, Mercury, Venus, Earth and Mars.

- Mars is making such a noise in the neighbourhood that he upsets the big fellow down the road, and he comes along to sort it out. And the biggest planet in the solar system is Jupiter.

- As Jupiter walks down the street you see that he has a white T-shirt on with a brilliant sun on the front. And of course SUN is short for Saturn, Uranus and Neptune.

- And then you notice a small dog yapping around his feet. And the little dog is called? Pluto.

So now we have Mercury, Venus, Earth, Mars, Jupiter, Saturn, Uranus, Neptune and Pluto. And if you've really done that visualization well, you'll always win a pint from friends when that question inevitably comes up in the pub quiz! Finally, go back to your sheet of paper and check how many you got right in the pre-test.

Visualization works extremely well for a wide range of applications – of course the trainer really needs to believe it so he or she can embroider the story with all sorts of details and realism.

5. Mnemonics

Mnemonics are a powerful way of remembering abstract or random information. Why not build into the design a session that asks the delegates to create their own mnemonic. Recognize these?

- Most Volcanoes Erupt Mulberry Jam Sandwiches Under Normal Pressure

- Every Good Boy Deserves Fun
- FACE
- Any Red Port Left?
- Take Vera to the Matinee and Doris to the Concert
- HOMES

In case you're stuck, they are:

- The order of the planets in our solar system.
- Musical notation EGBDF and FACE.
- The red light shows on the left (port) side of a ship or aircraft.
- The next one's for the navigation buffs – apply Variation to a True heading to convert it to Magnetic, and apply Deviation to convert Magnetic to a Compass heading.
- An easy way to remember the Great Lakes – Huron, Ontario, Michigan, Erie and Superior (that's another pub quiz question sorted).

6. Acting out a system

Assign people roles to play in a process or system and have them act out the whole process. This can be useful for teaching people concepts like handling a 999 (or 911) call.

7. Alternative presentations

Suggest that the trainer delivers a presentation as:

- a talk show;
- a news programme;
- a press conference (with learners planted with questions);
- a story hour;
- a bingo game (with learners having to complete information on bingo cards as new learning material is presented);

- a demonstration with people as props;
- a one-person skit, with the presenter depicting the situation he or she is in.

8. Articulation

Stop a presentation periodically and have partners talk to each other about the presentation, what it means to them, and how they can apply it in their life and work.

9. Collaborative pre-test

Give people 'the final exam' right at the start of the course/session. Ask them to collaborate with each other to see how much they already know or can figure out using the available reference material, ie reference guide and current knowledge.

10. Flowcharts/diagrams/drawings

Give delegates a text on an unfamiliar topic, for example management of a disciplinary case. Ask them to study the reference guide in pairs and then to produce a flowchart or diagram that summarizes the process described in the text.

11. Interrogating the text

- Give delegates an unfamiliar piece of text from the reference guide.
- In pairs or small groups they are asked to formulate important questions the text should be able to answer, or they hope the text will answer.
- Read the text, highlight key points, discuss the key points and agree answers to the questions formulated.

12. Key points

- Put delegates in groups and give them an unfamiliar piece of information from the reference guide.
- Ask them to read the text alone for a few minutes with an eye on the next task.

- The group identifies, say, five key points made by the text. (It helps if the number of key points is the same as the number of groups.)

- The trainer then asks each group to give one key point (that has not already been mentioned by another group).

13. Musical questions

- Give each learner a card. Ask them to print on the card a question relating to the material just covered, and not to write their name.

- While music plays, ask them to keep passing the question cards to the right until the music stops.

- Then give them a set amount of time to research the question card they are holding at that point, using any person or document in the room as a resource.

- Then debrief.

14. Treasure hunt

- Put people in teams.

- Give each team the same list of 10 or 20 items of information to gather in a set amount of time, using resources both inside and outside of the training room.

- Want to add an extra bit of fun? Give them Polaroid cameras and make it a 'Photo Treasure Hunt'.

15. Snowball

- Instead of 'telling', the trainer asks a question that leads to what the delegates have to learn.

- Each individual then writes down his or her thoughts without reference to others. Delegates then share what they have written in pairs or threes. Optionally, the pairs or threes combine to create larger groups, which again compare their answers, and then agree a group answer.

- The trainer asks each big group in turn for one idea they have had, and writes the useful ideas on the board, perhaps saying a little in support of each idea.

16. Stump your partner

Ask partners to ask each other five questions about what was just presented.

17. Learning by guided discovery

Ask 'diagnostic' questions and answers, and use any wrong answers to explore and correct misunderstandings.

Try to use thought-provoking tasks and questions, rather than simple recall, as these require more thought and processing.

18. Video/DVD

Using video/DVD can also be a very powerful way of transferring ideas or concepts, provided the content is really 'on target', short and to the point. From experience, video is a passive learning technique, as delegates quickly start 'switching off'. So use it in short bursts to demonstrate specific points, perhaps involving delegates with relevant activities where appropriate.

19. Whole body learning

Get people up on their feet and use their whole bodies in the learning process. For example, if you're trying to illustrate one of the many models that use two axes to describe behaviours, like 'social styles':

- Ask delegates to imagine a line on the floor – one end is 'task-focused' and the other 'people-focused'.

- Ask them to stand where they think they normally operate.

- Now introduce a second axis at right angles to the first axis – to the left go people who 'ask' and the right go people who 'tell'.

- Keeping their original positions along the first axis, ask delegates to move left or right by an appropriate amount to show how they influence people.

- Once the movement has stopped ask everyone to see where others are then open a discussion on the four different styles represented.

Before moving on it's worth taking a few minutes to review the last section and decide which approaches you could find useful.

0.20

Activity 9.2 Techniques for transferring ideas or concepts

Please take a few minutes to review the approaches and techniques we've explored so far.

❑Which of them are you using already?

❑Looking ahead to the course you're designing, are there any that seem to have potential?

'A' IS FOR APPLY THE LEARNING

It's one thing for delegates to know something – but quite different for them to know how to apply it. That's why this stage of STAR is so important: it's when the whole purpose of the learning process comes to fruition, and people start to change the way they work or behave. So your design needs to give delegates every opportunity to practise the skills, techniques or approaches in a realistic setting. In a later chapter we'll look at a lot of specific techniques you can use but for the moment let's stay with the principles.

Show me

Ask people to demonstrate their capability. Using the earlier example of the administrator the trainer could ask each delegate to demonstrate that they could carry out the task consistently 'error-free in 4 minutes or less'.

Simulations

Use games, projects, tasks or exercises that require delegates to show their mastery of the skills or techniques.

Collaborative working

Incorporate individual with team-based practice. Most of the things we do in this modern world require us to work with others to achieve our goals – there's very little we can do by ourselves. So give people the chance to show how they interact with others while applying their newly-developed skills.

TECHNIQUES FOR APPLYING THE LEARNING

1. Cross-training

- Form delegates into teams who become 'experts' on their specific topic (say A to C).
- Once they've had time to prepare, ask the delegates to re-form themselves into new teams so each of the new groups has at least one of the 'experts' (an A, a B and a C).
- Each 'expert' now trains the others on their specialist topic.

2. Role play or skill practice

Please see the next chapter for more detail.

3. Team discussion with feedback

Ask delegates to form teams and discuss how they will apply the ideas or skills back at work. Perhaps ask each team to report back on a different aspect so the team presentations are varied.

4. Correct the errors

- Delegates work in pairs.

- One introduces an error into a system and their partner needs to discover and correct it.

- Change roles and repeat the process, the 'errors' becoming more challenging.

5. Hat draw

Ask everyone to put a question in a hat. Then everyone picks one out and has five minutes to research the answer for the rest of the group.

6. Art contest

Have partners or teams create artwork to review learning material, colourful pictogram murals, three-dimensional displays, etc.

7. Buzz groups

- Students work in pairs or small groups to answer a question or series of questions using common sense, experience and prior learning.

- Students can all have the same questions, or can be given different questions on the same topic.

- This group discussion can last for literally a minute or less, or for 20 minutes or longer.

8. Concentration

Put people in pairs. Give each pair a pre-prepared deck of cards and lay out the cards face down. Students then play 'fish' and discuss the issues presented on the cards. You can stipulate one, two or more cards as the learning progresses.

9. Talk me through it

Ask people in pairs or small teams to reconstruct a model of a process, eg a sales interview, while talking aloud about what they are doing, why, and how everything works. (A facilitator could keep asking questions to draw them out while this is going on.) Use protocol cards or simply draw the answers.

10. Create materials

Divide learners into teams and instruct them to create learning materials for each other. This could include job aids, review games, learning exercises, models to manipulate, research projects or problem-solving exercises.

11. Peer teaching and review

- When teaching a hands-on process (eg dealing with a stuck lift), put people in pairs, one partner being A, the other B.

- Ask A to perform a process just learnt for B, as if B has never heard it before and is sight-impaired.

- A has to talk out loud in great detail about every step of the process while doing it, or shout instructions to a pair trapped in a lift.

12. Twenty questions

- Prepare a presentation and, before delivering it, put people in pairs.

- Ask everyone to prepare a 20-question oral (or written) examination for their partners based on what they are about to hear.

- At the end of the presentation, have partners administer their tests.

13. Problem-solving exercise

- At the start of the session put people in teams.

- Give them a problem to solve relating to the learning material.

- Ask them to use any resource they can imagine inside and outside the training room for solving it.

14. Thought experiment (or empathy)

Students are asked to imagine themselves in a given situation and are asked questions about the situation.

   For example, discussing poor performance during an appraisal interview might prompt questions such as 'How do you think the other person is feeling?' or 'What would your reaction be if he said… to you?'

15. Cooperative learning

- Learning teams answer questions on the resource material.

- Teams are asked to use the text to answer questions prepared by the trainer.

- These questions relate to the key points in the text and to the key lesson objectives. They should be thought-provoking.

- The answers to the questions should not appear in one place in the reference guide. Students should need to read, understand, and then think about the text to answer the questions.

- This requires students to construct their own understanding and not just repeat the text back to you.

16. Question/answer exercise

- After or during a presentation, have each person write down three or more questions they have about what was just covered.

- Then have them get up, wander around the room and ask each other their questions until they find the answers.

- Then debrief.

17. Quiz games

Use games based on ones that the learners are familiar with such as 'University Challenge' or 'Trivial Pursuit'.

Make sure that the teams are balanced and that no member of the team is ever left on their own to answer a question.

18. Making a video

Give delegates the basic equipment (camera, tripod and tape) and ask them to make a short video that summarizes the key points of what they've learnt or how they will apply it back in the workplace.

They will need about an hour to plan it, 30 minutes to shoot it, and 30 minutes to review and discuss it.

19. Walk about

This method is especially good for courses like health and safety. Having gone through the theory of, for example, safety hazards:

- Pair off your delegates.

- Ask them to walk about the training venue and look for safety hazards.

- Then hold a group debrief – you'll be horrified at what they've found!

Before moving on to the next section, it's worth taking a few minutes to review the last section and decide which approaches you could find useful. As you've probably realized, many of the techniques we've included in applying the learning can also be used for transferring ideas or concepts, and vice versa. Remember – these are 'tools', not 'rules'!

| 0.20 |

Activity 9.3 Techniques for applying the learning

Please take a few minutes to review the approaches and techniques we've explored so far.

❏Which of them are you using already?

❏Looking ahead to the course you're designing, are there any that seem to have potential?

'R' IS FOR REVIEW WHAT'S CHANGED

Any 'quality' programme has three main components:

1.   Say what you do.

2.   Do what you say.

3.   Prove it.

So, having completed the first two stages, the final one is to prove that your training or learning has made a sustained change to business performance. How do you do that? By measuring in a consistent way across a representative population. So the final stage in any learning process is to review what's changed as a result of the experience. Are people now able to do what we wanted them to do? Evaluating training is one of those topics that has been debated endlessly, and there are a variety of specific measures you can put in place to deliver some meaningful results. We'll look at each one in turn:

● To start with, you can measure changes to skills or knowledge after completing parts of the learning.

- At the next level you can measure what changes an individual has achieved having completed the learning.

- You can easily measure delegates' reactions to the learning.

- You can monitor what sustained changes delegates display several months after the learning.

- Taking a wider view, it's valuable to monitor changes to the business overall that have resulted from the training initiative.

- If possible evaluate the overall financial impact of the training, so the business can quantify the full benefits of training.

Measure changes during the learning

It is surprisingly easy to measure changes during the programme to see what has 'stuck' from the material that delegates have experienced. Many of the techniques we looked at in the 'Apply the learning' section will enable the trainer to see progress, but to get a more consistent measure it's helpful to build in progress tests or assessments as you go through.

One of the projects I've recently been involved with is a training programme that helps delegates to improve their ability to observe, record and transfer data accurately. We build into the programme regular assessments that record people's abilities before and after each of the main sessions. That way delegates can see for themselves how much their skills have changed after each session in the course.

Delegates are given short, focused assessments, which take about 10 minutes to complete. They then exchange their answers with those of a neighbour and they each score their partner's assessments using the 'solutions' given in the back of the manual. The trainer then holds a brief discussion to bring out common themes or 'sticking points'.

This approach is also used a lot in e-learning designs to monitor progress throughout the course so that learners can be redirected if they seem to be struggling with a particular section.

Measure changes following the learning

It can be immensely powerful to be able to prove the immediate benefit of any form of training as a way of deflecting any complaints about the time or money that training is costing the business.

To be able to clearly show tangible benefits, you need to measure delegates' ability both before and after the training intervention. The 'before' assessment is best done right at the start of the course as that way you can be sure that everyone is doing it, and that they are all doing it under the same conditions. In the programme I just mentioned, delegates are given a pre-course assessment in the first hour of the course, which takes them about 15 minutes to complete. This assessment tests them in all the key areas to be covered by the course and provides a reliable pre-course measure of ability.

The trainer collects the assessments and scores them. Once the results have been summarized for the whole course they are discussed with the delegates to show their initial state of competence. Grossing up the percentage errors found in the pre-course assessments, the trainer can show the overall effect of these errors when applied across the whole working day for one individual, then accumulated for all delegates on the course. The individual assessments are returned to delegates privately for people to see where their own competence level fits in with the group performance.

The last session of the course is devoted to a post-course assessment, which tests delegates in the same key areas covered by the pre-course equivalent. The trainer scores this assessment after the course and returns the results to the delegates individually. That way the trainer can assess the overall change in performance that has resulted from attending the course and report the summarized findings back to the sponsor. This approach of 'before' and 'after' assessment is also used to great effect with e-learning to show the learner how much he or she has learnt. The 'before' assessment has another important function in that it helps learners to steer their way through the course materials:

- It helps them identify topics or sections they are very confident or familiar with, which they may decide to completely bypass.

- It shows sections they may have knowledge of but need refreshing.

- It identifies sections they may be novices at and which may require more detailed study.

This navigational aspect of the pre-course assessment is an important element of the e-learning design. Once the delegate completes the post-course assessment, the learning system can then instantly show the individual how his or her knowledge or skill level has changed since starting the programme.

Measure delegates' reactions to the learning

Many people scoff at the traditional end-of-course questionnaires but personally I find them very useful. Most of the fundamental changes to my working practices as a trainer have come from comments delegates have made on these questionnaires. However, I have heard some trainers refer to them as the 'Happy sheets', and it's no wonder that they only collect superficial or unhelpful comments.

To make the questionnaires effective we would suggest a blend of direct and open questions. Direct questions focus on specific aspects of the course. Use a scale for delegates to record their degree of satisfaction, ensuring there isn't a mid-way mark for the fence-sitter to hop onto. Open questions invite delegates to record their own views on what happened and how they will benefit from it.

The end-of-course questionnaire in Figure 9.3, which includes these design features, gives you a template that you may wish to modify for your own situation.

Measuring sustained changes

The real challenge of any training programme is to be able to show that delegates have applied their learning not just in the first few days after the learning took place but that they continue to do so for months afterwards. You need to be able to prove that there have been irreversible changes in skills or behaviours. There are several approaches you can take but, because they tend to be time-consuming, they are often not done:

- Hold one-to-one discussions with delegates (and their line managers?) to see what sustained changes they are showing some three months after the learning took place. If the line manager has done a good job the changes could even be reflected in specific objectives, related to the main aspects of the role.

- Follow-up by e-mail to see what longer-term impact the learning/training had, and ask the delegate to give examples of sustained changes.

- An approach I've used with a client recently is to ask delegates to copy their manager with the specific changes they commit to make at the end of the course. The manager replies to the HR Director saying how they will support the individual.

- Three months after the course the HR Director then contacts the line manager and asks for a progress report on the specific action points. Figure 9.4 shows what the action planning sheet looks like.

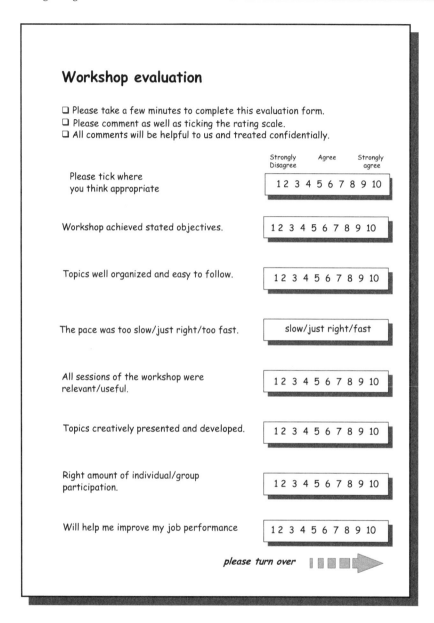

Figure 9.3 End-of-course questionnaire

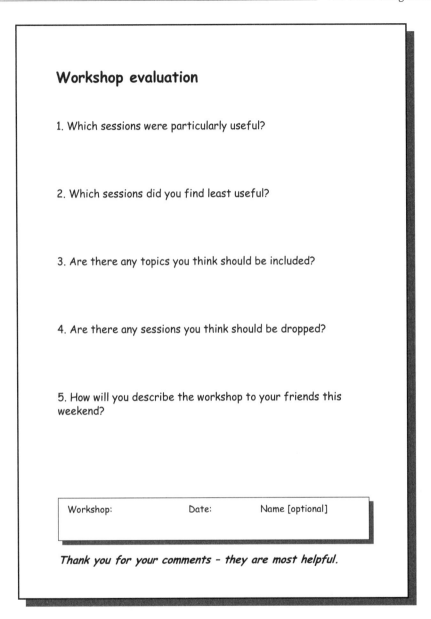

Workshop evaluation

1. Which sessions were particularly useful?

2. Which sessions did you find least useful?

3. Are there any topics you think should be included?

4. Are there any sessions you think should be dropped?

5. How will you describe the workshop to your friends this weekend?

| Workshop: | Date: | Name [optional] |

Thank you for your comments – they are most helpful.

Figure 9.3 End-of-course questionnaire (*continued*)

After this course I will …

Please review the course and identify a specific and measurable change in behaviour you intend to make.

❑ Please write the details here and be ready to share them with the other course members.
❑ After the course, please discuss with your manager what you intend to do. Your manager will be asked to return the tear-off slip at the bottom of the page.

> *I intend to …*

Name: Date course attended: /

To: AN Other
HR Director - Services

I confirm that one of my team,   , attended the
XXXXXXXXXX course on   /

Following the course I have discussed his/her proposed action plan and I confirm it has been recorded on their personal objectives.

I intend to support my team member in the following way:

Signed: Date: /

Figure 9.4 End-of-course planning

The difficulty everyone faces these days is that there's always so much pressure to get on with the next job that reviewing what's gone by is easily lost in the maelstrom. But it's worth doing if you can. If you can't monitor everyone, perhaps focus on a small number of 'critical' learning streams so you can at least be able to prove their worth.

Before we close this chapter you might want to think about what you may need to do to evaluate the effectiveness of the training programme you're designing.

0.20

Activity 9.4 Reviewing the effectiveness of your training programmes

Please take a few minutes to consider the way you intend to review the effectiveness of the training programme you're designing.

❑ Measuring changes to skills or knowledge during the learning.

❑ Measuring changes having completed the learning.

❑ Measuring delegates' reactions to the learning.

❑ Monitoring sustained changes several months after the learning.

10

Designing more complex activities

> - Designing workshop sessions
> - Reversed workshop sessions
> - Team-based projects
> - Role play or skill practices
> - Using actors

The last chapter explored a variety of ways you can transfer concepts or ideas, and which also help people to see how they can apply the learning from the course. All the methods outlined were fairly simple to implement and wouldn't require much organization or planning, but there may be times when you are asked to design a more complex session, for example when:

- Managers wish to disseminate a key message to a large number of staff.

- You wish to incorporate team-based activities into an event.

- You wish to develop interpersonal skills using role play.

- You decide to use actors.

DESIGNING WORKSHOP SESSIONS

Why use workshop sessions?

There may be times when it's necessary to design workshop sessions that will help to transfer ownership of the concepts being presented and make them 'come alive' for the delegates. But good workshop sessions don't just happen – they must be planned thoroughly and this section shows how. We have used a case study, based on an actual application in a factory, to illustrate how the principles were applied on a real assignment. There are many good reasons for using workshop sessions including:

- to build the delegates' commitment to an idea or proposal;

- to explore how an idea might be implemented or received;

- to change the pace and/or energy in an event;

- to strengthen relationships within or between groups;

- to have some fun or lighten the atmosphere in an otherwise 'heavy' session;

- to collect reactions to or suggestions on a particular topic.

There are at least two different approaches you can use for planning and managing workshop sessions: conventional workshop sessions and reversed workshop sessions. Each approach has its own merits and you will have to decide which approach is most appropriate for your needs. Conventional workshop sessions have these four steps:

1. Lead-in presentation.
2. Briefing for the workshop.
3. Workshop activity.
4. Feedback session.

Case study – introduction

To illustrate this process we will show how this model was used to plan and manage a complex communication event in a factory where the managers wanted to bring about a culture change among its 450 or so employees. The staff worked permanently in three shifts and were roughly equally distributed in terms of numbers. It was decided to hold a communication session with each shift to enable the factory managers to share their vision of the future with all members of staff. The session was broken into the following broad elements:

- Brief presentation by the factory manager on his vision of the future.

- Teams dispersed and, helped by trained facilitators, discussed three key questions.

- Teams returned to the main room and gave their responses table by table.

- Factory manager responded to the issues raised by the teams.

After outlining the guidelines for each step we will refer back to the factory setting and show how each part of the process was handled there.

Step 1. Lead-in presentation

For teams to be able to work effectively, particularly on a new topic or subject, they need some basic facts or background on which to base their discussions or activities. So, a useful preliminary is to have some form of presentation or input that gives the teams some facts or opinions on which they can base their discussions. It could be:

- a guest speaker who delivers a stimulating or motivational presentation;

- an industry 'expert' who shares some new research with the delegates;

- a senior manager who asks for a new level of commitment to change or new working practices.

By the end of this step the delegates should have a new level of knowledge or insight into the situation to enable them to go away and contribute meaningfully to the team-based activity, whatever it might be.

Case study – Step 1

The communication session opened with an address by the factory manager in which he:

- outlined the broad strategy being adopted by the factory management team;
- indicated what changes might occur and when they might be expected;
- discussed the future for the factory within the international group;
- asked for their full commitment.

The overall presentation lasted for 45 minutes and was repeated three times during the day, once for each shift: 10.45–11.30 pm for the night shift; 9.45–10.30 am for the morning shift and 2.45–3.30 pm for the afternoon shift. Incidentally, starting the whole process with the night shift was a novel feature by itself. Normally the night shift are forgotten altogether or seen last, which doesn't enhance their self-esteem. So involving them first in this process had a benefit all of its own.

Step 2. Briefing for the workshop

The delegates now have some new knowledge or insight and are ready to discuss implementation or how it might change their lives. To ensure the team-based work is productive and contributes effectively towards the overall objectives, they will need a full and comprehensive briefing. This is best accomplished using three media:

- Tell them in simple language what you want them to do.
- Show them the task, perhaps using slides or posters.
- Give them a handout that explains what outcomes you're expecting and what format they should be given in.

Case study – Step 2

After the factory manager's address the facilitator for the session briefed the staff for the next step in the process:

- He posed three key discussion questions for the teams.
- He outlined how delegates could participate in the discussions.

- He reminded people of the Post-it Note guarantee (that any issue raised would be answered within a given period of time).

- He described how the feedback should be given and mentioned that facilitators already had pre-prepared OHT acetates on which they could record their key points.

- He then invited team facilitators to take their groups away to start the discussions.

Step 3. Workshop activity

This is the moment when the teams actually get down to some work away from the main group. For them to be successful they need:

- A good briefing to ensure they start with the right objective and stay focused throughout their discussions.

- A suitable place to work together – free from distractions and with the right equipment.

- An optimum number of people, with a representative spread of views and opinions.

- Enough time to do justice to the topic – 50 minutes was given in our case study.

- A clear idea of the output(s) they were expected to produce.

- Ideally, their own facilitator to keep them on track.

- A set of ground rules they all agree to operate by.

Case study – Step 3

Having been briefed the delegates dispersed into 10 team areas, together with their own facilitator, who then led their groups through structured discussions:

- He kept the focus on the three key questions.

- They identified key points for the subsequent feedback session.

- They prepared slides for the feedback session.

- They helped the team to select a presenter who would give the feedback.

- Finally, they coached the presenter for their role.

The team rooms had all been prepared in advance so the facilitators knew that the discussion environment was right. Also, they had checked that equipment and materials were in place.

Step 4. Feedback session

The final part in the process is to gather all the staff back in the main room and collect their feedback. Juggling time is quite a challenge: spend too long on the feedback and the session can lose energy and people become bored; don't allow enough time and you will miss out on valuable feedback, and demotivate the delegates who have spent precious time debating your issues.

Once you have heard from all the teams you need to allow time to respond to the common issues or threads that have emerged. Again you will need to consider how to manage this without it seeming obvious that you have a pre-prepared response 'up your sleeve'.

Case study – Step 4

On the communications session the delegates had a refreshment break scheduled after their team discussions which, amongst other things, enabled the large plenary feedback session to start with everyone in place:

- The team presenters took turns to report their responses to the three questions.

- The factory manager listened to the views expressed.

- Once all groups had presented, the factory manager responded to the main issues.

- He guaranteed to reply personally to all the issues on Post-it Notes.

- Finally, he ended on a positive and uplifting note.

Altogether, something over an hour was scheduled for this closing plenary session, which allowed enough time for the teams to give their feedback, and still gave the factory manager some 20 minutes to respond to their comments and reactions. Overall the event was well received by all three shifts and led to a gradual and perceptible change in the culture within the factory.

REVERSED WORKSHOP SESSIONS

Another approach to designing workshop sessions is to juggle the sequence around so that you end with the expert's presentation instead of opening with it.

Case study – Introduction

The theme of this particular session was to explore ways in which computers and IT could be introduced to improve existing business practices. The guest speaker used a novel approach along the lines of the reversed workshop session.

Step 1. Introduction and briefing for the workshop

The overall leader for the session introduces him or herself to the teams and gives enough detail about the topic for the delegates to be able to contribute meaningfully to the workshop activity. This means that the topic should be one with which they are fairly familiar, and the facilitator is asking them to look at the issue from a novel or unusual angle. In addition to introducing the topic the session leader also briefs the delegates for the workshop activity, setting the task, team membership, timings, outputs, etc.

Case study – Step 1

Having introduced himself and the topic, the speaker told the delegates that they were to be introduced to an unusual business setting and they were to look for possible IT applications. He then showed a short (10-minute) video that explored the way that the international flower market has blossomed in Holland. It covered everything from growing, distribution and the way the auctions operated, through to final delivery to the end consumer.

Step 2. Workshop activity

This is pretty much the same as in the conventional workshop model – the teams go to their designated area and get stuck into the task. They produce the required outputs and prepare themselves to feedback to the main group.

Case study – Step 2

The teams dispersed, and explored possible IT applications in the flower market. Having produced the required outputs, they prepared their feedback to the main group.

Step 3. Feedback session

The teams return at the agreed time and share with the other teams the results of their discussions or activities. The session leader now acts as a facilitator, drawing out key points or underlying principles that he or she will develop in the final part of the session.

Case study – Step 3

The teams returned and shared their thoughts. The guest speaker facilitated drawing out key points to develop in the final part of the session.

Step 4. Concluding presentation

The session leader now takes centre stage and, using the outputs from the team discussions, develops the main themes of their presentation. If done well, this approach is highly effective, as the delegates see their ideas or conclusions being incorporated into the overall presentation. It must be done skilfully or the delegates may simply feel that they have been manipulated to produce results that fitted into a pre-ordained scheme. And that will alienate them – which is the total opposite to what you want!

Case study – Step 4

The speaker resumed control of the session and, using the outputs from the team discussions, developed the main themes of his presentation. He was able to show the delegates how their ideas could form the basis of a wider plan, and also how his particular expertise could exploit situations in ways they hadn't considered.

0.10

Activity 10.1 Workshop sessions

Can you see the need or value of using workshop sessions in your course or event?

If so, will you use the conventional structure, or the reversed style?

TEAM-BASED PROJECTS

Nothing cements people more effectively than asking them to work together in small teams on a specific task. Also, team-based projects change the whole basis of a course or workshop from being a one-way presentation of facts into a two-way, in-depth exploration of how delegates can use the new ideas or techniques. This section gives some ideas on how you can design light-hearted yet focused team activities, which can be used as stand-alone projects, or within courses, workshops or conferences to provide a motivating and energizing experience. A lot of the 'nuts and bolts' have already been covered in the last section so they won't be repeated.

You may well be asking yourself, 'What could we do?' To give you some ideas, here are some typical team projects, lasting from a few hours to several hours spread over a number of days. The specific examples given here are:

- Task 1 – to produce a video highlighting a new business opportunity.

- Task 2 – to produce a website for the department.

- Task 3 – to evaluate a CD ROM-based training package.

Task 1. Make a video

This particular task is a variant on a highly popular project, which challenges the team to produce a focused video in a very short period of time. They are given a basic video kit of camera and tripod, together with access to a range of materials and props. In this particular example there was additional pressure as the teams had to incorporate several fancy dress costumes, chosen at random, into the storyline. The whole team scored the resulting videos in a riotous after-dinner session, which resulted in the winning teams and individuals being presented with Oscars!

This type of 'make a video' project works very well for a wide range of applications as it is a *task within a task*. For example, if you're running a session on planning then you set the team the task of producing a video on the key elements of good planning. Not only do they have to focus their minds on what the key principles are, but they also get the opportunity to put the skills into action!

Task 2. Produce a website

This task unleashed a lot of creative energy. It made people really think about what they did and contributed to the organization, and how others might perceive them.

It's best if you can have some 'technical wizards' on hand to help the teams with the more technical aspects of developing the website, otherwise the available time can quickly be lost in dealing with the computing aspects.

The team sessions were scheduled over several days, which gave them sufficient time to develop really professional-looking websites. At the end of the overall programme the resulting websites were evaluated by a team of respected experts on several criteria, including creativity, innovation and overall impact.

Task 3. Evaluate a training package

This task presented the teams with the need to evaluate and report on a product that was relevant to their discipline or specialism. In this particular example the teams, all from the public affairs discipline, were asked to evaluate a CD ROM-based training programme. The teams were allocated several working sessions spread over a two-week period to complete the task. This was also a task within a task, as they were evaluating a product that provided media training, and so the very business of researching the product meant they were absorbing much of the content. The general approach works well for a wide variety of applications and people naturally take an interest in a subject that relates to their own work area.

When's the best time?

Lots of factors come into this but the obvious approach is to schedule these team projects at times when people's energy or interest levels are flagging. So schedule them at the end of the day and, if the event lasts over several days, schedule the team working sessions evenly throughout the programme. If you can arrange for the finale of the team sessions to occur towards the end of the event, perhaps with some humorous prizes, so much the better! Looking at the timing of the examples given in this unit:

- Task 1 – to make a video highlighting a new business opportunity. This was used at the end of a long and intensive first day of a two-day team building workshop. It released the tensions and provided a really fun and motivating experience in the run-up to dinner.

- Task 2 – to produce a website for a company. The teams were asked to produce their websites during three working sessions scheduled at the end of the formal business each day in a four-day training workshop. Getting together with team colleagues provided a light-hearted interlude in an otherwise busy programme.

- Task 3 – to evaluate a CD ROM-based training package. The teams were asked to evaluate this complex product over five working sessions scheduled during an extended two-week training programme. Returning to this task periodically helped to refresh key principles and also acted as an informal and quite unconscious training medium.

Design criteria

To secure the maximum degree of personal involvement, and hence success, it's worth checking your plan against these design criteria.

Task

- Make sure the task is relevant to the delegates' jobs.

- Provide a comprehensive briefing.

- Make the task challenging – put them under pressure.

- Provide all the necessary resources and give technical back-up.

The teams

- Keep the teams small – ideally five to seven people.

- Give each team its own dedicated work area.

- Give the team a sense of identity – team names, badges, logos, etc.

Timings

- Schedule the start time for the working session(s).

- Allow the participants to decide how long to work.

- If spread over several days, schedule the sessions late in the afternoon.

The spirit

- Keep the pace up – impart a sense of urgency!

- Make it competitive – tell them the success criteria at the start.

- Award prizes in a high-energy public setting.

- Have the teams produce outputs they can actually use after the event.

Using commercially available games and exercises

As you are well aware, there are a huge number of excellent games and exercises available commercially that have been carefully researched and designed to develop specific skills and behaviours. We're not intending to cover their use because they all come with excellent instructions. Do remember though when designing them into your programme that, as well as following the author's guidelines, you should also take account of the design criteria we've outlined above.

ROLE PLAY OR SKILL PRACTICES

Many of the courses you design will focus on developing specific skills, and an essential part of the learning process will be to give your delegates the opportunity to practise them in a safe environment.

Upfront, let's deal with the way you describe the sessions. For some reason people look horrified if told they'll be doing a 'role play' but seem to be quite happy when told they'll be doing a 'skill practice'.

Session design

The same overall design principles apply as we've covered in the previous sections:

- Step 1 – give a short linking presentation that clarifies the purpose and objectives of the session.

- Step 2 – briefing for skill practice – outline times, teams, roles, feedback guidelines, locations, etc.

- Step 3 – delegates undertake the skill practices.

- Step 4 – hold a feedback session to consolidate learning.

Team size

People seem most comfortable working in small teams, and probably the ideal number is three or four. For example, if they're practising interviewing skills, delegates can rotate around three roles: one person being the 'interviewer', one being the 'candidate' and the other one or two observing. After each 'round' they give feedback to the 'interviewer' before changing roles and doing it again, until they have all been the 'interviewer' and 'candidate'.

There are times when it's acceptable to work in a larger group. For example, when practising presentation skills most people realize that standing up in front of a larger number of people gives them a more realistic experience than presenting to two or three people.

Team membership

Generally, team memberships isn't an issue, but there are some potential problems to be aware of:

- Personality clashes. Occasionally you may become aware of personality clashes in the group that may influence team membership. My preference is generally to let delegates decide who they will work with, which means that folks with long-standing problems will avoid each other.

- The only time you may wish to break this rule is if the focus of the course or workshop is on, say, 'improving team working'. Then, forcing these people to work together gives them something very tangible to work with. And it may start to heal some of the underlying problems.

- The other common challenge arises if you have a manager and one or more of his or her staff in the same team. Whether this is a problem depends on the situation and the relationship between the people involved. If the manager is receptive to feedback, he or she will often receive valuable information normally denied to him or her. However, you often find that staff members feel inhibited by the presence of their manager so they contribute less and, as a result, benefit less from the course.

The scenario

Every skill practice needs a scenario that delegates can focus on – do you provide it or do you let delegates provide their own? There are valid arguments for each approach so you will need to decide what's right for you.

You provide scenarios – advantages

● Relevant topic – you know the focus of their sessions.

● Consistent focus – every course will focus on the same issues.

● Time saving – you save the time delegates need to think up and describe the situation.

You provide scenarios – disadvantages

● Topic relevance – not everyone may relate to the chosen topic.

● Playing a role – delegates may feel uncomfortable adopting a role that is foreign to them.

Delegates provide scenarios – advantages

● People get to practise situations they have to deal with.

● Very quickly the 'skill practice' feels real.

Delegates provide scenarios – disadvantages

● Panic – 'I can't think of a situation at the moment!'

● Time wasting – delegates need time to think of and describe the situation.

● Relevance – the topics may stray away from the main course theme.

A good middle course is to say that you'd prefer delegates to think of their own scenarios, but to have a selection of scenario briefings available that delegates can use if they can't think of their own topic. That way you cover both options. In a later chapter we'll explore the issue of good course materials.

Location

For skill practice sessions to be effective, the teams need somewhere quiet to prepare and then hold their sessions. If you have a large training room, you can possibly have two groups in there, provided they are well away from each other. Otherwise, you may need to include additional rooms in the venue specification to ensure you have the right amount of working areas.

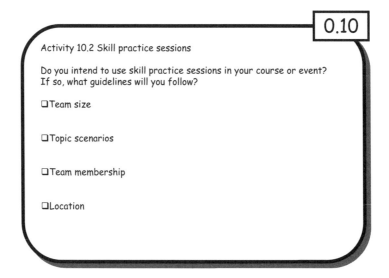

0.10

Activity 10.2 Skill practice sessions

Do you intend to use skill practice sessions in your course or event? If so, what guidelines will you follow?

❑Team size

❑Topic scenarios

❑Team membership

❑Location

USING ACTORS

One certain way you can overcome delegates' reluctance to take part in skill practice sessions is to use actors to play key roles. This way delegates are only ever asked to be natural and play themselves. Of course there are significant budget issues involved but, by careful scheduling, it is possible to spread the costs. I have had extensive experience of working with actors in training programmes, and giving two examples should illustrate the benefits.

When to use actors

One popular use is in recruitment courses when actors play the 'candidates'. By giving them a careful brief you can be certain that the 'interviewers' will all be presented with identical 'candidates'.

For example, when we have three actors I brief one of them to be 'pushy, over-confident and, when challenged, not as experienced as they portray'. Another is briefed to be 'quiet, unassuming, reasonably experienced but not assertive'. The final one is to be 'quietly confident, modest about achievements, well experienced for the job and focused on getting it'. That way the interviewing panels are all presented with the same evidence. It's interesting to see the different ways that people collect the evidence.

Another popular usage is in performance management courses when the actors play the staff members, leaving the course delegates to play themselves – the managers or team leaders. We generally ask the actors to work two main types of session during the course. The first is the introductory scene. Delegates are introduced to the actors and the wider scenario in a short scene, lasting perhaps 15 minutes. Delegates then have the opportunity to interact with the characters being played, and so learn more about the company setting and the roles the actors are playing. The course then breaks into a series of one-to-one performance discussions when each delegate has the opportunity to discuss performance with one character while other delegates observe. The timetable allows each delegate to hold at least one of these one-to-one sessions.

The actors have a clear briefing about their character and the issues they are facing, and will respond very realistically to the way they are handled by their 'manager'. Reflecting the sensitivity of the 'manager', I have seen one character come out of the one-to-one showing a growing sense of confidence about the future, while another 'manager' prompted a full mental breakdown!

Repeated over two days, the delegates experience a wide range of situations, both first hand and observing.

Benefits of actors

The overall benefits of using actors are:

- Delegates only have to be themselves – no role-playing involved.

- Consistent characters – depending on the quality of the briefing they are given.

- Natural responses to different ways of being 'managed'.

- Excellent, perceptive feedback to delegates on their performance.
- Brings an 'authentic' feel to a course or programme.

There are many sources of information on reputable companies that supply actors for this specific market. You could also ask your colleagues in other industries – you will quickly get a list of recommended companies… and those to avoid!

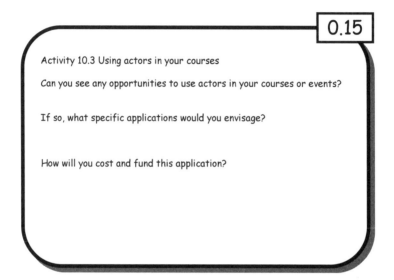

0.15

Activity 10.3 Using actors in your courses

Can you see any opportunities to use actors in your courses or events?

If so, what specific applications would you envisage?

How will you cost and fund this application?

11

Designing each session in detail

- Comply with company standards or policies
- The session plan
- Timings
- Session title
- Objectives
- Learning methods
- Administration and logistics
- A real example
- 'Diet' session plan
- Sponsor 'sign off'

COMPLY WITH COMPANY STANDARDS AND POLICIES

You are now well into the 'S' step of the DESIGN model we introduced in Chapter 3:

- In Chapter 8 you developed a logical flow and set the overall timings.

- In Chapter 9 you considered the most effective way to deliver each session, choosing from 38 different methods.

- In Chapter 10 you looked at designing workshop or team-based activities.

So now you are ready to design each session in detail and finalize the course time-table. As you start the process you must look outside your potentially 'narrow' training perspective and consider other factors that may influence your design. Depending on the topic there will be a varying amount of company-specific information, processes, standards or policies that must be incorporated into your design, and you need to find and use them. Failure to identify these 'givens' can cause you grief at a later stage in the design – at the very least you can waste valuable time while you gain the 'buy in' of people who 'own' the company standards. At worst they can derail your design process and insist that whole chunks of the course are redesigned.

For example, if you're designing a course on selling your company's products you must use exactly the same materials as are used elsewhere in the sales process. Contracts, specifications, conditions, prices, terminology, brand images, etc will all be defined by the relevant marketing teams and you must use them all, exactly as they are.

Delegates may also need to pass assessments or gain certification during or after the course to show they have met the requirements of appropriate certification boards. Some industries, for example financial services, are more strictly governed than others.

However, if you're designing a course on, for example, performance management, the situation will be more fluid. There will be many company standard procedures and policies that will have to be incorporated into the course, such as the company disciplinary procedure. There will also be many other aspects of performance management that are more generic, for example soft skills, and which can be imported as best practice from outside the company.

If you're designing a presentation skills course then the situation is likely to be different again. Apart from some general advice about using standard PowerPoint templates there will probably be little mandatory material to be incorporated. You will need to include all these materials, ideally in electronic format, so they can be used in your course design with the minimum amount of reworking. In many companies these materials exist in the company intranet.

One further aspect is to identify any other content that needs to be included in your training package. Perhaps there has been a recent directive or some new legislation that has to be stressed to all employees. For example, a recruitment and selection course would include a section on equal opportunities.

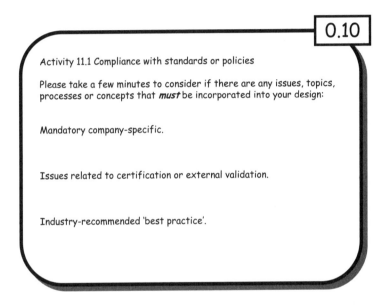

0.10

Activity 11.1 Compliance with standards or policies

Please take a few minutes to consider if there are any issues, topics, processes or concepts that *must* be incorporated into your design:

Mandatory company-specific.

Issues related to certification or external validation.

Industry-recommended 'best practice'.

THE SESSION PLAN

At the heart of every well-designed course or workshop is a detailed session plan that sets out exactly what the trainer will do, and when and how he or she will do it. Of course as trainers gather experience of a particular course they will need to refer to the session plan less, but it's always there as a back-up.

So what does a good session plan look like? We'll show you two formats – the 'traditional' tabular plan and a shortened 'diet' style. We'll start with the traditional plan, shown in Figure 11.1 and discussed in detail below.

				One-day Presentation Skills Course			
Start time	Finish time	Duration	Session title	Objectives	Learning methods	Admin & logistics
0900	0930	30	Welcome	Welcome delegates to the course. Clarify objectives. Safety & domestics. Introductions.	Trainer introduction. Delegates introduce themselves. Refer to pre-course work.	Delegate name cards. Workbooks. PowerPoint intro.
0930	1015	45	Designing your pre-sentation	Accept the need for preparation. Practice two visual techniques. Start design for own presentation.	Trainer-led discussion. Demonstrate two visual planning methods. Delegates practise on their own topics.	PP slides. A3 paper for Mind Maps. Plenty of Post-it Notes!

Figure 11.1 Draft session plan

TIMINGS

Start time

The start time is just that – when you expect this session to begin. Of course on the actual day the trainer may have a few 'no shows' at the published start time, so he or she may have to delay the start by a little. As trainers progress through the course they always have a guideline of what stage they should be at when they reach key milestones, such as morning break or lunchtime.

Finish time

Knowing the time that each session should finish gives the trainer a good reference point as he or she progresses through the course.

Duration

As the designer, you must recognize that the trainer will need to be flexible about the duration of each session as so much depends on the prior knowledge, skills or attitudes of the delegates. An experienced trainer will quickly assess which sessions can be whizzed through quite fast, or which may need more time than scheduled. Or perhaps there is a 'sticking point' that has to be dealt with before progress can be made on the course topic.

This often happens with internal courses, where there may be a 'hidden agenda' associated with the course or topic. For example, one of the clients I work for, in the electricity supply industry, relies on having 'suitably qualified and experienced people' (SQEP) at each of its sites, who become the 'experts' in particular disciplines or knowledge areas.

I remember being asked to deliver a series of courses to refresh the training and coaching skills of these SQEP, not realizing that there were considerable 'political' issues surrounding a proposed company-wide restructuring, which would involve significant redundancies or relocation. The delegates wanted to vent their frustration at the way the restructuring was being managed, and I had to devote a certain amount of time to this before we could make a start on the course content. A less experienced trainer might have tried to bypass these issues and stick to the session plan, not realizing that the group wouldn't want to learn anything until they were given the opportunity to air their grievances.

SESSION TITLE

Giving each session its own title helps everyone to see the shape and direction of the course:

- It helps to persuade the sponsor to 'sign off' the design, especially if you can use some of his or her key words or phrases in the session titles. Lots of Brownie points!

- A good session title then helps the trainer to see how he or she is progressing through the course, as the name of each session should illustrate the flow of the topics.

- Lastly, the session titles, if chosen well, should 'signpost' progress to the course delegates and help them see what stage they've reached.

OBJECTIVES

The next column in the session plan is devoted to objectives. Other than the welcome, the heading at the top of the column implies the following words: 'By the end of this session delegates should…'. It's very helpful to write focused objectives for each session that keep you, the designer, in touch with the fundamental reasons for having the course or workshop. Writing focused objectives is actually much harder than you think, so we'll take a few minutes to explore what's involved.

You may hear people talk about 'aims' and 'objectives' as though they are the same – but they're actually quite different. An 'aim' is a statement of general intent that gives a broad indication of the achievement required. For example: 'We aim to improve performance in the company.' An 'objective' on the other hand is a clearly defined milestone that is a step towards achieving an aim. It should specify what action is to be taken, how it will be measured, and when it will happen. For example: 'Our objective is to train managers in performance management and ensure that everyone has been trained by the end of the financial year.'

Three essential ingredients

So what should the objectives for your training sessions look like? One thing you can sure of – the better defined they are, the more able you will be to design training that works. And the 'tighter' your design, the more likely it is that people will actually deliver the required changes in performance. A good objective answers these three questions:

1. Performance – What do I want people to be able to do after the session?

2. Criteria – How well must they perform to meet operational requirements?

3. Conditions – In what context or situation must the skill be performed? Tools, resources, constraints, environment?

For example:

1. Performance: 'Administrators will enter all required delegate registration information…'

2. Criteria: '… error-free in 4 minutes or less…'

3. Conditions: '… using the company's standard word-processing system.'

Having this degree of detail for each session gives you a flying start to your design – for example, in this case you would know that this particular session would have to:

- Ensure that course delegates really understand what the minimum 'delegate registration information' actually is.

- Give them the opportunity to practise entering the information on the company's standard word-processing system.

- Provide opportunities for them to build their skills so they can show they can do it consistently error-free, in 4 minutes or less. So you'll need to build in time for them to show that they can do it.

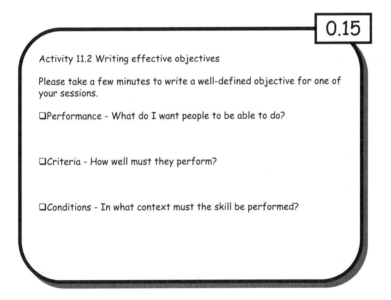

0.15

Activity 11.2 Writing effective objectives

Please take a few minutes to write a well-defined objective for one of your sessions.

❏Performance - What do I want people to be able to do?

❏Criteria - How well must they perform?

❏Conditions - In what context must the skill be performed?

LEARNING METHODS

By now you will have decided how you intend to deliver each session, so in the session plan you can record as much detail as you require. If you're doing the training yourself, all you need is enough to jog your memory. If someone else will be delivering the training, you will need to give enough detail to ensure that your design is followed consistently. This becomes even more important if the training is to be delivered by a number of trainers, at varying sites, and possibly in different countries. Remember the issues about cultural diversity we discussed in Chapter 3?

Whatever detailed methods you intend to use, remember that each session normally breaks down into three main 'chunks' – the beginning, the main body and the end. For a 45-minute session you might need 5 minutes for the beginning, 30–35 minutes for the main body and allow 5–10 minutes for the close.

The beginning

How the trainers open each session is vitally important as they need to quickly establish their own credibility before engaging the delegates' interest in the topic. This is critical, as the delegates need to believe in the trainer's skills, knowledge or expertise if they are to accept what they say. But there's a delicate balance to be struck. If trainers come over as being 'full of themselves' and bragging about their success or achievements, the audience may decide to take them down a peg or two. Conversely, if the trainers are too modest the audience may decide they don't have enough to offer and will not engage with them.

A well-known mnemonic for a good start is INTRO:

- I – Interest/Impact. Engage the delegates by asking a controversial question; or by making a provocative statement; or by telling them something startling; or by referring to a current 'hot' topic ('Did you see in today's paper…?')

- N – Need. Why should the delegates be there, let alone listen and learn? Put yourself in the delegates' shoes and see how you can make it relevant to them.

- T – Timing. Say how long each session will be, and how it fits into the overall plan for the course. 'This session lasts for 45 minutes, after which we'll be having the morning break.'

- R – Range. Briefly outline the range or scope of this session, and how it fits into the overall plan. Note the word 'briefly' – don't give too much detail at this stage.

- O – Objectives. Tell them specifically what they will take away from the session.

Of course the constituent parts of INTRO don't need to be said in exactly this order, so long as they are covered. There are also several other important things to remember about the opening, especially if it's the first session of the course or workshop.

'You're on before you're on'

Delegates form impressions of the trainer from the first moment they see him or her, and that may be quite some time before the course actually starts. Remind the trainer to be 'on parade' in terms of dress, organization and manner long before arriving at the training venue.

Workbooks or handouts

If you intend to give people materials tell them early on, to save them the chore of writing. If they have their heads down taking notes they will not be listening to the trainer. And they'll curse you for not telling them!

When to deal with questions

There are three options: answer them as you go through, leave them to the end, or both:

- Answering questions as you go can potentially distract the trainer from the thrust of the session, but has the advantage of involving the delegates right from the start. Participation is one of the most important underlying principles of good training.

- Leaving questions to the end will be very frustrating for people who cannot understand some key concept early on – they will disengage from the session.

- So the best solution is to take questions as and when they arise, and also allow time for questions at the end.

The main body

Much of what you do here will depend on the actual methodology you've selected to transfer the learning. Whatever you do ensure that you design a logical sequence, which will make it easier for the delegates to follow the learning points. If you're planning a conventional 'presentation' style then you might wish to use one of the following models:

- Chronological. Journey from the past, to the present and into the future.

- Spatial. Imagine describing the layout of your new house to your friends:

'You go in the front door and on the left is the kitchen – the stairs are straight ahead…'.

- Business project – the four Ps. Start with the Position or situation. Then describe the Problem or opportunities that arise. Next outline Possible solutions, before giving a firm Proposal.

- Product life cycle. Briefly go through the stages one by one – market research, development, production, marketing, distribution and sales.

- Problem solving. Start with the diagnostic phase – define the problem, collect data then search for root causes. Then enter the remedial phase – identify possible options, choose the best solution, then implement the solution with energy and review the outcomes.

Whatever you do, ensure it's relevant and interesting to the delegates, and that it also meets the session objectives. It's easy to get carried away with creative designs that, when tested against the objectives, miss the target.

There are various views about how many different concepts you should include in any one session. Many believe in the 'rule of three', which probably comes from sales training, where trainees are taught to have no more than three options on the table at any one time. Others believe in the 'six plus or minus two' rule, which suggests that people are best able to manage between four and eight ideas at any one time.

The best guideline is the topic itself. Imagine the flow from the delegates' point of view, especially when you consider what went before and what comes after. How much detail do you put in the session plan? As much as is required to ensure that the trainer follows the sequence you want, so that delegates gain the required amount of learning from the session.

The end

Every session will need a positive close when the trainer reviews what's happened, and clarifies any issues or concerns the delegates may have. We would suggest that you do this in two parts. First, build in time for questions and answers to clarify any outstanding issues or concerns, then close each session with a short summary of what the delegates should have learnt.

Why do it that way round when the normal approach is to give the summary before asking for questions? Simple really. If you leave the Q&A session to the very end, the trainer may be confronted with a question he or she can't answer. That way the session closes with the trainer saying: 'I'm sorry I don't know the answer to that.' Not a very good way to end. If you use the recommended approach, the last thing the delegates hear is the trainer's high-impact and succinct summary of what the session was about. And that's what they'll remember.

ADMINISTRATION AND LOGISTICS

Use the last column to record all the practical stuff the trainer needs to make it all happen, such as delegate name cards, materials, equipment, workbooks, Power-Point, flipcharts, etc. In the example we quoted earlier the trainer will need to have sufficient computer terminals for delegates to 'practise entering all required delegate registration information, error-free in 4 minutes or less'.

A REAL EXAMPLE

Having been through the theory in a fair amount of detail, now let's see how it works in practice. We'll use session six of a one-day presentation skills course, which focuses on course delegates using Post-it Notes to develop the sequence of their presentations. The session might break into the three chunks shown in Figure 11.2.

- The three 'timings' columns are self-explanatory.
- The 'title' for this session, 'Planning the flow of your presentation', clearly says what it's about.
- The 'objectives' column has been broken into the three chunks of the session, each dealing with different stages of the learning process.
- The 'methods' column shows how the three stages of the session will be delivered: trainer demonstration, practical experience and closing review.
- Finally the 'admin & logistics' column shows what the trainer will need for each phase of the session.

Why not design a session plan for one chunk of your training course to see how all the bits fit together?

'DIET' SESSION PLAN

The style of session plan we've just explored is good for newcomers to training, or for experienced trainers when delivering a session for the first time. But once you

Session Six - One-day Presentation Skills Course

Start time	Finish time	Duration	Session title	Objectives	Learning methods	Admin & logistics
1100	1145	5	Planning the flow of your presentation.	To introduce delegates to a visual planning technique.	Trainer demonstrates using Post-it Notes to develop a presentation.	PowerPoint slides.
		30		Delegates try out the techniques for themselves.	Delegates use the Post-it Notes to plan their own presentations.	Plenty of Post-it Notes!
		10		Consolidate the learning.	Trainer-led discussion – what went well? What could be better? How are the individual presentations shaping up?	Flipchart.

Figure 11.2 Detailed session plan

have some experience you will find that you can operate very effectively with a much simplified style of session plan, such as the one shown in Figure 11.3.

Session Six — Planning the flow of your presentation

❑ Introduce the topic and link to the earlier sessions.
❑ Stress that this session will help them put 'flesh on the bones' they developed using Mind Maps.
❑ Demonstrate using Post-it Notes for developing the presentation flow.
   ❑ Show the PowerPoint presentation
   ❑ Then illustrate using a real example.
❑ Give everyone some Post-it Notes and ask them to find their own 'pitch'.
❑ Confirm everyone has a topic to work on — offer to help anyone struggling.
❑ Set them going — walk around to help anyone who looks 'stuck'.
❑ After 15 minutes ask them to team up with a buddy and explain each other's plan.
❑ After 15 minutes reform the main group and hold a group discussion.
❑ Draw out their reactions to the method and when they might use the technique.

Timing: 45 minutes. 11.00-11.45.

Figure 11.3 'Diet' session plan

0.30

Activity 11.3 Drafting a session plan

Please draft a session plan for part of the course you've been designing.

Start time	Finish time	Duration	Session title	Objectives	Learning methods	Admin & logistics

SPONSOR 'SIGN OFF'

We've stressed all the way through the importance of getting the 'sign off' from your sponsor at every key stage of the design process, and this is a good moment to confirm that you're still on the right track. If you go ahead and do more detailed design without this approval you may have to do some time-consuming rework at a later, and more time-critical, stage.

So, is the sponsor satisfied with the outline design? If 'Yes', then you can proceed to develop partnership agreement(s), which can lead to drafting contracts or service agreements. If, however, the answer is 'No', then you will have to go back to the specification and rework the proposal based on your discussions. It's possible the project may not continue.

12

Designing course materials

- What might you need?
- Harmonize with company standards
- Sources for course content
- Displaying text effectively
- Delegate name cards or badges
- Workbooks for trainer-led courses
- Delegate handouts
- Exercise briefing notes
- Feedback sheets
- Course peripherals

WHAT MIGHT YOU NEED?

Initiate pilot programmes

By this stage you're ready to move into the fourth step of the DESIGN process when you take the agreed design proposal and, using appropriate design resources, create learning products ready for testing in the pilot/test courses (see Figure 3.5 on page 27). One of the key actions in this step is to plan and manage the development of learning materials. What will you need? To enable a course to run successfully there are lots of materials required – before, during and after the event.

Before

- Course joining instructions.

- Pre-course work or questionnaires.

- Room signs.

These items were covered in Chapter 9 (Stimulate interest, page 136), which you may wish to refer back to if you skimmed over it.

During

- Delegate name cards or badges.

- Pre-course assessments.

- Handouts.

- Workbooks.

- Exercise briefing notes.

- Activity recording sheets.

- Feedback sheets.

- Course peripherals, for example wall posters or desk displays.

- Any special handouts or 'goodies', for example mugs or pens.

- Interim progress assessments.

Pre-course and interim course assessments were covered in Chapter 9 (Review what's changed, page 158), which you may wish to refer back to if you skimmed over it.

After

- Post-course assessments.
- End-of-course evaluation sheets.

These items were covered in Chapter 9 (Review what's changed, page 159), which you may wish to refer back to if you skimmed over it.

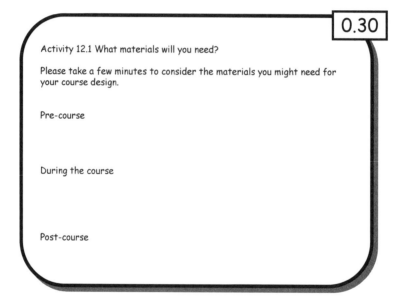

0.30

Activity 12.1 What materials will you need?

Please take a few minutes to consider the materials you might need for your course design.

Pre-course

During the course

Post-course

HARMONIZE WITH COMPANY STANDARDS

Before you start on detailed design you need to ensure that the materials you develop for your course are consistent with the company materials and standards. There are two separate but interlinked issues.

If you were developing a recruitment and selection course, for example, you would need to ensure that all the terms and content related to the topic were consistent with any existing text on the subject. You must also research and comply with all the physical design aspects of company materials, including fonts, colours, logos, templates, etc.

You may need to contact a wide range of people in the company to see if anything they have, or are responsible for, may impinge, however slightly, on the topic you are developing. Again it is time well spent – better to change something now than when many hours of development have been committed.

SOURCES FOR COURSE CONTENT

By this stage you will have identified materials you might use in your course design, or other sources you can call upon, but you may still have some topics for which you don't have an immediate source. So that's the next challenge – to plug those resource gaps.

The most obvious people to call on are subject matter experts who should have an up-to-date stock of resources or people to call on. Be certain to clarify who is going to source specific materials, when they will do it, and the format they intend to use. I remember working with one client where sourcing materials was a continual problem. People said they would supply items by certain times and didn't. Others did supply materials that turned out to be earlier, outdated versions of key documents. It all wastes time and causes unnecessary frustration.

If you're designing an e-learning course it also makes sense to have one central contact point in the software company who becomes the clearing house for information flows – both into and from the client company.

You also need to discuss issues such as copyright if you're relying on external people to source documents or materials. An excellent source is the internet – just type your topic in Google and watch the pages fill up. I was recently writing a training package and my partner suggested mentioning how a colony of monkeys developed new skills. Having explained the outline of the story she casually said, 'Why not try the internet?' So I did. I typed in '100 monkeys' and was blessed with pages of stories, reference material, analysis and books. Very helpful it was too! Now look at Activity 12.2 on p 200 on resource gaps.

DISPLAYING TEXT EFFECTIVELY

An important aspect of designing supporting materials is getting the right balance of text with graphics. Much will depend on the topic and the audience – some subjects will lend themselves more naturally to a 'textbook' approach, having

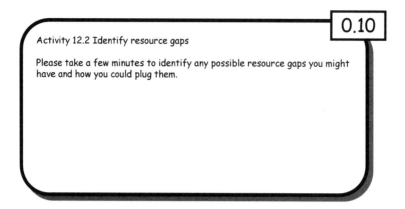

more text and fewer diagrams. Materials for most training courses for typical adult audiences will benefit from having more graphics and diagrams and less text. Designing good visuals is a subject all by itself and we have devoted Chapter 14 totally to this topic.

It's worth spending a few minutes considering how you can display text most effectively. Any good author will tell you that it's much better to 'show rather than tell', so here goes. Please work through these four examples and note how you feel as you try each one.

Justify or not?

Which style of text is easier on the eye?

Justified

Denim comes of age this season. British designers are breathing new life into a classic fabric, expanding the boundaries of the possible in the best traditions of British fashion design. The beauty of denim is its durability. Denim positively improves with age and regular washing as the fabric softens and moulds to the body. At the core of the original boom were well-made women's jeans in stretch fabrics. The new wave of denim fashion puts a similar emphasis on stretch. Although many women will always prefer wearing baggy men's jeans cinched in with a belt, the priority this year in fashion terms is very much fit – jeans, waistcoats and jackets that hug the contours of the body and leave nothing to the imagination.

Unjustified

Denim comes of age this season. British designers are breathing new life into a classic fabric, expanding the boundaries of the possible in the best traditions of British fashion design. The beauty of denim is its durability. Denim positively improves with age and regular washing as the fabric softens and moulds to the body. At the core of the original boom were well-made women's jeans in stretch fabrics. The new wave of denim fashion puts a similar emphasis on stretch. Although many women will always prefer wearing baggy men's jeans cinched in with a belt, the priority this year in fashion terms is very much fit – jeans, waistcoats and jackets that hug the contours of the body and leave nothing to the imagination.

Comments

- For many people reading unjustified text is easier, as the spacing between words remains constant, and so the eye follows the text more comfortably.

- One of the underlying principles of good typesetting is that the space between words should be less than the space between lines, or the eye may be 'fooled' and jump down a line.

- If you use justified text it may look neat but, with many word-processing systems, you end up with large rivers of white space running through the text, which can be distracting.

- Many people also consider that justified text can look rather heavy and overwhelming compared with unjustified, especially if there's a lot of text.

Italic?

Which is the easiest to read?

Italic text

We are writing to inform you that a further eyesight examination is now due, as recommended at your last consultation. Please call in or phone the practice to fix a convenient consultation time. Free examinations are still available to school children, students under 19 and those in receipt of Family Credit or Income Support. In addition, diabetics and those suffering from glaucoma or aged over 40 and related to a glaucoma sufferer are exempt charges. If you are not exempt then the charge for your examination will be £17.50. We hope, Ms Jones, that you will agree this is well worthwhile to ensure that your eyes are healthy and continue to perform at their best, either with or without spectacles.

Normal text

We are writing to inform you that a further eyesight examination is now due, as recommended at your last consultation. Please call in or phone the practice to fix a convenient consultation time. Free examinations are still available to school children, students under 19 and those in receipt of Family Credit or Income Support. In addition, diabetics and those suffering from glaucoma or aged over 40 and related to a glaucoma sufferer are exempt charges. If you are not exempt then the charge for your examination will be £17.50. We hope you will agree this is well worthwhile to ensure that your eyes are healthy and continue to perform at their best, either with or without spectacles.

Comments

- Excessive use of italic script is very hard on the eyes and most people will simply not read all of it.

- Not convinced? What was the patient's name? It was towards the end of the italic section!

- Please use italic very sparingly.

Capitals or lower case?

Which is the easiest to read quickly?

Capitals

A GIRL IN MY CLASS DECIDED AT THE AGE OF 8 THAT SHE WANTED TO BE A DENTIST WHEN SHE GREW UP. THE REST OF US HAD ALREADY CHOSEN OUR CAREERS, TOO. BUT WHILE WE WERE TORN BETWEEN ACCOUNT-ANCY AND BECOMING HOTEL MANAGERS, JANE WAS DREAMING OF MOLAR EXPLORATION. 'YOU'RE LOOPY' WE'D SAY HELPFULLY. 'ALL THAT SPIT AND STINKY BREATH! WHAT DO YOU WANT TO DO THAT FOR?' BESIDES, AS WE ALL KNOW, DENTISTS ARE SADISTS AND TORTURERS. 'YOU'LL HARDLY FEEL A THING – JUST A TINY STING,' THEY'D SAY. BUT WE ALL KNEW THE TRUTH. WASPS STUNG, BUT DENTISTS IMPALED YOUR GUMS WITH SHARPENED HARPOONS DIPPED IN JUNGLE POISON – AT LEAST, THAT'S HOW IT FELT. MY CLASSMATE JUNE ENDED UP RUNNING A DENTAL PRACTICE IN THE MIDLANDS, WHERE SHE SETTLED WITH HER HUSBAND. 'I CAN'T UNDERSTAND WHY PEOPLE DON'T LIKE DENTISTS,' SHE SAID WITH A SIGH WHEN WE LAST MET. 'SOME PEOPLE ONLY COME

TO US WHEN THEY'RE IN REAL AGONY.' YOU KNOW WHAT THEY SAY –
ABSCESS MAKES THE HEART GROW FONDER.

Lower case

A girl in my class decided at the age of 8 that she wanted to be a dentist when she
grew up. The rest of us had already chosen our careers, too. But while we were torn
between accountancy and becoming hotel managers, Jane was dreaming of molar
exploration. 'You're loopy,' we'd say helpfully. 'All that spit and stinky breath!
What do you want to do that for?' Besides, as we all know, dentists are sadists and
torturers. 'You'll hardly feel a thing – just a tiny sting,' they'd say. But we knew
the truth. Wasps stung, but dentists impaled your gums with sharpened harpoons
dipped in jungle poison – at least, that's how it felt. My classmate Jane ended up
running a dental practice in the Midlands, where she settled with her husband. 'I
can't understand why people don't like dentists,' she said with a sigh when we
last met. 'Some of them only come to see us when they're in real agony.' You know
what they say – abscess makes the heart grow fonder.

Comments

- Well, be honest, which did you find easiest to read? Most people will find lots
  of text in capital letters challenging.

- The reason why is very simple. Capital letters all look the same, whereas lower-
  case letters are different. As adults we don't read each word but scan the text
  and recognize the shape of the letters (which is why accurate proof reading is
  so difficult).

- Not convinced? Look around at public signage. On the roads, apart from HALT
  and STOP, all text signs are lower case.

- Did you read the whole section in capitals? If so, you will have found the
  deliberate mistake.

- The learning point? Use capital letters very sparingly.

Bullet points

Which of the following is easiest to understand?

Plain text

We are writing to inform you that a further eyesight examination is now due, as recommended at your last consultation. Please call in or phone the practice to fix a convenient consultation time. Free examinations are still available to school children, students under 19 and those in receipt of Family Credit or Income Support. In addition, diabetics and those suffering from glaucoma or aged over 40 and related to a glaucoma sufferer are exempt charges. If you are not exempt then the charge for your examination will be £17.50. We hope you will agree this is well worthwhile to ensure that your eyes are healthy and continue to perform at their best, either with or without spectacles.

Question – How many categories of people are eligible for free eye examinations?

Using bullet points

We are writing to inform you that a further eyesight examination is now due, as recommended at your last consultation. Please call in or phone the practice to fix a convenient consultation time. Free examinations are still available to:

- school children;
- students under 19;
- those in receipt of Family Credit or Income Support;
- diabetics;
- those suffering from glaucoma;
- people aged over 40 and related to a glaucoma sufferer.

If you are not exempt then the charge for your examination will be £17.50. We hope you will agree this is well worthwhile to ensure that your eyes are healthy and continue to perform at their best, either with or without spectacles.

Comments

- Having read the initial version, did you know how many categories of people are eligible for free eye examinations? Most people would have to read it several times to be able to say 'six' with any confidence.
- Bullet points draw your eyes to the key facts.

- You feel comfortable abbreviating the text and editing out unnecessary words in bullet points, so making it quicker to read.

General guidelines

To enable you to produce clear, easy to read documents you may wish to adopt some of these additional guidelines. But remember – they are 'tools' not 'rules'!

Font

Use a strong, simple typeface. If your company specifies Times New Roman or Arial then use it. Whenever possible I use Comic Sans, which is easy to read and looks a bit more informal. Avoid the temptation to use one of the fancy font choices on your computer, as many people will find them difficult to read. Once you have chosen your font – stick to it. At the most only use one other font style.

Font size

As a general rule, use 12 point. Don't drop to 10 point in order to squeeze text onto one page and, if you suspect your target audience may have difficulty reading, increase the standard font to 14 point.

Paragraphs

Separate paragraphs by double line spacing, or indent new paragraphs.

Signposting

Use headings to 'signpost' the way through your documents to make it easier for people to select the sections they want to read. Use a hierarchy of heading styles to show which sections individual pieces of text belong to.

Numbering systems

Numbering chapters, sections and paragraphs can be helpful to make it easier to refer to specific pieces of text – but keep the numbering system simple and easy to follow.

Emphasis

To emphasize a word it's best to use bold type. We've already demonstrated the drawbacks of CAPITALS and _italic_ text. In general, use underlining sparingly. Using underlining on more than headings is very wearing on the eyes and your delegates will be tempted to skim over the text – much like you are now!

Contrasts

In general use black text on white paper. A coloured type or background will make it harder to read and some colour combinations (red and green especially) will be very difficult for colour-blind people.

Page set-up

Aim for 25-millimetre margins either side of the page, and give lots of 'white space' on the page. Aim to have 8 to 12 average-length words per line, or about 70 to 80 characters (including spaces).

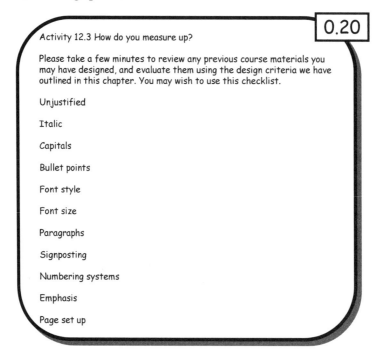

Activity 12.3 How do you measure up?

0.20

Please take a few minutes to review any previous course materials you may have designed, and evaluate them using the design criteria we have outlined in this chapter. You may wish to use this checklist.

Unjustified

Italic

Capitals

Bullet points

Font style

Font size

Paragraphs

Signposting

Numbering systems

Emphasis

Page set up

DELEGATE NAME CARDS OR BADGES

It's important for the trainer, and for other delegates, to get to know each other's names quickly and the best way to do this is to ask everyone to either have a name card in front of them or, if the course involves people moving around a lot, to wear a name badge. This can easily be designed into the 'arrival' process: delegates will probably have to 'sign in' on an attendance sheet and the trainer can ask them to write their own name on a name card – it's best to ask people to write their own instead of pre-preparing them from company data. You will often find that the company database is incorrect and name cards produced centrally are wrong, so Carole arrives to find her name card says 'Carol'. Not a good way to start.

People often use abbreviated names – if someone called out 'Anthony' I would look around to see where the guy is. I have been known as Tony all my adult life and I can't remember when someone last used my full name.

The only time you may find it difficult to get people to use name cards or badges is if you're designing an event for a closely knit team who all know each other. They won't see the need for cards or badges. The only advice to give the trainer is to draw a blank seating plan and, as people casually refer to each other, to surreptitiously fill in the blanks. It's also worth scribbling comments like 'Blue sweater' or 'Red hair' so that, when people are away from the table, you can still remember their names. Within 15 minutes or so the blanks will all be filled.

WORKBOOKS FOR TRAINER-LED COURSES

Why have a delegate workbook? There are several reasons.

First, a good training course will actively involve the learners throughout. They may be asked to complete tasks, or to sequence lists of options, or do other interactive activities. Of course you can write these on scraps of paper, but there is more value if these tasks are written in a workbook, which acts as a focus.

The workbook can also accumulate action points throughout the course. Any good course will generate lots of 'Ah ha!' moments – those sudden realizations or moments of truth that lead towards changes in behaviour or attitude. People need somewhere to write them down – or they quickly disappear.

Let's assume you've decided to have a delegate workbook – now you need to consider what it should contain.

The scope and coverage of the workbook

A workbook could potentially become very large so it's essential early on to decide the scope and coverage. You will need to be quite ruthless as there will be many types of topic competing for inclusion in the workbook, including:

- reinforcement of the key learning points;

- spaces for the learner to record the results of tests, case studies or other activities;

- spaces for the learner to record action points;

- the opportunity to reinforce key company messages or initiatives.

Reinforcement of the key learning points

This is a powerful way to drive home the key learning points of the course, and the challenge will be deciding what to include.

If you include too many topics, the workbook becomes bulky, and may lose some of its impact. If, however, you exclude too many of the learning points, people may find the workbook a bit 'lightweight' or not particularly helpful.

Spaces for the learner to record results

It is widely recognized that the value of a workbook, and therefore the course it's based on, is dramatically improved if the design actively encourages learners to interact with the programme and record their own thoughts, ideas or interpretation of the course materials.

So allow sufficient space for learners to effectively create their own course materials, within the overall structure of the course. As with the previous point, you need to strike a balance: too frequent recourse to this approach may cause irritation in the learner, whilst too infrequent loses the value of the intervention.

Spaces for the learner to record action points

Learning or understanding is one thing – knowing how to use the newly acquired skills or knowledge is something totally different. So the workbook should encourage learners to write their action points as they emerge during the course. Without this, the moment the programme ends, it's quite possible that the other messages competing for the learner's attention may drown all the learning gained from attending the course or workshop.

Reinforce key company messages or initiatives

A further category competing for inclusion may be key company messages related to the topic or related initiatives. For example, a course on performance management would present a superb opportunity to cascade the corporate messages on mission, vision, individual accountability, etc.

You need to be careful about how much of this type of information is included in both the course and the accompanying workbook. Too much, and it may turn learners off because of 'information overload'. They probably see the messages repeated in official documents, company newsletters, etc, and so may welcome the course as somewhere they can escape from these initiatives.

This type of information also tends to have a relatively short 'shelf life' and needs to be updated quite frequently. Modifying the workbook will be tiresome, but modifying the course, especially if delivered by e-learning, may become prohibitively expensive.

So, you will need to take a view on how large the workbook should be, and the relative amount of space allocated to the four topics outlined above.

DELEGATE HANDOUTS

If you use separate handouts, many of the design considerations apply as for the workbooks, and in addition:

- Will you give delegates a file or folder to hold the handouts as the course progresses?

- If not, they may have difficulty managing all the loose sheets of paper.

- How will you distribute the handouts? At the beginning of each session or at the end?

EXERCISE BRIEFING NOTES

If you are planning to use tasks, games or exercises during your course or workshop you will need to write suitable briefing notes. All the same design considerations apply as we've covered already and, in addition, you may need to note the following:

- Explain the task clearly and succinctly.

- What outcomes or outputs are delegates expected to produce?

- Explain any 'rules' or constraints.

- Mention any supporting materials or documents.

- Outline team size and membership.

- Give timings.

We've given you some practical examples of different types of tasks on the CD ROM so you can see the general approach. Remember, you may need to have briefing notes for the facilitator's eyes only!

FEEDBACK SHEETS

Many courses require delegates to give each other feedback, so you may wish to pre-prepare some standard feedback forms. The main benefit is that it directs the observers to the issues they need to be focusing on, so the trainer can be more certain about the quality and relevance of the feedback that will be given.

I developed another, more unusual style of feedback sheet for a team workshop I once ran. It had been an intense two days and I wanted the workshop to close with people having a final opportunity to give direct and personal feedback to individuals. So, at the end of the two days, I gave everyone an A3-sized personal feedback sheet on which they wrote their names. The feedback sheet was headed 'Our gift to you' and was broken into three sections, each with its own heading:

- 'You bring to the team…'

- 'We especially value…'

- 'You might try…'

Once everyone had stuck their sheet on the wall with Blu-tack, I started some appropriate music playing, then delegates walked around the room visiting every person's feedback sheet and writing comments in any of the three sections. After about 25 minutes the action started to die down so I invited people to return to their own sheet and see what people had said about them. It was a very powerful experience for everyone (me included – I had a sheet too!)

Many years later I visited the manager, Alan Dean, and after chatting about various topics the conversation drifted round to that workshop, which had been a really significant event. Reaching into his desk drawer, he pulled out his A3 feedback sheet, by now looking a bit dog-eared, and said that there were few weeks when he didn't look at it to remind himself how he needed to change.

COURSE PERIPHERALS

Much depends on the scale of the course or event, and the corresponding budget you can call upon, but some of the things to consider include:

- team clothing to strengthen team identity, or reinforce the 'big picture';

- 'dressing' the training rooms to match the overall theme;

- daily changes to keep the venue looking fresh, or link into changing themes;

- stimulating posters;

- promotional videos;

- personal name badges, table name plates and country/company flags on the tables;

- headed paper for course or workshop materials with the event logo;

- notepads and binders for delegates with the event logo;

- gift items, such as pen/pencil sets, clipboards;

- course photograph;

- daily news sheets highlighting key events or activities.

By now you will have noticed that I like to give personal examples, and here are two more.

Are you in control?

I once helped an internal audit team to develop a focused half-day course to show managers the value of the internal audit function. Originally the audit team had designed the course, and it was 'stodgy', with too much lecturing and theory. Course delegates had typically commented: 'Half a day is too long – can't it be reduced to one hour?' So we reworked it, making it much more participative and focused on the managers' needs. People loved it and many now said: 'Far too much material for half a day – it should be a full day!' The course theme was 'Are you in control?' and had a model based on a pyramid, much like the one shown in Figure 12.1.

As soon as I saw the PowerPoint slide I recognized immediately the opportunity to create a folding pyramid that delegates could take away from the course as a permanent reminder of the learning points. The pyramids were produced in sturdy, multicoloured card and given out at the end of the course; they quickly became a talking point around the company.

Jigsaw puzzle quiz

Another challenge was to design the opening session for a four-day international IT conference, which I was facilitating for a major UK company. The 80 delegates

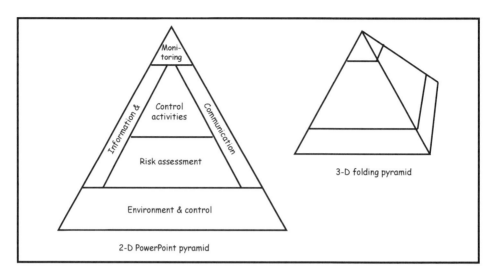

Figure 12.1 'Are you in control?' pyramid

would be travelling from all over the world and we needed a high-impact way to get them working together right from the start. We had designed team-working sessions into every day so I saw this as a good opportunity to form the teams and get them working together.

Each of the 10 teams was identified by one of the company's leading brands. I designed a 20-question general knowledge quiz that the teams would complete, with prizes for the winning team. Then I added a twist:

- The quiz was printed on the reverse side of 10 A2-sized cards, each one bearing a team's unique brand image, and colour-coded to make it easier to identify.

- The cards were then cut into eight pieces resembling a jigsaw puzzle. So there were now 10 sets of eight cards, one complete set for each team.

- Delegates were allocated to teams prior to arriving to get a good mixture of IT experience and geographical location within each team.

- The individual segments of each team's cards were now placed in a sealed envelope, which the delegates were given as they arrived, along with all the other conference materials.

- The envelope carried the message: 'Please bring this with you to the opening session. Not to be opened until instructed to do so!'

- The delegates all arrived, were given a welcoming drink, and encouraged to mingle and chat with their colleagues.

- At the appropriate moment I blew a whistle to attract everyone's attention and welcomed delegates to the conference. Having stressed that the conference was a working event, I then invited everyone to rip open their envelopes and get together with their team mates, who had the seven other pieces of their team jigsaw puzzle.

- Once they had assembled the puzzle, they turned it over and then did the general knowledge quiz, prizes being awarded to the winning team.

It was a very different way of starting the conference and began the process of team-bonding right from the first moment.

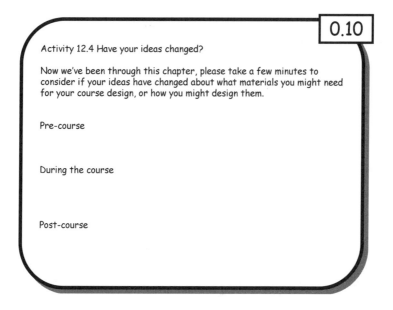

0.10

Activity 12.4 Have your ideas changed?

Now we've been through this chapter, please take a few minutes to consider if your ideas have changed about what materials you might need for your course design, or how you might design them.

Pre-course

During the course

Post-course

13

Using audio

- Why use audio?
- Some examples
- Slightly different uses
- Equipment needs

WHY USE AUDIO?

With the costs of shooting, editing and distributing video now much lower than they were just a few years ago, it's easy to dismiss audio as a second-rate training medium, but there are many applications for which it's still excellent. It's ideal for training staff who use telephones or radio a lot, for example receptionists, call-centre operators and the emergency services.

The advantages of using audio include:

- Variety – the novelty of hearing other voices adds variety and stimulation.

- Surprise – bringing some unexpected sound into the training room can catch people's attention.

- Authenticity – the audio 'clip' means that delegates hear messages under authentic conditions.

- Accessibility – making computer-based documents accessible for people with limited vision.

- Consistency – every training group will hear exactly the same message.

- Attention – having to listen, instead of seeing, perks up your attention.

- Can be used anywhere – we can listen to audio while doing virtually anything else – walking, driving, exercising, making... you get the idea!

- Minimum equipment – with the advent of gadgets like the iPod we can carry a massive amount of audio material in a tiny package.

- Cost – designing and developing audio materials is very cost-effective, especially when compared to video.

SOME EXAMPLES

Let's look at some of the ways that you can use audio; hopefully this will trigger some thoughts.

Accessibility

Using audio is a superb way to make all computer-based materials accessible to people with poor vision. We mentioned this in Chapter 3, and you might wish to revisit it if you skimmed over the materials earlier. We'll also cover using voiceovers in Chapter 15 when we look at designing e-learning materials.

Poor transactions

Play a recording of someone (a customer or patient) calling in for help (to a call-centre or reception desk) and getting a poor response. The delegates listen to the conversation and have to analyse what's going wrong and how it should have been handled. After the debrief it's useful to then play another version that illustrates the call being handled well. This positive reinforcement of good behaviours or skills is the right way to end the session.

Case studies

Delegates are paired off – one to be the caller and the other to receive the call. You need to prepare two briefing notes that emphasize the subtle differences between the two people's situations and that simulate the tensions that are often generated in real life. For example, when I'm training telephone techniques for hospital staff one of the scenarios I use is:

> *Ward sister:* You are working on a ward, it's the end of your shift and you're about to leave. You receive a call from a friend of a patient asking for details of their condition.
>
> The patient is terminally ill, but you have instructions not to discuss this with anyone but the immediate family, who are aware of the situation.
>
> *The caller:* You are calling the ward to find out about a patient. What the world doesn't know is that the patient is also your lover, and you have had an intimate relationship for 10 years.
>
> You are desperate to find out about their condition, as it's not possible for you to visit them in case you meet their family.

Taking messages

Delegates listen to someone calling in with a message and they have to record the key points to pass on a message to the intended recipient. Be sneaky – have a key fact given in the last sentence, almost as a 'throwaway' remark as, by that stage, most listeners will think they have captured all the important facts.

Ask everyone to write the message on A4 paper, which they post on the wall. Ask delegates to stand by someone else's message, so that as you replay the original audio recording they can 'score' the accuracy of their colleague's message.

Improving accuracy

There are many programmes designed to improve people's ability to handle facts and information accurately, and audio is used extensively. Delegates listen to a variety of information – messages, sets of numbers, names and addresses – and have to record them in the workbook. Delegates then change workbooks with their neighbour and score the results.

This technique was used in the Army to develop speed at 'reading' Morse Code. Soldiers had to listen to a series of transmissions in Morse and, once they were confident at that speed, they would listen to the next tape, which was at a slightly faster speed.

Learning on the move

Another excellent application for audio is learning on the move. As we said earlier, you can listen to audio while doing virtually anything else, and with modern MP3 players, equipment is no longer an issue. I have written material for a company that specializes in this type of learning (Journey Learning) and they produce a series of packages devoted to specific topics or issues; customers buy a set of CDs that give over five hours of training materials, recorded by two celebrity voices.

Extracts from commercial programmes

At times you may wish to play a short extract from commercially produced pro-grammes to illustrate a learning point, using either serious material or something humorous.

SLIGHTLY DIFFERENT USES

Here are some slightly different ways of using 'audio', which you might wish to consider when designing your courses.

Background music

Use appropriate music to create a mood or to change the pace of a course.

Concert reviews

An excellent way to review what you've covered in a busy day is to ask delegates to relax, then show the series of slides you have used, without any comment but accompanied by some gentle classical music. It gives people the opportunity to realize the range of learning points and make personal connections with the key points.

Blind walk

This is using 'audio' in a different way and is good for developing trust between delegates. Pair delegates up and ask one person from each pair to wear a blindfold.

The sighted person now guides the blindfolded colleague safely on a 10-minute walk around the venue and surrounding area.

Colour Blind

One superb exercise I use relies totally on 'audio' – it's a commercially produced product called 'Colour Blind'. Once all your delegates are wearing a blindfold you place in front of each person some unusually shaped pieces from some different-coloured sets. By only talking with each other the delegates have to discover which shapes you removed and what colour they are. This is an amazing experience and often reveals that the most unlikely people to have the ability to solve complex problems while denied the advantage of sight.

Assemble the pieces

Another fun challenge is to sit delegates back to back, one of them facing a desk or table. The person at the desk is given a set of pieces – his or her partner is given a diagram that shows how the pieces fit together (see Figure 13.1). The challenge is, by using speech alone, to enable the person at the desk to fit the pieces together correctly.

Figure 13.1 T shape

EQUIPMENT NEEDS

If you're going to be doing any significant amount of audio training, it's worth investing in the equipment to make the situations as real as possible. This doesn't need to be prohibitively expensive or fixed at one site. For example, I have a complete telephone training kit that fits into a standard briefcase, comprising two telephones, a cassette recorder, a control box with a loudspeaker, blank tapes and all the required leads. These kits are commercially available at sensible prices.

Using this kit I place one delegate (the caller) in a room with his or her own briefing notes. The person receiving the call sits in a separate room, again with his or her own situation briefing notes, which are different from the caller's. The other course delegates sit in the main room and listen in to the conversation through the loudspeaker. The caller starts the call, the colleague responds, while the others listen to what's happening (and the cassette recorder tapes the whole transaction for later replay).

This equipment is also good for recording your own audio demonstrations, for example the 'poor' and 'good' transactions we mentioned earlier.

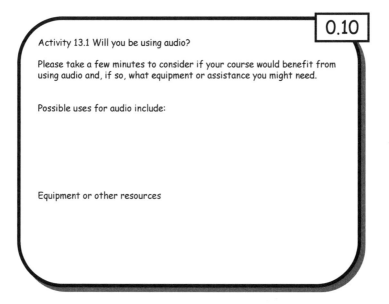

0.10

Activity 13.1 Will you be using audio?

Please take a few minutes to consider if your course would benefit from using audio and, if so, what equipment or assistance you might need.

Possible uses for audio include:

Equipment or other resources

14

Designing visual aids

- Why use visual aids?
- What visual aids can we use?
- Basic design principles
- Flipcharts
- Overhead transparencies
- Computer graphics
- Potential pitfalls
- Plan your visuals

WHY USE VISUAL AIDS?

Variety is the spice of life, and most people remember what they have seen more easily than what they have heard. But remember, visual aids can only make a good course better – they cannot transform a poor course into a good one. Visual aids are intended to enhance your ideas, not to relieve you of the responsibility for making them. Don't use visual aids for their own sake – each visual aid should have a specific purpose, and should emphasize or dramatize an important point.

Visual aids are a key element of any training course, whether it's the delegates' workbook or handouts, other course materials, or the trainer's presentation, so we'll devote a whole chapter to their design. First of all, why do we use visual aids? There are many reasons including:

- keeping the audience awake;

- helping to explain complex topics or diagrams;

- stimulating more of the senses;

- making the message more memorable;

- brightening up a less interesting topic;

- prompting the trainer – so he or she doesn't have to look at notes.

It's important to keep these in mind to ensure that the materials you produce really do aid the learning process and aren't there to impress or amuse. It's important to design the training first, then decide what visual aids you need to reinforce the messages. Avoid the temptation to start with a visual aid and then decide where you use it in the design. Wrong! As we go through the following design principles remember that these guidelines apply to the hard-copy materials you produce as well as the trainer's presentation.

WHAT VISUAL AIDS CAN WE USE?

We always talk about 'visual' aids but it's worth remembering that there are at least five human senses. We'll leave the spiritual sense out of the discussions for the moment – that's another book! So the ones we'll be focusing on are:

- Hearing – the easiest. We covered that in Chapter 13.

- Seeing – next easiest.

- Touching – getting harder.

- Smelling – a bit more challenging!

- Tasting – difficult for many courses or topics.

Some topics (and industries) lend themselves more easily to stimulating a wider range of senses – for example the catering industry. But for many mainstream topics you can struggle to get past the top two. So what visuals can we use? The following list covers the usual suspects and, remember, the higher up the list – the more senses are stimulated:

- The real thing. Walk into the Rolls-Royce training centre where engineers are trained to maintain their fleet of engines and you'll find an example of every current engine on trolleys. Stand alongside the Trent 900 and you wonder how an aircraft wing ever supports the weight!

- Models. Showing people a detailed model, for example of a power station or a new office complex, makes the subject 'come alive'.

- Parts of the real thing. It's often possible to bring parts or assemblies into the training room so that delegates can touch the equipment or components they'll be working with.

- Simulations. Flight simulators for pilot training are now so realistic that pilots converting onto other aircraft can almost do it without flying the real plane. On a more everyday level, simulated 'wounds' used in First Aid training are so real that the layman could feel faint just looking at them!

- Samples – eg packaging or products. Find items that delegates can touch and examine. A session on quality control for product packaging, for example, could be dull, but give delegates six samples and ask them to identify the production faults and it suddenly comes alive.

- Posters, photographs, or other peripherals. Display suitable material around the training room to stimulate interest in the topic. You may not notice much happening but people absorb so much information without realizing it.

- Computer visuals. Look how far down the list this appears. PowerPoint is good and Macromedia Flash offers superb animation.

- Overhead slides. Still a good stand-by for many situations.

- Hard-copy – for people to keep and write on.

BASIC DESIGN PRINCIPLES

Visual aids must be carefully designed (Figure 14.1), and following a few simple guidelines will improve their effectiveness dramatically:

Figure 14.1 Designing good visuals

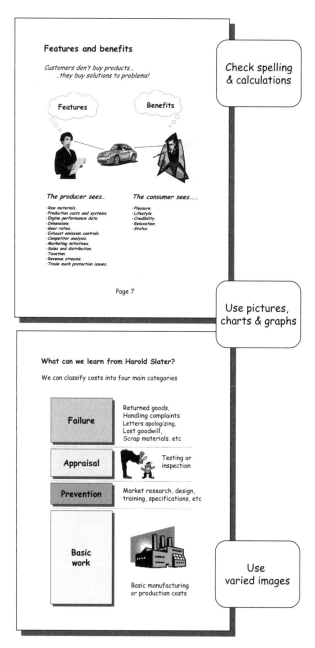

Figure 14.1 Designing good visuals (*continued*)

- Ideally, your visual aid should resemble a T-shirt. Big, clear images with few words. The image should be self-explanatory.

- Make bold and imaginative use of colour whenever possible.

- Be conscious that some colour contrasts will be difficult to read, especially red and green for colour-blind people (mainly men). Question – is that why traffic lights have an amber light between red and green?

- If you design non-pictorial visuals then make sure they are simple and easy to read.

- Try to avoid showing numbers as raw data – whenever possible display them as graphs, pie charts or histograms.

- Use the same font style throughout and develop a hierarchy of font sizes for headings and use it consistently.

- Check spelling carefully as people will notice errors.

- Where appropriate, vary the design template to avoid the MEGO effect (MEGO – my eyes glaze over!)

- Always check calculations carefully – people will automatically add columns or charts to check that totals are correct.

0.20

Activity 14.1 How do you rate your visuals?

Please take a few minutes to evaluate current visual aids - preferably some you have designed yourself.

❑Relevant - to the point being made.

❑Visible - can it be easily read?

❑Accurate - does it say what it's supposed to? Do the figures add up?

❑Interesting - will it seize and maintain interest?

❑Clear - does it make its point? Is it legible?

❑Emphasis - use colour and shading to good effect.

❑Content - don't have too many words or figures.

❑Drawings - simple and uncomplicated.

FLIPCHARTS

Flipcharts have been around for a long time and you will probably find some sessions in your course for which they are ideal.

Flipcharts – good points

- Flipcharts are easy to use, and enable you to add to your visual aid as the training session develops.

- They are also good for collecting ideas from people in real time.

- Being 'low tech', they are also immune to power failures!

Flipcharts – downsides

- Limited group size – the maximum is 14 to 16 delegates.

- Handwriting-dependent.

- If you produce lots of sheets – how will you display and extract information from them?

Preparing flipcharts

- If you want to create the flipchart live in front of the audience, lightly pencil the outline before the session.

- Similarly, you can write prompts or comments in light pencil on your flipchart, to remind you of key points during your presentation. The audience will not be able to see the pencil marks.

- Alternate your visuals with blank sheets of flipchart paper, so that the audience will not be distracted by the last visual.

- Use 'strong' colours like black, red, green, brown and blue. Avoid 'weak' colours like orange and yellow – the audience will not be able to read them.

OVERHEAD TRANSPARENCIES

Overhead transparencies are excellent for giving formal training sessions, or for addressing a large audience. They are easy to prepare and easy to read from a distance.

Overhead transparencies – good points

- Moderate quality image.

- Flexibility in sequencing.

- Easy to build up overlays.

- Medium tech – some risk.

Overhead transparencies – downsides

- Cannot modify the message.

- Slides can be bulky.

- Projectors are often heavy.

- Projectors – noise and bulbs.

Preparing an effective overhead transparency

- Always prepare a rough draft of the material and, if possible, consult in-house design or drawing office staff for advice.

- Resist the temptation to make an OHP slide from a photocopy of an A4 page of typed text – it will be unreadable for many people.

- Use overlays to build up a complex visual.

- Remember the '6, 7, 8 Rule'. Write a maximum of six words per line, on no more than seven lines per image, using letters 8 mm high.

- Leave adequate margins so that the complete image is projected.

- Write prompting comments around the mounting frame – you will be able to read them easily during the presentation.

- Try the readability test. Stand up and drop your OHP on the floor. Can you read it? If not, the chances are the audience won't be able to read it either.

COMPUTER GRAPHICS

Modern computer graphics packages like PowerPoint have revolutionized visual aids – in many ways the only limitation is your own creativity.

Computer graphics – good points

- High-quality image.

- Easy to modify the message and customize it to the audience.

- Limitless visual effects.

- Easy to carry around.

Computer graphics – downsides

- Limited sequencing flexibility.

- Projector and software compatibility – but getting better all the time.

- Risk of audience overload.

Hyperlinks

One drawback of PowerPoint is that, once you start a presentation, you have to follow the prepared sequence. If the trainer wishes to jump to another slide, in response to a delegate's question for example, it takes some effort (and presence of mind) to find the right slide in front of the audience. However, it's possible, using hyperlinks, to build-in some flexibility. Here's how it's done. Let's assume you have a session on personal presentation skills, for which you create four slides, which could look like Figure 14.2.

Creating hyperlinks on the first slide is easy:

- Select slide 1.

- Put your cursor on the 'words' icon and right click.

- Select 'Action settings'.

- Click 'Hyperlink to'.

- Select 'Slide' option.

- Specify 'Slide 2'.

- Click 'OK'.

Now repeat the process for slides 3 and 4, making the hyperlinks for each of the three icons; see Figure 14.3. Once you have selected 'slide show' you can move to slides 2, 3 or 4 by simply clicking the icon on slide 1.

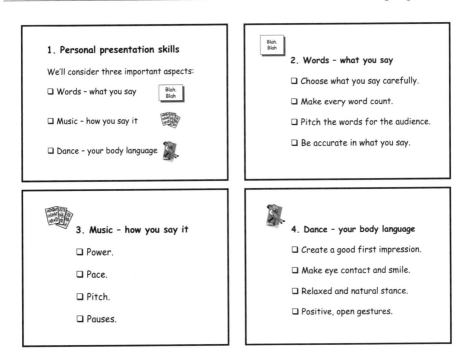

Figure 14.2 The four slides

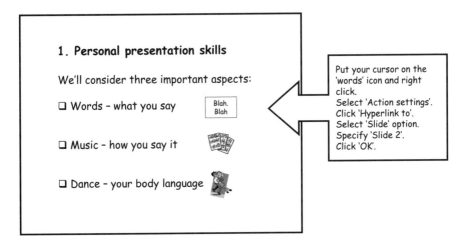

Figure 14.3 Creating the hyperlink

That sounds simple, but how do you return to the first slide easily? Here's how:

- Select slide 2.

- Select 'Autoshapes'.

- Select 'action buttons'.

- Choose the 'home' symbol.

- Position it on the slide.

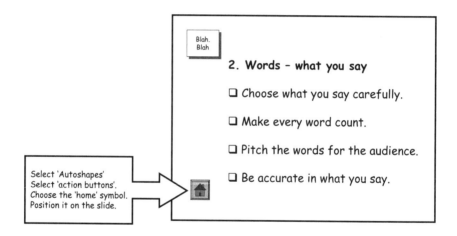

Figure 14.4 Returning to the home page

Once you have selected 'slide show' you can move back to the first slide (the home page) by clicking the 'home' icon on any slide.

Use familiar concepts

Look for opportunities to use familiar concepts or models in your training – it makes them more memorable. For example, when writing a book on recruitment techniques I developed a simple model to illustrate three types of questions, based on a traffic light (see Figure 14.5):

230

- Those on the red light have no place in a recruitment interview.

- Those on the amber light can be used with caution.

- Those on the green light can be used at all times.

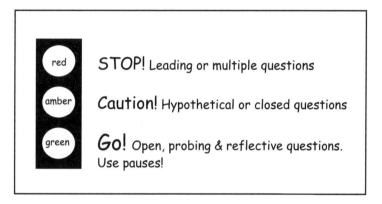

Figure 14.5 The traffic light

POTENTIAL PITFALLS

Too many slides

It's so easy with PowerPoint to keep adding more and more slides which, especially if they all look the same, can cause 'death by slide'. I helped one client to improve a one-day induction course that ran from 8 am to 5.30 pm and involved a large number of individual presenters. When we added all the proposed presentations together, the screen image would have changed every 75 seconds throughout the day. How much would delegates have remembered? Not a lot!

Tailor it to the audience

I worked with another client, a civil engineering company in the water industry, to develop a team of 'account managers' from their technical engineering staff. Typically they would pitch up to a client with masses of overhead slides, models and videos and they would subject the client to a standard two-hour, non-stop, multimedia presentation. And rarely get any contracts.

My programme lasted several weeks and finally led them to discover a new way to influence clients. They started with an interactive session to discover the client's needs, during which one of the presenting team was sitting at the back of the room discarding slides. They then gave a short presentation directed to the client's situation, which prompted a focused question-and-answer session. And they got new contracts!

Vary the format

Try to vary the images delegates see, especially if most people use a standard template. I remember one delegate on a presentation skills course who said: 'My problem is I'm one of a team of 13 internal auditors and we get together every quarter to share results of audits. After the third or fourth presentation people get bored looking at the same format. What can I do to make a greater impression?' I asked him for some typical findings, and his list included:

- 70 laptop computers – no insurance cover;
- broker's fees – halved from £20,000 to £10,000;
- most of our buildings are 50 per cent underinsured;
- our precious art collection is dramatically undervalued.

When redesigning the slides the underlying message is: 'Show, don't tell.'

Figure 14.6 shows some alternative ways you can give the same messages. Each slide shows how the image first appeared, then how it looked after some simple animation (some with sounds).

Check spelling and calculations

This sounds obvious, but you often see glaring errors. Columns of figures that don't add up... charts and graphs that are clearly inaccurate. All it needs is one simple error to undermine people's confidence in your whole session. Here's a classic example. I was delivering a presentation skills course for a water utility company and one delegate showed a slide that claimed to illustrate the water usage for the average domestic household (see Figure 14.7).

Figure 14.6 'Show', don't 'tell'

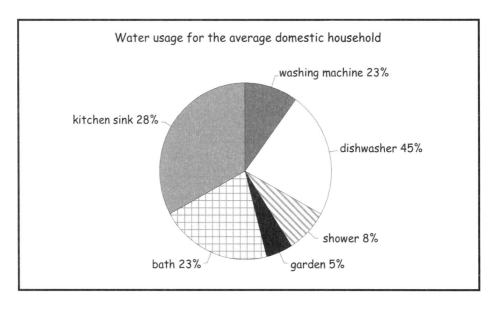

Figure 14.7 Get the numbers right

See anything wrong? First of all, the percentages don't add up to 100. Then you start to look harder. Do you really believe that a dishwasher accounts for 45 per cent of average domestic usage? But the dishwasher slice of the pie looks more like 25 per cent anyway.

You can imagine what happened to the presentation – absolute bedlam! What should the percentages be? Which slices are correct? His whole credibility was destroyed simply because he hadn't checked the numbers.

Keep it simple

Figure 14.8 shows some more examples of poorly designed visual aids. The person who presented these thought they were excellent – and you can clearly see that many hours went into their design.

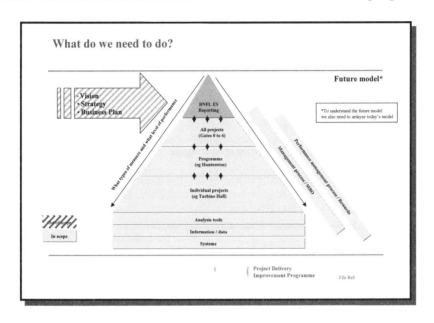

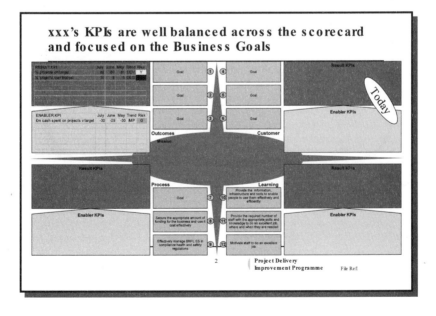

Figure 14.8 Poor visual aids

PLAN YOUR VISUALS

Now that you've reviewed the guidelines for success, and also seen some poor examples, it's time to plan what you will need. There are at least three main ingredients you may be considering:

1. The trainer's presentation.

2. Workbooks or handouts for delegates to use.

3. Posters, peripherals or other materials to 'dress' the training room.

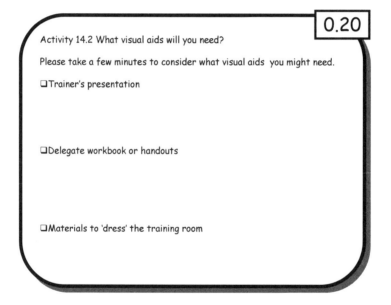

0.20

Activity 14.2 What visual aids will you need?

Please take a few minutes to consider what visual aids you might need.

❑ Trainer's presentation

❑ Delegate workbook or handouts

❑ Materials to 'dress' the training room

15

Designing e-learning

- Why e-learning?
- Managing the project
- The electronic learning system
- Using quizzes
- The course flow chart
- Building individual screens
- Creating the storyboards
- The trainer-led course
- The delegate workbook

WHY E-LEARNING?

For years people have been experimenting with computers as a training tool but the technology wasn't sophisticated enough. That's now changed – modern computers, coupled with intranets and the internet, mean that e-learning can take its place as a serious contender in the training armoury. E-learning has many benefits that can directly improve the competitive advantage of your company:

- Staff acquire new skills when they need them, instead of waiting for the next scheduled training course.
- People can break the learning into 'chunks' to fit the demands and time pressures of their own job.
- The time to learn underlying theory is minimized – people learn at different speeds, and may already know parts of the topic.
- Non-revenue-earning time is reduced, compared with traditional training courses, when the slowest person determines the pace.
- Any subsequent trainer-led course can focus on practising the skills, removing the need to explore underlying theories.
- Trainer-led courses are thus shorter, with reduced costs – trainers, facilities, overnight accommodation, etc.

So e-learning really can deliver 'more for less' – greater skill levels with reduced costs. For e-learning to be effective, people need to experience three stages:

1. Grasp the theory. They undertake a self-study e-learning course, supported by other learning resources, for example books or videos.
2. Practise the skills. Learners practise their skills in a short, intensive trainer-led course.
3. Apply the learning. They apply all the learning to reach new levels of business performance, supported by online coaching.

This chapter will show you what's different about designing e-learning compared with conventional training. Where appropriate we have given examples of materials and courseware on the CD ROM.

MANAGING THE PROJECT

Select and brief a software supplier

You will need to select a software company to provide the electronic learning system for your course and, as you shortlist them:

- Ensure you see their learning system in operation on a typical course.

- Try it out yourself and see how 'user-friendly' the whole package is.

- Judge whether the technology enhances learning or gets in the way.

- Try accessing their learning materials using your own network, not on a CD. That way you will sense how slow or frustrating the system may be for your own staff as they work through the modules.

The project team

Add two important people to your project team: someone from your in-house IT department who can advise on technical interface issues between the company's system and the electronic learning system, and a representative of the software company who knows the learning system thoroughly.

Specify your needs

To ensure success you'd be well advised to use a project specification document such as you can find on the CD ROM. Please take a few minutes to look through the general style and format, as this document can act as the reference for all parties during the life cycle of the project, especially during the periodic review meetings:

1. Introduction. Brief description of the project.

2. Format. Specify the format to be used, which is compatible with existing IT systems or other electronic learning systems.

3. Target groups. Who the training is primarily intended for, with perhaps secondary groups who may also benefit.

4. Target countries. The countries in which the electronic learning system is to be used. There are several considerations here:

   - technical compatibility of the learning systems;

   - language for on-screen text and voiceovers;

   - will cultural differences make a message unacceptable or confusing in another country?

   - internal funding, if costs are to be shared by several operating companies.

5. Learning aims. What is the training designed to change?

6. Structure. Outline the course chapters.

7. Learning outcomes. Detail the changes in knowledge, skills or attitudes the learning needs to bring about.

8. Platform. This is when your own IT person and the representative from the software company will leave everyone feeling in the cold as they revel in the joys of technical specifications. Ensure that what's being proposed is compatible and involves the minimum additional IT budget.

9. Training duration. Specify broadly how long the training should last end to end, but remember it's for guidance only, as people will progress through the course at different rates. However, clarifying whether it's a one-hour or a two-hour course helps to focus minds.

10. Notes. Record any notes for unusual aspects of the project.

11. Schedule. Outline the schedule for the whole project, which drives all the subsequent activities.

Book the review meetings early to ensure that the key people can attend. If the meeting's not required… it frees up welcome space in people's diaries. Allow sufficient time for internal 'sign off' at different stages. You just need one or two key people to be unavailable and suddenly the five-day 'window' for client sign off stretches to two weeks or longer. Then it's no good blaming your contractors when the project starts to seriously slip.

You may also need informal intermediate progress reviews. For example, I like to have the client 'sign off' the content and sequence of screen images before starting work on storyboards.

THE ELECTRONIC LEARNING SYSTEM

Discover the strengths and limitations of the learning system so that you know what you can and cannot do with the actual training materials.

For example, if you ask the learner to rearrange a series of items on a particular screen, how easy will it be to display them on a later screen, and comment on the order the learner has selected? What limitations are there when asking a learner to carry out a task, then having the results displayed on a later screen?

You may not know all the questions to ask right at the start and, as you begin to develop the course materials, you will need to consult with the software designers to check out specific ideas before they are implemented to avoid wasted effort.

> **0.20**
>
> Activity 15.1 E-learning project specification
>
> Which elements of the project specification would be helpful when managing your e-learning project?
>
> 1. Introduction - brief description.
>
> ☐2. IT format.
>
> ☐3. Target groups – primary and secondary.
>
> ☐4. Target countries.
>
> ☐5. Learning aims.
>
> ☐6. Structure - outline chapters.
>
> ☐7. Learning outcomes.
>
> ☐8. IT platform.
>
> ☐9. Training duration.
>
> ☐10. Notes - any unusual aspects.
>
> ☐11. Schedule.

Screen layout and navigation buttons

How will the materials be presented to the learner? What will the screen actually look like? Every software provider will have slightly different approaches to the screen appearance and you need to discuss and agree how they will use the available space. Your corporate relations people will guide you on displaying the company logo, as well as colours for borders and fonts.

Imagine the learners looking at their computer screen. The usable screen area in the centre will generally be sandwiched between an upper and lower border. The upper border is often used to tell learners exactly where they are at that moment. The components are typically:

- the company logo and name;
- the course title;
- the current chapter title;
- the actual page or screen number.

The lower border is often used for navigational icons, which enable the learner to move around the course:

- a right arrow – go to the next page;
- a left arrow – go to the previous page;
- a home sign – go to the home page;
- a '?' – which takes you to Help;
- a printer icon – print that page.

Of course there may be more, depending on your software provider and what you agree in your contract. The usable screen area starts to shrink quite dramatically, so you need to resist the temptation to have too much on any particular screen.

On-screen tasks, questions and activities

Your design must keep the learners motivated and interested as they work through the course. No matter how exciting the screen image or the impact of the material that's presented, the attention span of a typical adult learner is quite short. So keep them interested by changing the screen appearance and the types of tasks they are asked to complete. A course that simply presents screen after screen of text or pictures will quickly lose the learner's interest. So the secret of success when designing e-learning is just the same as when designing trainer-led courses – active and meaningful participation. And lots of it!

There are many different ways to achieve this, including:

- click and drag answers;
- rearrange items on the screen;
- type in responses to questions;
- quizzes;
- responding to multiple-choice questions;
- use of short video clips;
- case studies.

Ask the software providers to recommend what works best with their learning system, and remember that the range is continually expanding as the software becomes ever more sophisticated, so keeping the learner turning the page.

Accessing the e-learning system

How will learners access the learning system:

- Directly by selecting the appropriate drive?

- Only after they have 'enrolled' with HR?

- Through another internal gateway?

This apparently simple decision may involve a variety of departments and budget holders, and needs to be sorted out internally before selecting the software supplier. Depending on the speed of the network, you may also wish to make the courseware available on CD ROM so that people with slow links or limited computer access can still use the course.

Tracking individual progress

Will staff be able to access the e-learning programme only after they have 'enrolled' on the course with the HR department?

- Unrestricted access leaves the HR team unaware of how many people have worked through the course and with what results.

- This could be a problem if you have an internal system for charging departments for the training.

- It would also be difficult to link usage of training and training needs recorded in individual personal development plans.

HR will probably wish to know who has started the course, and which parts they have completed. This will be important to ensure that staff enrolling for a trainer-led course have completed the relevant e-learning course.

Learning system usage

The company may wish to monitor the overall success of the e-learning system, and the contribution it's making to achieving corporate objectives. Data you may wish to collect includes:

- how many start the course, by department and grade/rank;

- the proportion of staff who do not complete the course, by department and grade/rank;

- the time taken to work through individual chapters, which might indicate the degree of challenge each chapter presents;

- the percentage who fail to complete each chapter, which might indicate those that are most challenging or least interesting;

- the time taken to complete the whole course, or parts of the course, as an indicator of the cost-effectiveness of e-learning;

- the time from an individual learner starting the course to completing it, or abandoning it;

- feedback from individuals on which parts they found most interesting or useful, and those parts they found least helpful;

- the impact of the e-learning system on the company's IT system overall;

- the quality of service experienced by individuals in different locations – does the internal network operate sufficiently fast over all sites?

You can quickly appreciate that there's lots of information you might need to collect and it may be difficult and/or costly to build it in retrospectively.

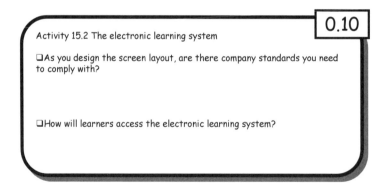

0.10

Activity 15.2 The electronic learning system

❑As you design the screen layout, are there company standards you need to comply with?

❑How will learners access the electronic learning system?

USING QUIZZES

E-learning offers the potential to assess learners' progress by testing their knowledge or skills before they start the programme, and then giving them a similar test at the end to see what they've learnt. Quizzes, or self-assessment exercises, also enable learners to control their own learning, by focusing on the sections they need to explore and bypassing the material they are already familiar with.

Of course you don't necessarily need a quiz to do this – you could simply ask learners to select the modules they think they need to experience. But using a quiz to select and deselect the appropriate modules is likely to give a more objective result, depending on the quiz of course.

When could you use quizzes?

- At the start of the course to assess the learner's knowledge or to select the course modules he or she needs to complete.

- At the end of the course to evaluate how much he or she has learnt.

- At any stage to highlight specific learning points, or to carry out interim self-assessments.

End-of-course assessment

If you're planning to use the 'before' and 'after' quiz to evaluate the effectiveness of the course, you will need to consider what questions to ask. If you repeat exactly the same quiz at the end as at the beginning you can, in theory, get a precise measurement of learning. But the smart learner could 'cheat', so giving a false impression of acquired learning.

Perhaps the best approach for the closing quiz is to mix some of the original questions, rephrased or presented in a slightly differently way, so the learner doesn't just repeat the answers from the opening quiz. You could also balance the repeated questions with some new questions, so that the closing quiz looks and feels quite different.

Are there 'right' answers?

When drafting quizzes, be careful about the types of question you ask. You can easily demotivate learners by making them choose what you believe are 'correct' answers, when they may believe there are a variety of 'appropriate' answers.

'Right' answers

Obviously there are many topics for which there are 'right' and 'wrong' answers. For example, if the course was on aviation meteorology, one question could be:

245

Buys Ballot's law states that, in the Northern hemisphere, if you stand with your back to the wind, the area of lower pressure is:

A. On the right.
B. On the left.
C. Ahead.

There is only one correct answer and it's B. In the Northern hemisphere, if you're flying towards an area of low pressure the aircraft will drift to the right, as the wind is coming from your left.

'Recommended' answers

There are many topics that have 'recommended' answers. For example, if the course was on Health and Safety you could ask the following question on RIDDOR, the legal framework for Reporting of Injuries, Diseases and Dangerous Occurrences Regulations, 1995:

How and when should incidents be notified under RIDDOR?

The answer would be: this notification must be by the quickest practicable means and this is usually by telephone. The notification must be followed by a written report within 10 days and this is usually done using Form F2508.

Note the word 'usually', which implies that this is what is expected, but is not mandatory. There may be situations when the 'usual' approach is not appropriate.

Best practice

Finally, there are many topics for which there may be 'best practice' depending on the situation. For example, a quiz on 'problem solving' could ask:

What logical steps would you work through to ensure a problem is solved effectively?

The recommended steps might be:

1. Define the problem.

2. Collect relevant data.

3. Identify the root cause(s) of the problem.

4. Identify possible solutions.

5. Choose the best solution(s).

6. Implement and review.

However, there could be good reasons for inserting additional steps, or skipping steps, depending on the actual situation. Imposing one 'right' sequence on learners might risk alienating them. You can see why you need to be careful. If you try to 'upgrade' what is a recommended approach and impose it as a 'right' answer, you risk alienating your learners right at the very beginning of the course.

Detailed quiz design

Having decided the strategy, you can then design each quiz or self-assessment task:

- Start by selecting topics that are relevant to the course material, and represent the main stream of the course.

- Then decide how to present the questions, aiming for variety to keep the learner interested.

- For example, multiple-choice questions or rearranging a range of possible answers, can be interspersed with more conventional methods.

As you design the quiz or self-assessment tools, bear in mind how you will score the learner's answers, and how the results will be displayed and referred to later in the course. In the CD ROM we've shown you a sample opening quiz so you can get the feel of what to do. Having asked the questions, the learning system must record the learner's responses and display them at an appropriate moment.

Designing a closing quiz

Having designed the opening quiz, you can then consider what sort of closing quiz to have. This is best done once you have designed the rest of the course material, so it may be one of the last tasks you complete.

Who will see the results?

Another important issue to consider is who will see the results and how they will be used. This topic can become quite 'hot', exposing a wide range of views in the planning team. There will also no doubt be lots of discussion about which 'results' are being considered. Are they solely the 'before' and 'after' quiz results, or are any other measurable results generated during the e-learning course?

Are the results purely for the learner's benefit to show them progress? Should the results be available to the professionals who manage the e-learning courses to show how effective the courses are, and which parts seem to be most challenging and so may need redesigning?

This information also reveals the percentages of learners who abandon the course, the average time taken to complete the course, and an indication of the 'take up' of e-learning in different parts of the business.

Of course there are different cost implications for the two different approaches.

Learner's use only

The learning management system will need to store the results from each session, and be able to display them again each time the learner logs on to the system, especially if the quiz results are to be used to select the route through the course.

Wider publication

If the results are to be used more widely, the electronic learning system will need to transfer the data to the HR administration system. All this comes at a cost, not only for the software, but also for people to be trained to administer the system and publish the results.

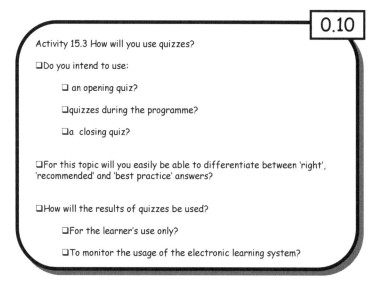

0.10

Activity 15.3 How will you use quizzes?

❑Do you intend to use:

❑ an opening quiz?

❑quizzes during the programme?

❑a closing quiz?

❑For this topic will you easily be able to differentiate between 'right', 'recommended' and 'best practice' answers?

❑How will the results of quizzes be used?

❑For the learner's use only?

❑To monitor the usage of the electronic learning system?

THE COURSE FLOW CHART

Before designing the course we recommend you develop a flow chart, as this helps:

- to clarify the route through the course;

- you to stay on track as you do the detailed design;

- the software design team to understand how the various elements all relate to each other, and the links between individual storyboards.

The flow chart may become complex as the course materials develop. Figure 15.1 shows the flow chart for the Managing Meetings course – let's walk through the main elements.

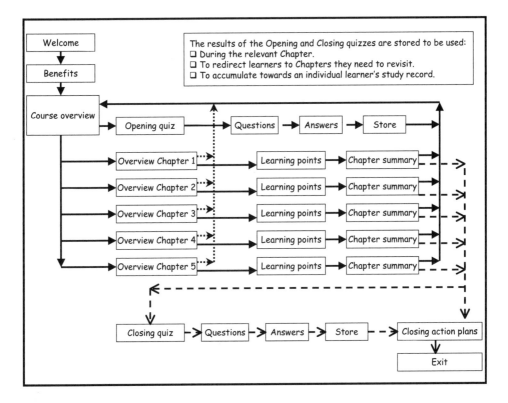

Figure 15.1 Course flow chart

Welcome

- Starts at the Welcome page, learn the Benefits of the course, before reaching the Course overview.

- The Course Overview lists the Chapters and enables the learner to discover more about each Chapter.

- The learner can go directly to the Chapter to start work, or return to the Course Overview.

- The final option from the Course overview is to go to the Opening quiz.

Opening quiz

The results of the Opening quiz are stored, so that the results can be:

- referred to during the relevant chapter;

- used to redirect a learner to a part of the course he or she seems to have struggled with;

- accumulated to track a learner's progress, or simply collect statistics for overall course usage.

Chapters

- The learner starts working through the chosen Chapter.

- Each Chapter ends with a Summary and an invitation to do some action planning.

- Link to the learner's workbook throughout the Chapters, to reinforce key messages, or to involve the learner in practical tasks.

- Having completed the Chapter, the learner chooses to return to the Course overview to select another Chapter, complete the Closing quiz, or Exit the course.

Closing quiz

The results of the Closing quiz are stored, so that the results can:

- redirect a learner to a part of the course they seem to have struggled with;

- be accumulated to track individual learners, or simply collect statistics for overall course usage.

Having completed the Closing quiz, the learner does some final Action planning, before Exiting the course.

Closing action plans

- Before finally exiting, the learner reviews the learning points from the course, and records them in the workbook.

- Highlight what comes next – is there a trainer-led course they can attend to practise their skills?

- Mention other resources, for example books or video tapes/DVDs.

0.30

Activity 15.4 Develop a course flow chart

Using a sheet of A3 paper, why not start drafting your course flow chart? Don't worry if it looks 'messy' to start with – the shape will gradually develop with time.

BUILDING INDIVIDUAL SCREENS

Designing the individual screens that deliver the specific learning points for the course, highlights one of the major differences between e-learning and a trainer-led course. A trainer gets continual feedback on how well delegates are grasping the ideas or concepts, and responds by inserting additional ideas or models to help overcome any blocks or barriers. With e-learning this cannot easily be achieved without regular tests or assessments, which can be tiresome for the learner.

Your learning materials must be comprehensive and make no assumptions about the learner's current level of knowledge or ability. Each screen of information needs to lead naturally to the next, drawing the learner through a logical, developing story. Once you have settled on the content you can then decide how to present your information and, if you think of the guidelines you would follow for designing visual aids, you won't go far wrong.

Using text

- Limit the text on the screen or it looks very 'busy' and may turn off the learner.

- Use large-sized fonts so the course doesn't become an eyesight test.
- Ideally, use one font – is there a corporate standard?
- Use stronger font colours – you may have to adhere to corporate standards.
- Be careful with contrasting colours, especially red and green.

Using images

- A picture tells a thousand words, so they say, but ensure it's the right picture!
- Every image should have a positive learning point – avoid using images just because they're funky or striking.
- Ensure images can't inadvertently offend people – what may be fun to you may cause embarrassment or offence to others.
- Don't have too many visual gimmicks; they quickly become tiresome and distracting.

Blend of text and images

- Blend text with images to keep the learner interested.
- Vary the way you present your text and images.

Graphs and charts

- Follow all the usual rules about presenting figures and graphs.
- For example, a pie chart or a bar chart will have more impact than a table of figures, especially when coupled with appropriate use of colour.

Maximum participation

An important aspect of designing e-learning is to keep every learner interested. Just because you find your own topic interesting, you can't assume that everyone else will share your enthusiasm. Your quest for engaging delegates will only be limited by:

- Your own creativity.

- The budget – some great ideas will suck up large amounts of money, but will add little value to the course.

- Technology – learning management systems are constantly widening the horizons (but at a price!)

- Time – always keep an eye on how long the modules will take to work through.

Approaches to try

Display text and images

- Simply show the text, together with any appropriate images.

- Avoid too many 'runs' of this type of display or the learner may lose interest.

Specific questions

- Pose a question and the learner enters his or her responses on the screen.

- The next screen shows the 'right' answer, and explores differences between the responses.

Audio

- Use an audio demonstration and ask the learner to choose between several options.

- For example, you could ask the learner to listen to three examples and decide which was spoken assertively, which was aggressive and which was passive.

- The learner clicks and drags the box to the number.

- A later screen would show the 'right' answer.

Another excellent use is to demonstrate the optimum speech rate when giving a presentation. The voiceover repeats the same paragraph at different speeds, and the learner chooses which is the most appropriate.

Rearrange options

- You present a list of options and invite them to decide which order they would choose.

- For example, the screen could ask learners to decide how they would deal with a disruptive person at a meeting, by rearranging the options into their preferred sequence.

- The next screen would show the recommended order compared with the learner's choice.

Case studies

- You introduce a person or team, giving sufficient background information to enable the learner to make informed judgements.

- Then you introduce several alternatives and ask the learner to decide which is most appropriate.

- Add continuity by using one or a series of case studies throughout the course, which you can refer to periodically to illustrate specific learning points.

- This approach is particularly useful for in-house programmes using industry-specific case studies.

Simulated conversations

- The learner overhears several versions of a conversation, and has to decide which is the most appropriate for the given situation.

- The subsequent screen would reveal the recommended way, and discuss its merits.

- If the learner picks the less effective options, he or she can be directed to a short audio clip that demonstrates why that approach works less well.

Video clips

- The underlying approach is similar to simulated conversation – the learner watches a short video clip demonstrating a variety of approaches.

- The subsequent screen would reveal the recommended way, and discuss its merits.

- If the learner picks the less effective options, he or she can be directed to a short video clip that demonstrates why that approach works less well.

- This approach is very flexible and realistic, but also costs significantly more to develop.

Animations

- Use diagrams or cartoons to bring otherwise dull or complex issues to life.

- For example, build up a complex diagram of a piece of equipment or plant, from initial outline to the full picture.

- The learner can see how the component parts of a complex machine move together to operate effectively.

- Develop a 'route map' showing how to progress through a variety of steps to reach an end goal, for example how a team works through key steps to manage a complex project.

Link to the learner's workbook

Keep the learner actively involved by asking him or her to undertake tasks in the workbook that accompanies the e-learning course.

hours

Activity 15.5 Start creating the screens

So you know the theory – now it's time to put it into practice and start developing your screens. You don't have to start at the beginning – just pick one screen you're confident about developing.

❑Create a PowerPoint file and start playing with text and images until you get something that looks reasonable.

❑Then move on to another screen and repeat the process.

❑Once you've tried six or seven screens you'll be getting the idea and will want to go back to improve the first ones you did.

❑Then just keep going until you have illustrated all the learning points needed for your course.

❑Once you have completed the first pass review the learning techniques you've employed and see if you can introduce more variety.

❑All the time imagine you're the learner – what will they feel like working through your materials? Challenged? Motivated? Intrigued? Stimulated? Wanting more?

❑If not ... change it!

CREATING THE STORYBOARDS

The project reaches a critical stage when you hand it over to the software design team to transform your creative ideas into stimulating, enjoyable and productive electronic learning. To enable the learning points and the 'flavour' of the course to be accurately translated, the software designers will require a detailed briefing on every screen that needs to be created. You do this by designing a suite of story-boards, much like those a film company uses to explain the development of the plot in a movie. So the final stage in development is to convert all the individual screens into their equivalent storyboards. For a one-hour Meetings Skills courses there could be about 120 separate screens.

In addition to the storyboards the software designers will also need the course flow chart to enable them to confirm the route the learner needs to take through the material.

Storyboard components

Make no mistake: the storyboards are, in effect, the contract you have with the software designer – the quality of the final course will be a reflection of the quality of the storyboards. A sample storyboard is shown in Figure 15.2. Let's go through each element in more detail.

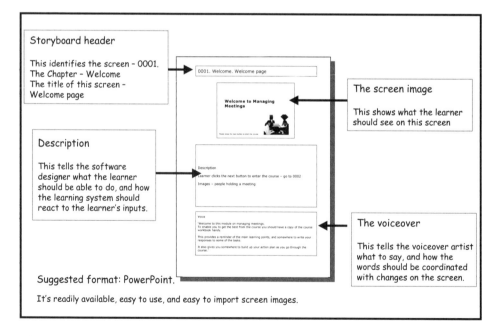

Figure 15.2 Sample storyboard

Storyboard header

At the top of the page, the header conveys some key information.

Screen number: the number 0001 shows this is the first in the package. The numbers run sequentially to the end of the course. If adding a screen after '1021', make it '1021a'; if deleting a screen, simply drop the number.

Chapter title

The Chapter title identifies where you are in the course. It normally appears in the border along the top of the screen.

Screen title

The title of this screen is the 'Welcome page' and again this would normally appear in the top border of the learner's screen.

The screen image

The next box shows the designer the required screen image. It shows what the learner should see on this screen, which is much easier than trying to describe what you want.

Show images and any text, together with the relative positions you would like to achieve. Using PowerPoint you can show a certain amount of animation, or how the images should develop.

Having defined what the learner should see, and the broad parameters you want to apply, you must now leave the software designer to interpret the screen within the technical limitations of the learning system. This is why it's so important for you to have a good working relationship with the software designers.

The description

The 'description' box tells the software designer some other important information:

- what should happen with the text and images, with timings and sequences;
- what learners should be able to do while at that screen, and what they should not be able to do;
- how the learning system should react to the learners' inputs;
- where they go next when they leave this screen.

- If any information needs to be stored, when it will be required again and in what format.

The voiceover

The final box on the storyboard details any voiceover that's required. It's not mandatory to have a voiceover but it certainly helps the learner to stay interested in what's happening. Remember accessibility?

The voiceover shouldn't contain any information not on the screen, as it's possible that many learners will switch the voiceover off. They may be in a noisy environment (so can't hear it) or a quiet environment (distracting others). The ideal speed for the voiceover speech is about 140 to 150 words per minute.

The voiceover box tells the voiceover artist(s):

- what to say;

- how to harmonize the words with changes on the screen;

- specific instructions about tone of voice, pace, emphasis, pauses, etc.

I usually add some extra advice to the voiceover artist along the lines of: 'Please feel free to make small changes to the language or words to make the voiceover more natural, without changing the meaning or substance of the course.'

How to build the storyboards

Please look at the CD ROM, where we show several examples of storyboards. You will quickly grasp the idea. There are no shortcuts – it's a screen-by-screen job, requiring intense attention to detail, constantly checking where the learner needs to go to next and signposting it clearly for the software designer.

The examples should give you ideas for designing the storyboards. When working with your own materials you will quickly get a feel for what works and develop your own style and approach. It's essential to develop a good working relationship with the software designers so that they feel comfortable about ringing you to ask: 'On page 114 you say you want us to do... Do you really mean that?'

Designing the storyboards is intense, tiring work and you will make mistakes in logic or detail however hard you try not to. So allow plenty of time for proof-reading and, ideally, ask someone who has not had any contact with the project to read it for you. They will see errors and omissions much better than you ever will!

Activity 15.6 Create your storyboards

As before, it's time to put theory into practice and start creating your storyboards. This time it's best to start at the beginning with number 0001.

❑Create a template using PowerPoint and build the appropriate boxes.

❑Enter the details in the 'storyboard header' box.

❑Then import the screen image and size it to fit in the 'screen image' box.

❑Now turn your attention to the 'description' box and write a concise account of what should happen at this screen.

    ❑What should the learner be able to do, and how should the system react?
    ❑What should the learner not be able to do?
    ❑Where does the learner go next?
    ❑Refer to the course flow chart to make sure everything is consistent.
    ❑Any other special instructions? Animation? Timings?

❑Finally, plan what you want the voiceover artist to say.

    ❑Any special emphasis?
    ❑Any special timings?
    ❑Harmonizing with animation?

❑Congratulations! You've done number 0001 ... now move on to 0002 and repeat the process until you have designed all your storyboards. It'll take a few hours!

THE TRAINER-LED COURSE

Will your e-learning students be attending a trainer-led course to practise their skills? If the answer is 'yes', you can now start designing the trainer-led course. As we've discovered, there are many advantages to using blended training but, like everything in life, it's not all roses. There are certain potential challenges you will need to be aware of and prepare for.

Varied amount of preparation

Sadly, not every learner will approach the e-learning course with the same degree of motivation. Personal commitments, coupled with the pressure at work or frustrations with the performance of the IT network, mean that delegates arrive with varying degrees of knowledge. But no matter how many 'health warnings' appear in the course joining instructions, typically the trainer will find in a group of eight delegates:

- Only three or four people will have completed the course fully.
- Perhaps three or four people will have completed most of the course, but with some gaps.
- At least one person will have either attempted no more than 50 per cent of the course material, or studied the course so long ago that their recall of the content is poor.

Identify the skills to be practised

Early on, you grouped your course learning points into two piles: acquiring knowledge would be part of the e-learning course, and practising skills should be included in the trainer-led course. But take time to review your ideas as things may have changed – a topic that seemed ideal for e-learning may need, based on feedback, to be included in the trainer-led course. You may be surprised by the variety of other resources you already have, including:

- books and training packs;
- published articles;
- video tapes;
- DVDs;
- audio tapes;
- interactive videos;
- computer-based training;
- existing course designs and materials;
- one-to-one discussions;
- visits.

You probably won't use these resources during the trainer-led course, but you can recommend them to learners as additional sources of learning.

It's useful at this stage to decide which models, techniques or skills are critical for success and need to be reinforced in the trainer-led course. Keep your mind open and just identify possible sessions for the course, recognizing that some of them may be dropped once you start to look at the time available.

Course duration

In most cases a one-day course should be sufficient to practise new skills and receive some meaningful feedback, depending on the number of delegates attending the course. Let's look at a practical example.

Most people have attended a Presentation Skills course at some stage in their career, which probably lasted two days with a maximum of eight delegates on the course. This format gives enough time to explore the theory, and allows each delegate to deliver three presentations during the rest of the course. By using e-learning to explore the theory you can reduce the trainer-led course to one day and still allow time for meaningful skill enhancement.

In most cases one day should be sufficient to replace a two-day course, otherwise there is no convincing reason for the expense of creating the e-learning component.

How many delegates?

To have an effective one-day course you will need to limit the number of delegates. As the numbers increase, the amount of individual attention each delegate receives obviously falls, so limiting the overall value of the experience.

Most courses will work best with a maximum of eight delegates, while the minimum number depends on the course content, but in most cases it would be four.

Key milestones

You also need to manage some practical issues to ensure you have a successful pilot event. One of the big advantages of e-learning is that learners can do it when they want, where they want, and spend as much time as they need. For the trainer-led course they must all be together, for the agreed duration, in one place. So you will need to:

- Book an appropriately sized and equipped venue.
- Ensure a suitably qualified trainer is available.
- Design the workbooks and trainer presentations.
- Confirm all your learners are available.

Sounds easy – and it is, provided you do it early enough! This is why you need the course administrator in the project team. Remember also that this is the pilot course and you may need to make some changes, however small, before the course can be put on general release. This may be particularly important if you're harmonizing the course with some planned strategic initiative, so the sooner these dates are booked, the better.

If possible, schedule a review meeting the morning immediately after the pilot course. That way you get everyone together while the course is fresh in everyone's mind, and you don't lose any time preparing for the next course. It keeps the momentum going.

Finalize the budget

The final item for the agenda – agree the budgets for the courses and the development work. Looking through the paragraphs above will trigger thoughts about the various provisions you need to make.

Using a refresher quiz

It's important to ensure that both components of the learning experience, the e-learning and the trainer-led course, are not only consistent but clearly linked so that they appear to be part of a continuous learning path. We've stressed all the way through the need to ensure that you use the same language, models, fonts, images, etc as these all reinforce a consistent approach.

Inevitably there will be a time delay between any particular person finishing the e-learning course and attending the trainer-led course, and that this elapsed time will vary from person to person. There are two easy ways you can link the two learning experiences together: 1) use a refresher quiz during the course; 2) develop a delegate workbook.

The one-day trainer-led course will be very busy so we strongly recommend using a refresher quiz early in the course to:

- Refresh the theoretical concepts covered in the e-learning.

- Break the ice – encourage delegates to talk to each other.

- Highlight any outstanding issues or concerns delegates may have.

- Help the trainer to discover any potential barriers or individual learning needs before the day starts.

Designing a refresher quiz

If you're using a refresher quiz, you could follow these guidelines.

Time

Decide how much time to allow for the refresher quiz session. We would recommend in total 45 minutes – 15 minutes for delegates to discuss the questions with a partner, followed by 30 minutes' group discussion facilitated by the trainer. Using more time than this seriously eats into the time available for practising the skills.

Topics

Review the e-learning course and decide which topics you need to refresh before you start the practice sessions. Using Post-it Notes gives you flexibility and doesn't inhibit the creative juices flowing. Simply look through the e-learning course and jot a Post-it Note every time you find a potentially useful question.

Select the questions

Having looked at a list of possible questions select and discount them until you have the number you require. We recommend a maximum of 10 questions for the available time, and accept that not everyone will answer all the questions. They are there mainly to prompt discussion.

Write the answers

The final step is to write an answer sheet the trainer can distribute following the group discussion.

Pilot the refresher quiz

Remember to try out the refresher quiz on a typical group who have completed the e-learning course. Their feedback will be most helpful. You can find an example of a refresher quiz, based on a presentation skills course, on the CD ROM.

1.30

Activity 15.7 Design the trainer-led course

Will your e-learning students be attending a trainer-led course to practise their skills? If 'yes' then this is a good moment to put your initial thoughts together on what the course might look like.

Review all the ideas we've suggested in this chapter and start your initial design.

Duration? One day maximum? How many delegates?

Will you be using a Refresher Quiz? If so, you might want to select some suitable topics.

How can you make links to the e-learning course and the delegate workbooks?

THE DELEGATE WORKBOOK

A workbook to accompany an e-learning course offers two main benefits. First, working through an e-learning course should be interesting and help the learner to acquire lots of knowledge and skills, but without a permanent reminder of the topics the retention rate can easily fall dramatically once the screen is switched off.

Another issue is continuity. It's very unlikely that the learner will work through the course end to end in one session. It's more likely that the course will be done in chunks, with varying amounts of time between sessions. A workbook will remind learners where they got to in the previous session and so kick off the latest session more productively.

Consistency with the on-screen image

It's important that the workbook should mirror exactly what the learner sees on the e-learning screen. So design the workbook and e-learning materials in parallel, and ensure that any changes or modifications to either are carried over into the complementary medium:

- The sequence and flow needs to be the same.

- Use identical concepts or models.

- Use the same characters in case studies – same names, sex, appearance, etc.

- Use identical industries and settings.

Clarify the format and style of the workbook

Agree the role the workbook plays in achieving the overall goal of improving performance. The issues to consider include:

- How does the workbook fit alongside the course?

- What balance of content do you want?

- How large should it be – both size and number of pages?

- How does this workbook relate to the workbook learners will get when they attend the trainer-led course?

Detailed design

Once these wider issues are settled you can begin the detailed workbook design. Of course much will depend on the actual topic being presented, but there are still many common themes, including:

- front page – develop a consistent style across all the e-learning products;
- 'welcome' page;
- balance of text and graphics;
- how to refer to e-learning pages and other resources, eg company intranet;
- consistency with existing hard-copy documents;
- style – for example, using plain English;
- action planning page – consistent with existing style.

How will learners access the workbook?

A final aspect to consider is how learners will access the workbook; there are at least two possible approaches. You can either produce the workbooks in bulk and send one to learners as they commence the course, or allow learners to print their own workbook on demand locally.

0.45

Activity 15.8 Design the course workbook

A useful way to reinforce the e-learning is to give students a workbook to accompany the course. Some of the design issues to consider are:

❑How does the workbook fit alongside the course?
❑What balance of content do you want?
❑How large should it be - both size and pages?
❑How does this workbook relate to the workbook learners will get when they attend the trainer-led course?

Remember that this workbook must be consistent with the e-learning screen image and any workbooks you develop to accompany any trainer-led course.

16

Train the trainers

> - Write a Trainer's Guide
> - Train the trainers
> - Trainer-led courses for blended learning

WRITE A TRAINER'S GUIDE

An important element of any training programme is ensuring consistency and, for any trainer-led course, a good starting point is to write a comprehensive Trainer's Guide, followed by some form of train-the-trainer training. In this chapter we'll take you through the steps you can follow to ensure your trainers are competent to deliver your course. On the CD ROM is a sample Trainer's Guide for a trainer-led course that would follow an e-learning course on presentation skills.

Brainstorm the contents

Start by brainstorming the contents of your Trainer's Guide and (surprise!) we recommend using Post-it Notes to collect your initial ideas. From experience we would suggest that the Trainer's Guide should include at least the following.

Section 1. Welcome to the course

- Welcome – set out the purpose of the Trainer's Guide and outline the contents.

- Course objectives or benefits – clarify what the course should achieve.

- Course delegates – discuss maximum and minimum numbers.

- Venue – minimum requirements.

- Course materials and equipment – what you need to run the course.

- Consistency – stress need for trainer to follow the programme and model the techniques.

Section 2. Course timetable

The course outline – overall structure of the day.

Section 3. Detailed tutor guide

Detailed session notes giving advice on how to deliver each session, which could include the following information:

- session title;

- purpose;

- time;

- materials and resources;

- preparation;

- how do I do it?

Section 4. Copies of the course documents

These could include:

- venue specification;

- course joining instructions;

- refresher quiz – if used;

- materials or equipment requirements;

- briefing notes for specific sessions;
- end-of-course questionnaire.

Write the first draft

Once you have the ideas you can quickly assemble them into a logical order, before writing the draft Trainer's Guide. Prior to finalizing the Guide, invite comments or suggestions from trainers who might run the courses. Get their input – it will be very helpful and starts to build their ownership of the course.

Design any extra materials you may need to use during the practical sessions, and the guideline here is to keep them to the barest minimum. What sort of materials? You might need any of the following:

- sheets for giving focused feedback;
- briefing sheets for skill practice sessions;
- case study scenarios for exercises;
- action planning sheets;
- end-of-course questionnaire.

Computer graphics

Most people these days use PowerPoint graphics to illustrate their presentations or courses, and you may wish to invest the time to transfer some of the background materials for each course onto this medium. Remember to include the hardware and software requirements in your course specification.

Delivering the courses

You may still not be convinced of the need to write a Trainer's Guide. When trainers start delivering a new course they will often need to refer to the detailed session notes in Section 3 of the Guide to ensure they cover all the key points. Then, as experience with the material grows, trainers will find that they only need to refer to the outline timetable (in Section 2) to keep themselves on track. Once they are completely familiar with a programme, experienced trainers will be able to confidently deliver a course by simply referring to a PowerPoint presentation or the delegate workbook.

> 0.10
>
> Activity 16.1 Do you need a Trainer's Guide?
>
> Please take a few minutes to consider your needs for a Trainer's Guide.
>
> How much detail will you need to give?
>
> ☐ Section 1 - Welcome to the course
>
> ☐ Section 2 - Course timetable
>
> ☐ Section 3 - Detailed tutor guide
>
> ☐ Section 4 - Copies of the course documents

TRAIN THE TRAINERS

Once you have written your Trainer's Guide you can select and then train the trainers who will run the courses. Sometimes you can use the training process to help you identify potential trainers for your programmes. There are two separate but interlinked issues here. First, you need to be sure that trainers are familiar with the course materials. But knowing is one thing – doing is quite another, so you may need your potential trainers to demonstrate their competence to deliver the programme. The best way of doing this is to hold some form of train the trainer event, which we can best illustrate with a real example.

Inexperienced trainers

One of my clients, a leading printing house, decided that it needed to improve the customer service given by all its staff at its various sites. It decided that site managers would train all the staff using my Customer Care Pack as the core training materials. So we designed a two-day course that enabled the potential trainers to become familiar with the training pack, before demonstrating their ability to deliver specific sessions. In outline, the course offered the following sessions.

Day 1

1. Welcome to the course.

269

2. Gain the delegates' buy in to the course.

3. Profile of the successful trainer.

4 and 5. Walk through the selected Customer Care modules.

6. How people learn.

7. Tutor demonstrates one module.

8. Brief delegates for day 2.

9. Delegates prepare their 45-minute sessions.

Day 2

10. Welcome to Day 2.

11 and 12. Sessions delivered by delegates 1 to 4.

13 and 14. Sessions delivered by delegates 5 to 8.

15 and 16. Sessions delivered by delegates 9 to 12.

17. Other factors for success.

18. Close the course.

This programme enabled 12 delegates to explore the core training materials, deliver one session with partner, and watch five other modules being delivered. Overall it was very successful and delegates left the course feeling confident to return to their sites and train their staff to improve their customer service.

More experienced trainers

If you're intending to use experienced trainers who are simply unfamiliar with the course materials you can adopt another approach:

- First, hold a short familiarization session where you take the trainers through the materials, session by session.

- Then ask them to sit in and observe you deliver the course, so they can see the materials 'come alive'.

- If the individuals are still feeling a little unsure of their ability to deliver the course then you can always suggest they attend a further course, when they share the workload and deliver some sessions themselves.

0.15

Activity 16.2 Train the trainers

❑Do you need to design and/or deliver any form of train the trainer event?

❑If so, will it be for experienced or inexperienced trainers?

❑Do you anticipate asking managers to deliver training sessions? If so, how will you train them?

TRAINER-LED COURSES FOR BLENDED LEARNING

In the last chapter we showed how designing e-learning courses differs from conventional training and, not surprisingly, the same applies to delivering trainer-led courses as part of a 'blended learning' package. Ideally the preparation should have started much earlier, involving some of the trainers in designing the e-learning course materials. The Trainer's Guide we introduced earlier gives you a flavour of what needs to be done.

Customize the training

Your trainers' experience will determine how much time and preparation they need to become confident to deliver the course:

- Everyone will need to work through the complete e-learning course before attending the train the trainer session so they are familiar with the materials.

- Trainers who are used to working with e-learning and/or the topic may need half a day to walk through the Trainer's Guide with you, exploring how they will deliver each session.

- Trainers who are not familiar with working with e-learning and/or the topic may need a full day to walk through the Trainer's Guide with you, and then deliver a few sessions so you can be confident about their style and approach.

Special considerations

In addition to the usual preparatory work prior to running any new course you will need to emphasize to your trainers that there are several important issues they need to accept, especially if they have limited experience of delivering the 'blended learning' type of course.

Keep to the script

When presenting the course it is essential that they do not deviate in any way from the concepts and ideas presented in the programme, even if they don't agree with all of them.

No new materials or models

The one-day timetable is already very 'tight' and there simply is no time to introduce any new materials or concepts.

Put aside their own preferred ways of working

Recognize that they, as experienced trainers, have their own approach to the topic and it is quite possible that certain skills or behaviours may be presented differently from how they would do it themselves. However, to avoid confusing the delegates, and to ensure the course is delivered consistently you should ask them to:

- Put aside their own personal preferences or styles and deliver the course as designed.

- Respond to any questions in a way that is consistent with the materials in the e-learning course.

- Project themselves as a role model for all the course concepts, demonstrating them consistently throughout the day.

By the end of the train the trainer event you should have a list of people who you are confident will deliver the courses consistently and energetically. Ideally, 'pencil in' some possible training dates while you have them on site!

17

Select and manage the venue

> - Draft the venue specification
> - Manage the venue

DRAFT THE VENUE SPECIFICATION

Much of the success of a course relies on the venue – if the setting is wrong, or perhaps the room is cramped, then it will be an additional barrier for the trainer to overcome. An easy way to minimize the risk of this happening is to define the 'ideal' venue and use this specification when searching for the course venue. This chapter has been written on the basis that the course will be residential – clearly, things will be much simpler if the course is a 'day job'.

Make sure someone visits the venue, preferably the trainer delivering the course. To give an example of how badly this can go wrong, I arrived at a hotel that had been booked for a two-day participative senior management workshop. The main room booked was the boardroom, which, although looking very elegant, barely had enough room for people to squeeze behind the chairs once others were seated. By good fortune they had also booked two team rooms where, although they were only marginally larger, we were able to strip out the furniture, leaving only the chairs around the edges of the room. No room for screens for PowerPoint – we could just squeeze in two flipchart stands.

The moral of the story: suggest the trainer visits it and imagines being in the room for the course duration. Each course will be different in terms of the venue, but the following general principles apply.

Room size

Insist on a generously sized room as most hotels or conference centres will offer you a room that is far too small. This may be OK if you are sitting around a table holding a short meeting, but not for a participative day-long training course. For a course with 12 delegates, specify a room at least 7 metres square.

Environment

Ideally your room should have natural daylight and air conditioning.

Room layout

Every trainer has his or her own preferred approach but we would recommend:

- Up to six delegates – sit around one table, set out board room style.

- Seven to eight delegates – use two tables, with three or four delegates per table, café style.

- Nine to 12 delegates – use three tables, with three or four delegates per table, café style.

- Thirteen delegates upwards – use four tables, with three or four delegates per table, café style.

Supply the venue with a room plan, such as the one shown in Figure 17.1, to minimize 'misunderstandings'.

Tutor's needs

The tutor will require a chair at the front of the room, and a side table for course materials and equipment.

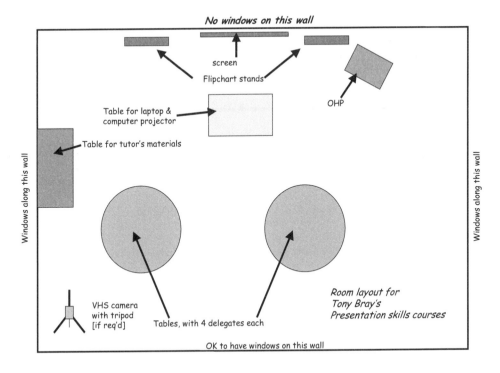

Figure 17.1 Room layout

Training equipment

- Sufficient free-standing flipchart stands with a good supply of flipchart paper and pens.

- An OHP projector, with a pack of blank OHP acetates and a good supply of OHP pens, together with a screen.

- If you're using PowerPoint you'll need a screen and projector – who will bring the laptop?

- Check the availability of sockets and extension cables.

Refreshments

Ask the venue to supply water, orange juice, etc, as well as tea and coffee at the formal breaks. Clarify the catering arrangements – don't leave anything to guesswork.

0.20

Activity 17.1 Draft an outline venue specification

Please take a few minutes to consider what sort of venue you might need for your course.

MANAGE THE VENUE

Once you have selected the venue, the next challenge is to manage things for best effect. Please look through the following guidelines to see which might apply to you.

Venue management team

- Confirm names and telephone, mobile and fax numbers of key personnel in the venue management team.

- Confirm who has authority to authorize expenditure and the limits.

- Request written confirmation of the agreed programme, including the proposed rates and charges.

General venue facilities

- Confirm what the venue can provide, eg restaurants, leisure facilities.

- Collect copies of venue brochure to send to delegates.

- Confirm the broad numbers attending, dates of arrival and departure.

- Agree what will be charged to the main account, and what individual delegates will be required to pay.

- If working outside the UK, try a test video to ensure the video format presents no problems.

- Do the bedrooms have computer access for e-mail?

Delegates

- Who should delegates contact to confirm attendance?

- Confirm if delegates require smoking or non-smoking rooms.

- Confirm any special dietary requirements.

- Are there any special accessibility issues?

- Confirm delegate rate – what's included/excluded?

- Request venue to allocate specific rooms by day, date and time, so that you can notify all delegates who's where and deliver welcome packs.

- Programme of arrivals and departures for non-resident delegates to be finalized.

- Confirm dress code.

Support services

Check what the venue can provide by way of the following support services:

- Typing/word processing.

- Incoming/outgoing messages. During/outside normal hours?

- Production of OHP foils.

- Photocopying – mostly routine but occasionally at very short notice.

Breakfast

When and where will this be available (bearing in mind possible early morning starts)? Can delegates have breakfast in their room at no extra charge?

Tea and coffee breaks

- Request tea, coffee and fruit juice for all refreshment breaks.

- Is it possible to have them constantly available throughout the day, rather than set times?

- Venue needs to be flexible about times.

- Some breaks may be served in the main room or, at other times, in syndicate rooms.

Lunch breaks

- Specify type of meal required – for example, hot/cold buffet or silver service.

- Agree when the menu is to be finalized.

- Confirm time, place and seating arrangements.

Evening meals

Normal evenings

- Specify initial requirements – subject to later confirmation.

- Menu and drinks to be agreed.

- On any evenings when delegates may be going out for dinner – can the venue suggest any local attractions?

Formal end-of-course event

- Pre-dinner drinks. Time, location, numbers, drinks, nibbles, etc.

- Agree timings.

- Agree the menu – vegetarian alternative?

- Wines and after-dinner drinks?

- Arrangements for hosting VIP guests.

- Seating plan.

- After-dinner speaker? Selection. Briefing. Hosting. Accommodation. Departure.

- Any special 'thank you' gifts for key personnel?

Main training room

- Specify when the room is to be available and when it can be released.

- Confirm that the room is not to be used for any other activities overnight. Some venues 'sell' a room for overnight usage, and return it back to its original state by early morning.

- Agree the room layout – and supply a diagram.

- Specify types of table with numbers of delegates at each table.

- Check location and number of power points – on walls or floors?

- Audio/visual equipment. What's currently available? What could be ordered in from external suppliers?

- Are you aware of any unusual needs by trainers/presenters?

- Discuss decoration of the conference tables and rooms.

- Sufficient flipcharts for the main room and team rooms.

- PA equipment – button or radio mikes?

- Dressing and refreshing the training rooms throughout the day.

Other issues

- Supplies of miscellaneous stationery items.
- Pigeonholes for posting delegates' materials.
- Photographs of the conference sessions.
- Video recording of keynote speakers?
- Key venue contacts – day and night.
- Overnight security – what are the arrangements?

Syndicate/team rooms

- Specify when the rooms are to be available and when they can be released.
- Confirm that the rooms are not to be used for any other activities overnight.
- Overnight security – what are the arrangements?
- Check they will be large enough to seat the numbers of delegates in comfort.
- Specify any visual aids and/or computer access or facilities.

End-of-course arrangements

- Closing individual and overall venue accounts.
- Luggage on final morning.
- Onward travel to airports, etc.
- Overnight accommodation for delayed delegates.

External presenters

- If possible, meet all the external presenters on site to discuss their sessions.
- Walk through individual session briefing notes.
- Confirm objectives, workshop requirements, outputs, etc.

- Discuss specialized audio/visual/computing requirements.

- Confirm their agreement to be recorded on video (if appropriate).

Costs and accounts

- Clarify the costs and how they will be billed.

- Do you have an outline agreement or even previously agreed corporate rates for the venue concerned?

- Ask for written quotes for each aspect of the event, especially anything that may have to be subcontracted to external suppliers.

You will also need to clarify:

- What will be charged to the main account.

- To whom and in what detail the final main account should be submitted.

- Who has authority to commit expenditure to be charged to the main account.

- What will be charged to individual delegate's rooms, for them to pay on departure.

- Whether the accounts will be subject to any extra taxes. If so, how much?

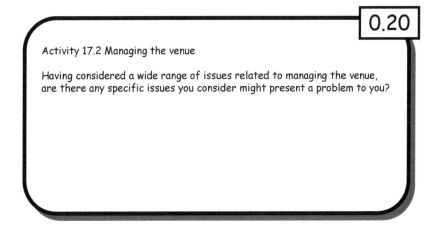

0.20

Activity 17.2 Managing the venue

Having considered a wide range of issues related to managing the venue, are there any specific issues you consider might present a problem to you?

18

Pilot the course

- Plan the pilot
- Pilots for blended learning
- Deliver the pilot
- Evaluate the pilot
- Sponsor 'sign off'

PLAN THE PILOT

You have now reached stage 'I' of the DESIGN process, when you initiate your pilot programmes. All the design work has been done, the key people have been involved along the journey... and it's very tempting to steam into full-scale production. But, however thorough the design work, you would be well advised to try it out on a group of 'real' delegates and see how well the course actually works. Does it deliver the promised changes in business performance? As you enter this phase of the project it could be helpful to discuss with the sponsor exactly what he or she would like to see by way of 'evidence' to convince them that the project can be safely 'signed off' at the end of this stage.

The right balance

An important issue easily overlooked is the need to strike the right balance of people to take part in the pilot course or courses. Make sure you get a representative 'slice' of people across the target audience – all sites, all shifts, all grades, all countries, etc. That way you not only collect feedback that is fully representative of the whole target market, but you also retain the 'buy in' of all these key groups. The last thing you need is one site or group of staff rejecting the final product because they were not involved in the pilots.

Not too many 'experts'

Sometimes it's tempting to have a mixture of delegates on the pilot, intermingling 'ordinary' delegates with people from the HR or training department. Quite naturally, the 'experts' want to come along to see how the pilot works, and to be able to give their feedback during the review meeting.

However, try to keep the proportion of 'experts' low, as the presence of these knowledgeable people disrupts the flow of the course. This can easily lead to the pilot course being quite different from what it would have been if the delegates were 'ordinary' operational people.

Because their focus is on the course itself rather than just practising the skills, they can also divert the discussions towards how the course needs to be improved, instead of how individual delegates need to change their skills or behaviours.

0.15

Activity 18.1 Planning your pilot events

Please take a few minutes to plan how you intend to pilot the course you've been developing.

❑ Will you need more than one event to ensure you collect feedback from a representative 'slice' of the
target audience?

❑ When and where will it/they be delivered?

❑ Who will be invited to attend as delegates?

❑ Who will deliver, and who else might attend to evaluate the product?

❑ Will you need to trial any 'pre-production' equipment or materials? Is so, how can you produce the 'mock ups' while still preserving their functionality?

❑ What evidence will the sponsor require to 'sign off' the programme as being roadworthy?

PILOTS FOR BLENDED LEARNING

Because blended learning involves upfront commitment of significant amounts of resources, it's worth devoting extra time to the piloting process. We suggest you do it in three phases.

1. Initial evaluation

Top Tip! Pilot your e-learning course content, ideally before it gets anywhere near a piece of software. Once you have developed the initial 'screens', it's worth trying out the course materials on some typical delegates who form the target audience for the course. Obviously the course materials are not in their final format, but you will receive some very helpful feedback. Here's how to simulate the 'real thing' as best you can at this stage of development:

- Do it in a one-to-one session, working through the materials with a typical learner.

- Starting with the course workbook allows learners to familiarize themselves with its contents.

- Then ask them to start working through the planned online materials, going through each screen in turn.

- As you're testing the suitability of the on-screen material to be self-explanatory, you should only comment if the learner is obviously unable to grasp the learning points. This can be very difficult, as the natural tendency is to comment or expand on the course materials.

- The most you can to is to simulate the intended voiceover for each screen.

- You will also need to act the part of the learning management system, telling them what will happen at different stages of the course. For example, you might say to them: 'If you click Continue at this point you will jump to page XX, so let's go there and see what happens then.'

- As they work through the course you should note any areas that seem to be confusing or where the flow could be improved, and seek the learners' comments on what they think should be different.

- Keep an eye on timings – it will give you an idea of how long the course will take to complete.

- At the end of each session summarize your notes and ask the learners for any additional comments or suggestions.

Once the materials have been tried on a selected group of delegates you can then take stock of all their comments, and decide how the course materials need to be improved. Their comments will:

- Show where the flow needs to be changed. Simply rearranging the order of some screens may make the materials easier to understand, or a topic to 'come alive' more.

- Tell you where you need to insert additional screens because, perhaps, the concepts are not sufficiently well explained. You may have made assumptions about people's knowledge or understanding.

- Show you which screens are redundant and can be removed.

- Give you some idea about how interesting they found the materials, and which parts need to be injected with additional interest or participation.

- Indicate how successful the course is overall in equipping them with additional skills or confidence.

2. Pilot the e-learning course

Once the software designers give you the complete e-learning course it's a good idea to pilot this before making it available to the wider target audience:

- This will give you valuable feedback on how people react to the course materials in their final form.

- It will also tell you how 'user-friendly' the target audience find the electronic learning management system.

- You will also learn how fast or slow your existing IT network is, and the amount of frustration learners sometimes suffer if the network is slow. This may highlight the need to upgrade the IT services to certain sites or locations if e-learning is to become popular and widely accepted.

- Depending on how much you incorporate the course into your existing IT system, you may also collect valuable feedback on how effective the learning management system is in tracking individual learners, as well as collecting overall statistics.

After trying out the courseware on a selected group of learners, at a representative number of sites, you should hold the next project review meeting when all of these topics can be discussed. If you've done the earlier reviews thoroughly then the number of changes resulting from these pilot events should be small and therefore not too costly.

3. Pilot the trainer-led course

The final pilot stage for a blended learning programme is to pilot the trainer-led course. How effectively did it reinforce the e-learning course? Once these two key components, the e-learning and the trainer-led course, have been piloted and finalized, you will be in a position to consider the wider launch of the whole e-learning training programme.

0.15

Activity 18.2 Pilots for blended learning

If you're piloting an e-learning or blended learning programme please consider:

❑How will you gain feedback on your initial ideas before committing significant software design resources?

❑When, where and how will the first pre-production e-learning materials be piloted?

❑How, when and where will the trainer-led course be piloted?

❑Who will be invited to act as delegates for either/both components?

DELIVER THE PILOT

Once you've decided who to invite, schedule and deliver the pilot course as a normal event. You want to test your design under normal operational conditions so that you know what, if anything, needs changing. Try to ensure that delegates experience an event that is as much like the final product as possible. Clearly, you may have items that are expensive to produce and which you can only acquire once you know the design is sound. This may mean that on the pilot you use some materials or equipment that are 'mock ups' and only resemble the final production versions.

EVALUATE THE PILOT

Get feedback

At the end of the course it's essential to ask individual delegates to complete an end-of-course questionnaire as you normally would. If the course lasts more than one day it's useful to do this evaluation at the end of each day while things are fresh in delegates' minds. Lots of people scoff at these forms but, if you make it clear that you do take them seriously, people will often give you constructive, and sometimes painful, feedback. I can look back on many years of training experience and readily admit that many of the good ideas I have developed have arisen from delegate feedback.

At the end of the pilot course it's also valuable to ask the delegates to give some group feedback, and you can do this very easily:

- Use two flipcharts, one headed 'This went well' and the other 'This could be better'.

- Split the delegates into two groups, one standing at each flipchart.

- Now ask them to list on the flipchart anything they want to relating to the heading.

- After 5 minutes or so, ask them to change flipcharts and add any extra ideas to the other one.

- Finally, ask everyone to gather round the 'This went well' flipchart and invite the 'author' of each comment to briefly say why it's important to them.

- Change flipcharts and all stand round the 'This could be better' list and again ask the 'author' of each comment to briefly say why it's important to them.

This process will give you lots of good ideas about what needs to be changed to make the pilot really effective, as well as stroking your self-esteem! Summarize the feedback and send it quickly (ideally by e-mail) to all the interested parties so everyone knows what's been said.

Schedule review meetings

If at all possible, schedule a review meeting for early on the day immediately after the pilot course, so all the key people can review what happened while it's fresh in their minds. You can then decide what changes need to be made and get going on the modifications. Some of the topics for discussion could include:

- delegates' comments and feedback;

- trainer's comments and suggestions for improvement;

- the pace, timings, contents and flow;

- was there too much/just right/too little in the day?

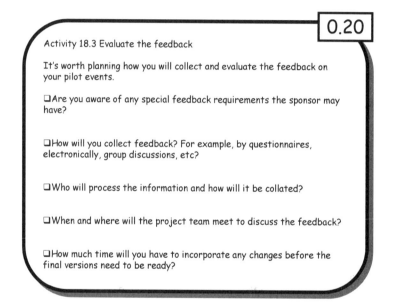

0.20

Activity 18.3 Evaluate the feedback

It's worth planning how you will collect and evaluate the feedback on your pilot events.

❑Are you aware of any special feedback requirements the sponsor may have?

❑How will you collect feedback? For example, by questionnaires, electronically, group discussions, etc?

❑Who will process the information and how will it be collated?

❑When and where will the project team meet to discuss the feedback?

❑How much time will you have to incorporate any changes before the final versions need to be ready?

SPONSOR 'SIGN OFF'

Decision time! Having conducted the pilot and reviewed what changes need to be made you must now meet the sponsor and share the results.

Is the product fully acceptable to the sponsor and can it go into production for delivery across the target market? If the answer is 'Yes', then go ahead and make it available to all operational training units. If the answer is 'No', then you will need to make the required changes and re-pilot as necessary.

19

Go live

- Confirm ownership
- Identify resources and materials
- Market the programme
- Deliver the programme
- Follow up
- What could go wrong?

CONFIRM OWNERSHIP

You've now reached a significant step in the DESIGN process, where you move your newly designed and tested product into sustainable delivery. This can be quite an emotional time as you have to hand over what has until now been your 'baby' to the care of someone else. Will they treat it with the devotion you would like?

The first step along the route is to confirm exactly who will take ownership of the new product and, hopefully, the sponsor will already have someone in mind. This issue becomes more complicated if the product is to be released globally, as you may find that ownership is being delegated to individual end-market operating companies each with differing operational priorities. Only time will tell. Of course if you're the 'product owner' life is so much easier!

Life cycle management

Once you have confirmed ownership you can then discuss the life cycle management of the product. In addition to clarifying who will be responsible for it initially you will also need to discuss who will manage it in the longer term, and make decisions about the product's life cycle:

- Some training programmes will have been developed to support a specific initiative, for example launching a new product, and so by their nature have a short life.

- Other training programmes will have been designed to develop mainstream skills and so can be expected to have a longer shelf life.

- The final category are the programmes that can be expected to last for a longer period because they deal with less 'volatile' topics, like meetings skills, or have involved considerable expense, for example e-learning.

The important point here is to ensure that someone takes specific responsibility for monitoring the effectiveness and condition of each of the training programmes to ensure that they are all delivering what was expected of them.

IDENTIFY RESOURCES AND MATERIALS

You can now hold meaningful discussions with the new owner about how they will roll out the product into sustained delivery. Administration and logistics will feature large in the discussions:

- How many delegates are to be trained in the given timescale?

- How many courses need to be delivered – do they have sufficient trainers and suitable venues?

- How do they want the product transferred? Hard copy or electronic, or a mixture of the two?

- Will you need to supply any supporting equipment or materials, for example delegates' folders, posters or videotapes?

- Will materials be sourced centrally (giving economies of scale) or locally (giving increased flexibility)?

This sounds very mundane yet is vitally important for the success of the programme. It doesn't matter how brilliant the original course design was if the delegates can't fit their handouts into the flash 'high impact' delegate folder. If a training programme has to be implemented within a specific 'window', for example to launch a new product, then it's easy for people to underestimate the sheer scale of the administration required. Courses won't run full – you generally have 'no shows', and they can't always be shoehorned into the remaining courses without adversely affecting the learning experience.

So insist on getting the administration well planned or there may be a disaster. And you can guess who they'll blame – yes, that's right, the course designer!

0.15

Activity 19.1 Life cycle manager

Look ahead to when you reach this stage in the DESIGN process.

❑ Who is likely to be responsible for managing the product throughout its life cycle ?

❑ What projected lifespan will the product have?

❑ Will you be asked to give any administrative support? If so, what?

MARKET THE PROGRAMME

Never too soon to close

Having organized the programme, all that remains is to make the complete course available to all appropriate units and departments. Sounds easy, doesn't it, but we all know that there's a lot to effective marketing. Take a tip from a salesperson's toolkit – it's never too soon to close a sale.

So, from the moment you start the DESIGN process always be looking to talk about what you're doing and winning people over. Throughout the design process it's worth putting some energy into raising awareness of the new training programme and, especially if you're introducing e-learning, overcoming the very natural reluctance some people may have. Developing a strategy for 'selling' your programme into the business will be easier if you've actively involved managers and users throughout the design process.

If you're promoting a combination of e-learning with a shorter trainer-led course, you must expect that some people need some encouragement to embrace it willingly. Consider internal magazines, newsletters, the company intranet and notice boards. Also be aware of when managers will be discussing annual appraisals so that e-learning becomes one of the possible development options.

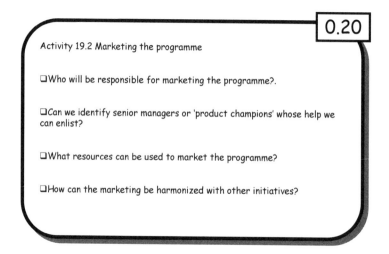

0.20

Activity 19.2 Marketing the programme

❑Who will be responsible for marketing the programme?.

❑Can we identify senior managers or 'product champions' whose help we can enlist?

❑What resources can be used to market the programme?

❑How can the marketing be harmonized with other initiatives?

DELIVER THE PROGRAMME

Select the venue

Using the criteria in the draft venue specification, select a suitable venue and confirm the date. Don't skimp on the venue – it's a key ingredient for success. There's nothing more demotivating than being cooped up all day with a group of people in a claustrophobically small room. It can undermine everything that's gone before:

- It sounds obvious but, whenever possible, visit the venue in advance to ensure it really does meet your needs.

- At the very least, ask the venue to send you a detailed room plan showing measurements, and the locations of windows, doors and power sockets.

- Look for any built in (and unmovable) training aids, eg screens for projectors and wall-mounted flipchart stands.

- Check out the size and location of any syndicate rooms you want.

Lead times on venues can be quite long and coming to an understanding relationship with nearby conference and training venues can relieve lots of pressure. The ideal would be to have dates 'pencilled in' but leaving you free to cancel if the number of delegates is insufficient to run the courses as scheduled.

Collect nominations for the course

So the marketing's under way and people are showing an interest in the course. Review the wait-list and schedule an event once the minimum number has been reached. This sounds easier than it often is in reality:

- You reach the minimum number and seek a venue.

- They give you a date that you test out with your delegates – and find that not all can attend that day.

- You ask when they could attend, so you check out that date with the venue – only they are fully booked that day!

And so it goes on! But eventually you will find a date when your delegates can attend, the venue has a suitable room... and the trainer is free! Obviously, a key element in managing this whole process is having a database that allows you to easily monitor potential delegates and their availability.

Issue course joining instructions

The course joining instructions may be your first formal contact with your delegates so they need to be:

- Timely. Far enough in advance to give reasonable warning, but not so far that people lose them.

- Complete. Make sure you include all the information people need.

- Accurate. It's easy to get addresses or telephone numbers wrong.

- Inviting. Make them look exciting and stimulate interest.

You probably have your own format, but you might want to look at the example given in Chapter 9. Ask delegates to confirm attendance and monitor the take-up to ensure the minimum numbers are met. Let's briefly go through the main elements.

Welcome

- Welcomes the delegate to the course.

- Outline what needs to be do prior to attending.

- Stresses that attending is conditional upon completing the full e-learning component (if appropriate).

Benefits of the course

Tells the delegates how they can expect to benefit by attending.

About the course

- Stress the need to arrive on time and give full commitment.

- Ask for mobile phones to be switched off for the whole day.

- Give outline timings.

The venue

- Give full details of the venue.

- Contact person's details at the venue.

- Directions on how to travel to the venue.

- Parking, security, refreshments, lunch, etc.

Pre-course work

Detail any pre-course work.

Course tutor

Say when the tutor will be available at the venue, and that they welcome any questions delegates may have.

Dress code

State the dress code for the course, normally smart casual.

Can't attend?

Stress the need to give maximum notice if they can't attend so the place can be offered to another delegate.

Any queries?

Offer a contact if the delegate has any queries.

Sign off

Sign off in a friendly way –'We look forward to meeting you on the day' – with a name people can read.

Pre-course preparation

Just before the scheduled date send course materials and equipment to the venue, clearly labelled for the trainer, with the name of the training room and date. The times I have spent frantic minutes on the morning of the course searching hotels for a box of materials!

- Finalize the administrative details with the venue managers.
- Confirm the number of delegates and trainers, timings and any special dietary requirements.
- Finally, confirm the date and venue with the trainer(s), together with travel directions and the name of the training room.

> ### 0.20
>
> Activity 19.3 Delivering the programme
>
> Please take a few minutes to develop your own checklist of materials, resources, people, locations, equipment or anything else you will need to ensure success.

FOLLOW UP

Assess learners' improved skills and effectiveness

We started this journey looking at the three phases people work through to improve their skills or confidence:

1. Grasp the theory. Delegates may undertake a self-study e-learning course, supported by other learning resources, for example books or videos.

2. Practise the skills. Learners come together with colleagues to practise their skills in a trainer-led course.

3. Apply the learning. They apply all the learning to reach new levels of business performance, supported by coaching.

Delegates will return to their workplace after attending the trainer-led course and begin to implement their action plans. This is a potential danger period as they may get swamped by 'business as usual' when they return to their desks, and it's quite possible for all their good intentions from the course to get lost!

In an ideal world each delegate will have discussed the outcome from the course with their line manager, who will, of course, show an interest in their action plans. It's vital that the action points learners develop as they both grasp the theory and practise the skills are SMART in every way:

- Specific – they identify specific tasks or activities to focus on.

- Measurable – if they can't measure it they won't know how well they're currently doing and, worse still, they won't know when they've met the new standard.

- Achievable – a balance is required here. A goal that's too easy is no motivation, while one that's unattainable is an immediate turn-off.

- Relevant – both the learner and the line manager must see the objective as relevant to the job in hand.

- Timely – give it a date and time, and you have something real to achieve.

It will be important to develop some meaningful measurements to really determine the true improvement in individual skills or behaviours, especially if you want to compare changes across different parts of the business, or at different sites.

Offer coaching to reinforce learning

The line manager needs to discreetly monitor the learner's progress against the action plans written at the end of the course. Depending on their response, they might need coaching, which can be given in at least two ways. First, there is the traditional method, where the line manager sits with the learner and gives one-to-one coaching on specific skills or behaviours. Secondly, there is online coaching, when the trainer who delivered the trainer-led course offers remote coaching via the internet or the company intranet.

Whichever approach is adopted, you must ensure delegates get every bit of help and encouragement to implement their action plans. One additional advantage of the second approach is that the central HR department has a continuing relationship with people who have passed through the e-learning system, so enabling them to monitor its ongoing effectiveness more realistically.

Online coaching

If online coaching is an option, it needs to be mentioned at each stage of the process to reinforce its value to learners and to ensure a reasonable take-up of the service. Online coaching is quite different from the normal form of coaching and, for it to be successful, there are some additional elements to be taken into account:

- Ideally the online coach needs to have been involved in the trainer-led course so he or she has seen the individual 'in action'.

- The online coach needs to have a copy of the action plan completed at the end of the trainer-led course, and be brought up to date with progress by the learner.

- It will be important to specify the maximum amount of online coaching the individual will receive, perhaps eight hours.

- It's useful to give a commitment about response time; for example: 'To contact your personal coach, send an e-mail with your particular question to coach@XXX. com. We will normally respond within one working day although we endeavour to reply within a few hours.'

It's also worth considering establishing a form of automated follow-up whereby the learner receives a series of reminder messages at specified periods after attending the trainer-led course. The various forms the messages could take include:

- top tips;

- frequently asked questions;

- action plan reminders.

> **0.20**
>
> Activity 19.4 Follow up
>
> An important part of any programme is providing support to delegates after the course to ensure they apply their learning.
>
> ❑ How will you involve line managers in supporting their staff as they apply their learning?
>
> ❑ Do you intend to give any direct support (after-sales service) to your delegates? If so, how will it be given?
>
> ❑ Is it possibile to contact delegates after the course to offer top tips, frequently asked questions or action plan reminders?

WHAT COULD GO WRONG?

Rolling the programme out for wider distribution, especially as it will doubtless involve other people, means there are plenty of opportunities for things to go wrong. But with a bit of forethought it's possible to counteract many of these potential problems. To close this chapter we'll invite you to do a risk assessment; see Figure 19.1. First of all, let's walk through the process step by step.

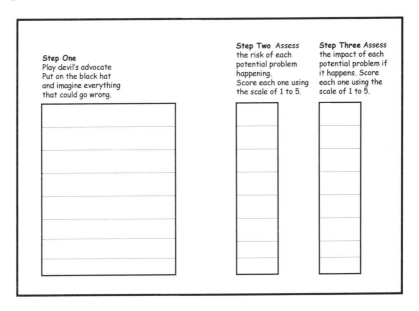

Figure 19.1 Risk assessment

Step 1. Play devil's advocate

Put on the black hat and imagine everything that could go wrong. This is difficult for a natural optimist (like me) but very important to do. List your thoughts in the first column.

Step 2. Assess the risk

Assess the risk of each potential problem happening. Score each one, using the following scale of 1 to 5, and enter the result in the second column. You can classify the risk as:

5 – Almost certain

4 – Likely

3 – Possible

2 – Unlikely

1 – Rare

Step 3. Assess the impact

Next assess the impact of each potential problem if it happens. Score each one using the following scale of 1 to 5, and enter the results in the second column. You can assess the impact as:

5 – Catastrophic

4 – Major

3 – Moderate

2 – Minor

1 – Insignificant

Step 4. Evaluate the results

Now you can combine the scores and evaluate the probable mitigation required for the identified and estimated risks. Use the risk analysis chart in Figure 19.2 and plot the potential problems in the appropriate boxes.

- Avoid – potential problems that fall into these boxes present serious risks, especially those in the 'High:High' box. You must look for every opportunity to minimize the risk – redesign things to avoid the problem. In the worst-case scenario you might even decide the risk is too high and stop it altogether.

- Recover – potential problems falling in here should be positively avoided if at all possible, or develop rugged contingency plans.

- Absorb – potential problems in this category should be able to be absorbed once people realize the problem exists.

Having grasped the theory, now it's time for you to apply the learning and see how it works for the course you've been designing.

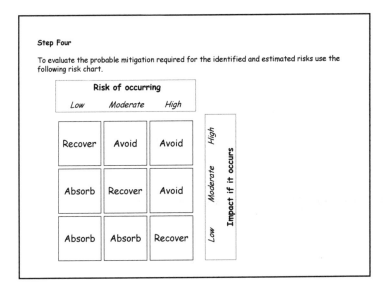

Figure 19.2 Risk analysis

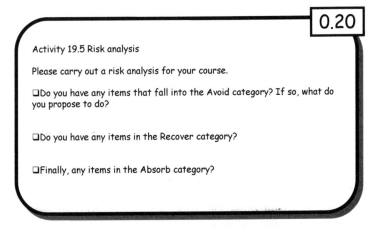

20

Review and relaunch

- Review what's changed
- Sources of feedback
- Measuring wider business impact
- Time for decision
- The end of the journey

REVIEW WHAT'S CHANGED

So now you've reached the final step of the DESIGN model where you review the continued relevance and effectiveness of your learning and/or training programme, and decide its longer-term future. In practice this validation needs to be a continuous activity enabling you to report back with confidence to the stakeholders on the success of the venture. If the expected level of performance is not being delivered, you can modify the training programme accordingly. It's important to note that, although the review and relaunch step is the last in the DESIGN cycle, you need to be working on this aspect throughout the whole design process. A well-organized project team will have decided the success criteria many months earlier, so that relevant data can be collected from the very start of the initiative.

Many years ago when I first became involved in quality management systems, I was amazed by the huge manuals that always seemed to accompany the workshops. Overcome by the sheer volume of material I was expected to become familiar with, I asked one of the experts what the underlying principles were. The expert said that any good quality management system had essentially three main components:

1. Say what you do. Write a clear, simple statement of exactly what you intend to do.

2. Do what you say. Put in place the people, equipment, materials, tools, training and other resources to enable you to do what you've said you would do.

3. Prove it. Take consistent and reliable measures that prove that you do what you said you would do – first time, every time.

So, once people have completed any parts of the formal training programme and have applied their skills, perhaps having received some coaching along the way, you can look back and confirm what's actually changed. This review process is essential, not only for the specific course you've been developing so you can change or tweak parts to make it even more effective, but also in the future as you develop other courses or workshops.

SOURCES OF FEEDBACK

There's a wide range of feedback you can collect to help you carry out a balanced review of the training course or programme, so that your final conclusions will be supported by both factual and anecdotal evidence:

- Review all the feedback you have collected from learners, for both trainer-led and self-study courses, together with feedback from training and HR professionals. Does it suggest any changes to the programme are required?

- Review current or projected changes to the commercial environment – does anything impact on the overall programme?

- Are there any other internal/external factors that may impact on the programme?

- Even if the contents are sound, could the programme benefit from a formal relaunch to recaptivate interest in the target market?

MEASURING WIDER BUSINESS IMPACT

Customer-supplier surveys

Measuring the wider impact of training programmes across the business is more difficult because other factors come into play. For example, if the company had 'sheep dipped' everybody in a series of customer-focus workshops, followed up by specific project-based work designed to improve product delivery, one would think that by a comprehensive series of 'before' and 'after' customer surveys you would be able to show the success of the programme.

Given general market stability that should be the case, but then other factors come into play. Market forces affect the way that companies operate and improvements in customer service could be swamped by sudden changes in legislation, raw materials and fuel costs, wars, mergers and take-overs.

However, the longer-term value of training can still be proved by these 'before' and 'after' surveys – you just have to recognize the potential pitfalls. External surveys of customers and suppliers carried out over a period of time will reveal trends, which could be the results of training initiatives. Similarly, internal staff surveys done at frequent intervals will show trends in attitudes, which could be ascribed to specific initiatives, as well the prevailing market forces.

Return on investment

Wouldn't it great to be able to show the return on investment that results from your training programme? Undertaking this type of study could be very time-consuming, but the following approach might give you a 'rough and ready' answer.

Step 1

Select some performance indicators you believe your training programme should improve, such as increased sales; reduced errors; reduced turnover; increased number of new accounts; higher productivity.

Step 2

After the training programme, periodically monitor the performance data for these indicators: sales reports; employee error records; turnover data; records of new accounts; productivity reports, etc. Although a variety of factors could bring about an improvement in performance, a noticeable change in any specific indicator following a training programme designed to target that indicator, could be evidence that the training has worked.

Step 3

Calculate average revenue increases or cost savings for the performance indicators that might have been affected by the training intervention, such as: additional sales per employee multiplied by the average revenue per sale; average cost per error; average cost of a new employee (estimated recruitment, training, lost productivity costs, etc); average revenue per account; percentage increase in productivity multiplied by cost per employee; etc.

Step 4

Gross up the figures. Multiply each average revenue increase or cost saving by the number of employees, accounts, employees retained, total errors avoided, or any other numerical value that shows the extent of the revenue increase or cost savings for the performance indicator throughout the company.

Step 5

Calculate the net worth. Add the different revenue increases or costs savings for the whole company, then subtract the total costs of implementing the training programme.

Although this can only be a 'rough and ready' estimate, the resulting numbers will show the amount of additional revenue, or reduced costs produced by the training programme. This process, while not exact, is an efficient and effective alternative to a time-consuming large-scale investigation. And it is better than not attempting to calculate the return on investment at all.

TIME FOR DECISION

Now that you have collected and evaluated all the data, it's time to meet the course sponsor and discuss:

- Is the product still acceptable?

- Is it delivering the required changes in business performance?

- Are there any other markets, globally, where it might be required?

> **0.15**
>
> Activity 20.1 Sources of feedback
>
> Look ahead to when you reach this stage in the DESIGN process.
>
> ❑ What sources of feedback will be available to you?
>
> ❑ Are there any industry-specific forms of feedback you could use?
>
> ❑ How will you be able to assess the wider effectiveness of your programme?

If the answer is 'Yes', then consider relaunching the product to retain staff awareness, or launch it in the new markets, using the evidence of success to encourage interest. Market the product more energetically, using all internal communication media, focusing on benefits and sustained improvements to business performance.

If the answer is 'No', then how will you react? If the product is still valid but in need of updating or a 'makeover', make the necessary changes and relaunch. If the product is no longer valid, discuss with the sponsor what action to take.

> **0.15**
>
> Activity 20.2 Review and relaunch
>
> Schedule a meeting with your sponsor soon to discuss how he or she will wish to manage the final part of the DESIGN process.
>
> What evidence will he or she want to consider and evaluate?
>
> ❑ What will convince him or her of the programme's continued value to the organization?
>
> ❑ Does he or she know of any other initiatives or programmes that might impact on what you're doing?

THE END OF THE JOURNEY

Well, now we've reached the end of our journey together. We hope that you have not only gained some new insights into the fascinating world of designing training, but also designed a course or workshop along the way. The activities we've included in the book were designed to transfer practical skills and approaches, and we trust we've been successful. Please let us know – is there anything we have missed that should have been in the book, or any topic that should have been developed differently?

Review and relaunch yourself!

Everything we do is an opportunity to discover more about the world around us, and learn how effectively we respond to the pressures and challenges we encounter. In the first chapter we mentioned a few ways in which buying the book might benefit you:

- Perhaps you've been delivering training courses that other people have designed, and you'd like to be able to do it yourself.

- You might have been told that you'll soon be asked to design a course and you haven't a clue where to start.

- You may be an experienced training course designer and perhaps feel the need to refresh your existing skills.

- Perhaps you've designed many courses but some of them may be a bit 'jaded' or need re-energizing.

- You may be taking on a new role as a training 'consultant' and want to be able to project a more professional image with your client departments.

At the most modest level we hope that the book has enabled you to meet the needs you started out with, but our expectations go higher than that. Now that you have worked through these 20 chapters, has the book encouraged you to see yourself, and your future, with a fresh perspective?

- Will you take on wider training design roles?

- Do you see yourself moving to a different role?

- Can you see other avenues in the wider training or development profession?

- Perhaps you feel motivated to make a more fundamental change.

So there it is. Best of luck with whatever route you take. The training and development profession is truly worthwhile – helping people to overcome their anxieties, or to develop confidence with unfamiliar subjects, is a great privilege and, as we all know, the role of the 'trainer' is not for the faint-hearted. If you can derive a fraction of the pleasure I have from both designing training and writing this book about it, you will be a truly contented person.

Index